# OUR OWN METAPHOR

ADVANCES IN SYSTEMS THEORY, COMPLEXITY,
AND THE HUMAN SCIENCES

Alfonso Montuori, Series Editor

Mind and Nature: A Necessary Unity
*Gregory Bateson*

Angels Fear: Towards an Epistemology of the Sacred
*Gregory Bateson and Mary Catherine Bateson*

Our Own Metaphor
*Mary Catherine Bateson*

The Narrative Universe
*Gianluca Bocchi and Mauro Ceruti*

Mind in Time
   The Dynamics of Thought, Reality, and Consciousness
*Allan Combs, Mark Germine, & Ben Goertzel (eds.)*

Politics, Persuasion and Polity
   A Theory of Democratic Self-Organization
*Gus diZerega*

Evolution: The Grand Synthesis
*Ervin Laszlo*

The Systems View of the World
*Ervin Laszlo*

Homeland Earth: A Manifesto for the New Millennium
*Edgar Morin and Anne Brigitte Kern*

A Tripartite Seed
*Gordon Rowland*

New Paradigms, Culture and Subjectivity
*Dora Fried Schnitman (ed.)*

# OUR OWN METAPHOR

A PERSONAL ACCOUNT OF A CONFERENCE ON THE
EFFECTS OF CONSCIOUS PURPOSE ON
HUMAN ADAPTATION

## MARY CATHERINE BATESON

WITH A NEW FOREWORD AND AFTERWORD BY THE AUTHOR

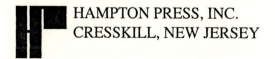
HAMPTON PRESS, INC.
CRESSKILL, NEW JERSEY

Copyright © 2005 by Hampton Press, Inc. and
The Institute for Intercultural Studies

Printed in the United States of America

PRINTING HISTORY
Alfred A. Knopf edition published 1972
Smithsonian Institution Press edition published 1991

**Library of Congress Cataloging-in-Publication Data**

Bateson, Mary Catherine
 Our own metaphor : a personal account of a conference on the effects
of conscious purpose on human adaptation / Mary Catherine Bateson; with
a new foreword and afterword by the author.
  p. cm. -- (Advances in systems theory, complexity, and the human sciences)
Account of a conference held in 1968 at Burg Wartenstein, Austria.
Originally published: New York: Knopf, 1972. With new foreword and
 afterword.
Includes bibliographical references and index.
ISBN 1-57273-601-1
1. Human ecology--Congresses. 2. Mind and body--Congresses. 3.
Cybernetics--Congresses. I. Title. II. Series.
GF23.B3 2005
304.2--dc22

2004051479

Hampton Press, Inc.
23 Broadway
Cresskill, NJ 07626

This book

is dedicated in memory of

Warren McCulloch, 1898–1969,

and

Martin Kassarjian, 1968

# CONTENTS

A DARKNESS UNOBSCURED

[*The Last Two Days*]

# FOREWORD 1991

This book is based on a conference that took place over two decades ago, yet the ideas that dominated that conference are still working their way into our understanding. At that time, in 1968, awareness of the depth and complexity of impending ecological crisis was confined to a rather small circle of people, but a major shift in attitudes had begun.

Although a commitment to conservation and to the preservation of wilderness goes back to the nineteenth century, public concern about pollution, one of many kinds of danger to the natural environment, can perhaps be tied to Rachel Carson's book, *Silent Spring*, which appeared in 1962 and led to scrutiny of the effect of pesticides and to the limitation and then prohibition of DDT. Other concerns followed. The blue-green portrait of earth as seen from space was published in 1968, and the first *Whole Earth Catalog* appeared the same year. By the end of the sixties, environmental worries were sufficiently widespread and well informed that the National Environmental Policy Act of 1969 could be passed and the first Earth Day in 1970 could win popular success.

The general level of consciousness about environmental issues has risen since then, yet we still lack an adequate, integrative vision of the nature of the problem that is responsive to the vision of the planet. The twentieth anniversary of Earth Day in 1990 took place in a context of great concern and growing readiness to act. The environment had been established as a major item on the American political agenda, and Green political movements had gained influence in many countries. However, actual achievements in that twenty-year period were limited. There had been a slowing of certain kinds of pollution and environmental degradation, a few species preserved at least for a time, a stay of execution for a few wetlands, but no real change in the pattern. For all the environmental legislation and regulations, approaches remain piecemeal.

New hazards continue to be discovered. In 1968 we knew nothing of the thinning of the ozone layer, nor did we foresee acid rain. The increase of carbon dioxide in the atmosphere, threatening world climate, had been pointed out, but it still seemed very abstract. Even then, however, the time was ripe for recognizing a multitude of dangers as different aspects of a single problem: a destructive mismatch between human behavior and the characteristics of the biosphere within which human beings live and on which we depend. This is a mismatch rooted, not in the mistakes of particular chemists or the wastefulness of hunters or farmers, but in the human capacity to think about natural systems and act on that knowledge. The time was ripe for a new kind of awareness, made possible by the confluence of several trends: the accumulating collection of environmental horror stories, the maturation of the disciplines of ecology and systems theory (or cybernetics), and an increased openness to interdisciplinary thinking.

The first step toward this awareness was to recognize that our drift toward ecological disaster is a systemic problem. At a more abstract level, however, the systemic problem can be recognized as an epistemological problem, a deficit in what we are able to know and think. I believe that this recognition has still not been fully incorporated into even very sophisticated discussions of environmental issues, although some of the specific epistemological ideas that were novel twenty years ago, such as the association between ecological irresponsibility and mind-body dualism or the differential impact of intellectual strategies of reductionism and holism, are familiar today.

In 1968 my father, Gregory Bateson, began to explore the nature of this mismatch between natural processes and human mental capacities. He hypothesized that we act in the world on the basis of a systematically distorted understanding of the effects of our actions, a sort of blindness to cybernetic circuitry leading to deficits as pervasive as those produced by color blindness, but far more serious. This distortion in understanding he associated with the capacity for conscious purpose in combination with technology. To discuss this idea, he called together a group of scientists and thinkers for a conference titled "The Effects of Conscious Purpose on Human Adaptation." Participants were chosen with the hope that each one would contribute special knowledge about how human beings think and learn or how human groups communicate and make decisions or would offer a descriptive insight into the structures of the natural systems that we need to understand. In initiating that intellectual exchange, Gregory set a process in motion that changed forever our understanding of the questions. This book is about that process and, therefore, about the process of epistemological change that is still so deeply needed.

Being at that conference was an essential step in my own development, both intellectual and personal. My account of it was designed to give the reader a chance to share not so much in the conclusions as in the experience itself, to encounter within the compass of a few chapters the sense of approaching disaster, the vertigo of epistemological change, the inadequacy of some of humankind's loftiest ideas, and the recognition of formal similarity between different kinds of error. The title of this book is derived from two very key ideas that emerged in our thinking: that a change in one's way of viewing the world must be rooted at the most personal level in a change in ways of viewing oneself—for each individual, his or her own central metaphor—and that an understanding of natural process could be achieved through a diverse and impassioned group process—a metaphor shared. These are the themes that I will develop in the Afterword.

This book has been a victim of some of the same epistemological problems it explored, for what it attempted to integrate, convention separates. Sales personnel were perplexed about the subject and where it should fit into the compartmentalization of knowledge reflected in the procedures of bookstores and were uneasy with the intermingling of analysis and emotion. They felt that the book was too difficult for the ordinary reader, for whom even the word *ecology* then seemed somewhat abstruse. Over the years, however, an increasing number of readers have used this book as a way to learn to understand systems. It has been photocopied, borrowed back and forth, and, alas, stolen from libraries. I believe it still provides an entry to ways of thinking we have not yet sufficiently learned to teach.

When *Our Own Metaphor* appeared in 1972, I did not fully understand the genre into which the book had evolved in my hands. It is conventional for foundations that support conferences to try to arrange for their publication; but it is typical for publishers and buyers to regard the edited proceedings of conferences as "nonbooks," appropriate for libraries, sometimes usable as readers or anthologies, but not designed, as this book is, to be read. Most conference volumes simply bind together what the different participants bring with them, often unaltered. Indeed, in any gathering of specialists only a minority actually listen to each other and learn from what is said. Few go home changed. Our conference was better than most in this regard, composed of an extraordinary and versatile group. But for me, younger than anyone else there, the conference was a whole education, and I did not think of myself as a specialist. The two ideas I focused on, the notion that a whole family of intellectual errors have the same form and the notion of the self as a metaphor for other systems, came to me as totally new insights; developing from these rough early phrasings, they have remained pivotal in my thinking. This book is an invitation to come with me through an intellectual rite de passage, on the one hand an initiation, on the other a voyage of discovery.

It may be helpful to locate the conversations in this book in the context of other unfolding awarenesses. The optimistic social activism of the early sixties had already been shadowed: 1968 was the year that Martin Luther King, Jr., was assassinated, and Lyndon Johnson had responded to bitter agitation against the war in Vietnam by announcing that he would not run again for president. *The Feminine Mystique* had been published in 1963, but the realization was only beginning that the struggles against bigotry and war and the struggle for the environment dealt with related issues. Today there is a growing understanding that every system that depends on domination reinforces all the other kinds of domination, including the notion of the mind ruling the body, or of humankind ruling nature, or of men ruling women. We had just begun to speak then in terms of multiple liberations and were becoming conscious that domination has built into it a systematic blindness on the part of the dominator to dependence upon the object of exploitation.

A recognition of such formal similarities makes it possible to set different stories side by side, each serving as a parable of the other. The story of Lake Erie is important in itself, but it stands in this text as an example of many such tragedies caused by human interference with natural systems. We have gotten used to the idea of the devastation of Lake Erie, so it is no longer news, though this particular problem, dwarfed by so many others, remains unsolved. Like the problem of the ozone layer, it represents a convergence of multiple processes, including some that we regard as necessary and constructive. There are parables of learning here, in the training of horses, the patterns of child rearing, and the behavior of cargo cults. Anatol Holt's presentation on formal descriptions of process has been absorbed in his subsequent work and that of others, but it still provides an introduction to the existence of alternative forms of description.

One of the examples of human habits of thought used here meant that when this book was first offered to publishers, it was rejected repeatedly; this was Barry Commoner's critique of DNA theory. DNA theory continues, of course, to be fundamental in biology, but some of the arrogance of the early formulations that Barry criticized has been moderated—indeed, some biologists claim their rhetoric was not meant literally in the first place. Nevertheless, modes of expression that are easily dismissed as rhetorical may set a pervasive style. In 1968, Barry had to search for obscure examples of cases where specificity was not solely determined by DNA. Today, most readers are familiar with the then unknown phenomenon of retroviruses, where the determination of specificity is preempted by RNA; the best known retrovirus is HIV, the virus that leads to AIDS. There is a curious resonance here between a moment of intellectual arrogance and a rediscovery of human vulnerability to natural process.

Barry's purpose was not to give a full discussion of molecular biology but to display and criticize the tendency to look for single causes. He urged the necessity of focusing on interactive systems in which the whole is more than the sum of the parts. In 1968, the word holistic was relatively little known. Now it is widely known but sometimes misused. In relation to medicine, it often refers to all forms of healing that stand outside of establishment practices, including many with narrow and magical foci. Ironically, there has been an increasing acknowledgment within the medical community that health or disease do depend upon the interaction of multiple factors.

It was at Burg Wartenstein that I learned the intellectual tools for thinking about stability and sustainability, although some members of the group were already challenging the emphasis on homeostasis and self-correction and looking beyond them to models for nondestructive systemic change. Scientists have since developed a range of new approaches to thinking about change, and particularly about change that is neither degenerative nor deterministic, that were not part of the conversation at Burg Wartenstein. The concept of equilibrium is, now as then, an essential element in a critique of the direction of modern society; yet an overemphasis on equilibrium has worked against the environmental movement, for our planet is not a closed system. All of the systems we spoke of, whether single organisms, forests, or societies, are characterized by change as well as balance. Most of us would still warn against unlimited population growth and the belief that technological solutions can be found to every shortage, but we increasingly admit that a sensitivity to natural balance can produce an untenable insistence on stasis.

The development of ways of functioning that will not destroy the viability of our planetary home will depend on conversation, understood in its widest sense: individuals in interaction manipulating words and tools, the symbols of economic exchange, political power, and passionate belief. Over time, there is a need to develop an ecology of ideas that will allow diversity and change and permit individuals to identify with the larger systems to which they belong. The conversations of this conference, including its quarrels and confusions, are a parable for the worldwide conversation that lies ahead of us.

M. C. B.

*Fairfax, Virginia*

# FOREWORD

# TO THE FIRST EDITION

THIS BOOK is an account of a conference and of the effects of that conference on my own thought and feeling. I believe the story is worth telling because I came away with both a new understanding and a new concern about the human condition. I wish to share these, not by summarizing conclusions, but by inviting others to join with me in this context of learning. The learning at the conference came about through the interweaving of ideas expressed by all who were present. An attempt by me to summarize them would be hopelessly shallow and even the things I said myself at the time would make little sense torn out of context. This is itself part of the message of this book: the process of the conference is a metaphor of what the conference was about.

I am deeply grateful to all the participants in the conference: Frederick Attneave, Barry Commoner, Gertrude Hendrix, Anatol Holt, W. T. Jones, Bert Kaplan, Peter H. Klopfer, Warren McCulloch, Horst Mittelstaedt, Gordon Pask, Bernard Raxlen, and Theodore Schwartz, and to the organizer, my father, Gregory Bateson. Without the ideas they brought with them and their response to each other, my own experience would not have been possible. They have allowed me to proceed in a very unusual way with this manuscript, using their words and excerpts from their writing, with their real names attached but in a way which is entirely my own responsibility. In the final hours of our meeting, I outlined my proposed procedure and received their agreement: I would take the tape recordings of our sessions and the papers written in advance and operate in complete freedom to produce a personal account of the human event of our meeting, trying to share that experience, with its humor and conflict and muddle, with the reader, in a way that is not typical of the usual published conference "proceedings." Everything that appears in quotes corresponds to something that was actually said, edited to produce a reasonable dialogue; but the editing is my own. The participants all saw an early draft of this manuscript, but, as we had agreed, were not asked to edit or approve. I may unwittingly have introduced errors by my editorial changes, set remarks in inappropriate contexts, or misheard key technical terms on the tape; the same is even more likely where I have paraphrased or described presentations in my own terms. The participants have been uniformly helpful in answering my queries, but there may be many questionable points that I did not know enough to query, and for these I take full responsibility. I am sure that no member of the group will be in full agreement with me on my interpretation of the event, or fully satisfied with his own face or voice as it is recorded in these pages. I can only say that few people are happy with their own voice and face on tape or film and that, however different the images here may be from each person's favored public image, I became very fond of every member of the group and I feel sure that the account of each of these personalities, as it appears here, includes my own affection. My principal regret is that I have had to leave out many fascinating and important things that were said that did not enter directly into my own sense of illumination.

My father, Gregory Bateson, read first one draft and then another, giving me the concrete criticism and suggestions that carried me through to completion. Others who have read the manuscript and given detailed comments and criticism include my husband, J. Barkev Kassarjian, and my mother, Margaret

Mead. Without the proddings of Angus Cameron, of the editorial department at Knopf, the book would never have undergone the final reshaping needed to make it just that: a book, rather than a report.

In addition to sponsoring the conference in the summer of 1968, the major clerical expenses of preparing the manuscript were borne by the Wenner-Gren Foundation for Anthropological Research. I would like to express what I know are the feelings of all the participants, that the foundation and especially its Director of Research, Mrs. Lita Osmundsen, have acted with great generosity and imagination. The foundation showed its further interest in these discussions by sponsoring a follow-up conference entitled, "The Moral and Aesthetic Structure of Human Adaptation."

During part of the preparation period of this manuscript I was supported by National Science Foundation Post-Doctoral Training Fellowship #48072.

M. C. B.

*Cambridge, Mass.*

# A NOTE ON FORMAT

THE CHRONOLOGY of the conference, as recorded here, corresponds to that of the actual event only at the beginning and end of our deliberations, and even there I have taken the liberty of rearranging brief sections for greater coherence. Readers interested in the dynamics of such events know from experience how discussions of this kind often begin from a common point, go through a period of divergence, and then converge at the end. Chapter 15, "Our Own Metaphor," follows the order of the discussion almost exactly, recording an enchanted time when the comments of different people dovetailed with an intoxicating felicity, except that the discussion actually began at noon on one day and continued until the coffee break the following morning. Gordon Pask was unavoidably absent during the middle period of the conference and so had no opportunity to participate in the discussions reported in Chapters 4–8 and 13–14. Excerpts from written materials prepared in advance are interspersed through the text, and are set in a different typeface so they can easily be distinguished from quoted speech.

# OUR OWN METAPHOR

# Prologue

WHEN I WAS A CHILD I used to tell questioning adults that my father was a scientist. In those days, science meant for me his knowledge of the woods and the streams, slugs found in the backyard, butterflies, and especially the tiny creatures of the New Hampshire lake nearby. By the time I was old enough to call him an anthropologist, it was already difficult even for adults to untangle just what this might mean from a long skein of interdisciplinary interests. He had been trained as a naturalist and then, in 1927, he went to do anthropological research in New Guinea, and later in Bali. By the beginning of the war he had completed his field work among exotic cultures, bringing back several ideas that fit very precisely into the intellectual structure that was then being built for the discussion of such complex wholes as individual organisms, societies, or the network of interdependent animal and plant life. Many kinds of observed patterns of balance and development began to be compared in discussing these systems, often using as the skeleton for the comparison the formal notions of cybernetics or information theory. These were the things that my parents, Gregory Bateson and Margaret Mead, were talking about when I was a child. It was during the first summer of peace, when I was six, that my father and I collected insects and looked at plant cells through the microscope; my father was reading Von Neumann's *Theory of Games* to himself and *Alice in Wonderland* and *The Rime of the Ancient Mariner* out loud to me.

Those years after the war were also the period when a new kind of seriousness about the human species gradually emerged. It took some time to see that the immense power of thermonuclear weapons would involve a total rethinking of human adaptation. Since that time, of course, we have gradually become aware that the danger of thermonuclear war is only a special case of the human potential for destruction. "Population explosion" became a familiar term in the early fifties. Ten years later, people began to be systematically concerned about environmental pollution, realizing that lifeless water in the streams and deadly gases in the air would destroy first the loveliness and then very quickly, because it is related, the viability of this planet. Within this concern, the ability to look carefully at a leaf or a snail or a dragonfly, the study of rituals in New Guinea, and the command of lean mathematical formalisms are found to be interlocked. I have grown to adulthood in a world where we can only take sufficient care of what we value through the kind of awareness of many interlocking factors that has been formalized in cybernetics.

I remember one very early lesson I was given in cybernetics, without the frightening name applied. It must have been when I was eight or nine years old. My father had gone to live in California, but was in New York on a visit, and we went down to lower Manhattan to shop for an aquarium: a huge tank, sand, plants, fish, and a thermostat-heater combination. He explained to me that the flamboyant fighting fish were used to living in tropical waters, so I remembered the descriptions my mother had given me of the climate in Burma where he was during the war, and imagined him looking down at red and blue fish in a warm stream. A heater, immersed in the tank, would raise the temperature of the water, but if it were heating the water constantly the fish would die—and there would be no way to keep the temperature in the tank steady as doors and windows were opened and closed and the seasons changed.

Some of the heat conducted through the water from the heater, however, would warm a metal bar in the thermostat, and as it heated it would curve, since it was made of two metals with different rates of thermal expansion. When the aquarium got above a certain temperature this curved bar would switch off the heat; when it cooled to below a particular temperature the bar would straighten and the heat would go on again. The temperature would be going up and down constantly between these two limits, but because they were quite close together, I would not be able to notice the variation with my finger dipped in the water and the fish would not be disturbed. Practically, the temperature was kept steady, a process of homeostasis. The effect of the rising temperature was looped back to govern the heater itself.

This was what I later learned to think of as controlled oscillation. The thermostat controlling it is called a servomechanism and the control depends on negative feedback: the heater does not switch until after the temperature has deviated from the ideal, and it is this error which controls a continuing back-and-forth swing. The thermostat, when you consider it, is responsive to differences and depends on an analogy between the difference between actual and ideal temperature and the difference in thermal expansion between two metals.

The first aquarium was difficult to maintain, because the Siamese fighting fish persisted for some time in killing their mates, responding to the strange females as they would to another male. When two males meet, they engage in competitive display that rapidly escalates into conflict; one threatens and this stimulates the other to a further, exaggerated threat, until finally they attack one another. In this kind of runaway, feedback, instead of leading to equilibrium, leads to an increased imbalance; it is as if the thermostat, instead of limiting the heat, were increasing it as the water became hotter, so that the temperature went up faster and faster until the glass sides of the tank shattered. Fighting fish are bred for conflict and will fight to the death.

My father had discovered this kind of feedback, regenerative feedback that leads to the destruction of the system, when he was writing up his early field work among the New Guinea Iatmul.[1] There he observed that the men were as flamboyant as Siamese fighting fish, threatening and swaggering, inventing proud new hairdos and boasting of their ancestry and the esoteric knowledge to which it gave them a claim; the women, on the other hand, were muted and plain, admiring the swagger of the men. My father observed that these two styles were so antagonistic that one wondered why the two sexes did not develop into extremes of belligerence and submission that would destroy all communication between them and the unified life of the culture. This tendency toward increased polarization he termed schismogenesis, and it was a household word in my very early childhood until my father replaced it with the cybernetic term, positive or regenerative feedback.

After the venture with the fighting fish, the aquarium stood empty for a year or so and then we went down to Canal Street again to restock it. This time we bought five or six different kinds of fish: swordtails and guppies that I might be able to breed, graceful black and gray angel fish that blanched when the water was disturbed, and a brown, mustached catfish to lurk in the bottom of the tank. The idea this time was to establish a mixed community of fish and plants in a balance. I never had a filter or an air bubbler in my aquarium, so the fish were always dependent on the green plants for the oxygen they breathed, and their numbers had to be small. The catfish scavenged on the floor of the tank, snails moved sedately up and down the sides controlling the algae, and the water stayed fresh and clear without being changed, year after year. Indeed, as long as the sun shone through the window and water and food and heat were supplied as needed, the fish flourished. A tiny ecosystem was balanced, as a number of different circular systems went on simultaneously: plants and bacteria were nourished by what the fish left, the fish nibbled on the plants, and oxygen and carbon dioxide passed back and forth.

The tropical fish were the first living things for whose care I was responsible. The aquarium, both sheltered and exposed by its glass walls, had a certain elusive self-sufficiency. I sat beside it by the hour and brooded on the relationships between the fish and on the balances that would have to be maintained in order for them to live. Sometimes, indeed, I interfered in ways that disrupted the balance in the tank, adding too many fish, uprooting the plants to rearrange them, or dosing the aquarium with tonic. It was the community I learned to care for, self-contained to a degree, and yet dependent on me and on our household on Perry Street, so that the lives of those fish depended on the peace and continuity of our lives, just as our own peace depended on a wider political peace in those early years of the Cold War. The aquarium was a world within a world within a world, connected to these wider systems through my capacity to understand and respond to its needs. This kind of relationship between such complex wholes as an aquarium, a household, and a nation is spoken of in cybernetic terms as a coupling of systems.

When I had had the aquarium for two or three years, it had to be moved one summer and somehow was disrupted so that almost everything died. It had been a beautiful thing, standing in front of a high window, the light barely filtered through the thin white curtains at one end of the long living room. My mother, looking through the water past the water grasses at the early morning light, used to say it reminded her of the sun rising over a reef in the South Pacific.

Norbert Wiener's book on cybernetics[2] came out in 1948; I was only eight and I did not read it, so it was a long time before I realized it was related to my aquarium, but it was already of central concern to the adults around me. The first of the Macy Foundation Conferences on Cybernetics was held in 1946 and for a decade both of my parents attended these and then the Macy meetings on Group Processes.[3] Year after year, a small core group would gather to link their abstractions, arguing fiercely and discovering curious parallelisms in research done quite separately. Those were the years when the whole concept of interdisciplinary work was growing rapidly, partly because of imaginative foundation executives like Frank Fremont-Smith and Larry Frank. Since Larry also owned the brownstone in New York where my mother and I lived and we spent our summers near him in New Hampshire, interdisciplinary conversation and conferences dominated life year round. In New Hampshire, especially, a dozen different households were linked by intellectual effort; these formed a community in which the children explored the woods and played pirates and the adolescents fell in and out of love with one another, while together we would play charades and sit for long hours singing around a campfire. The adults were talking about group process and child development, and meanwhile Larry Frank and his wife, Mary, and my mother were working to keep the adults and the children in one community. We played games that were designed by my mother so that the adults—the anthropologists and psychoanalysts and mathematicians—would never be bored and the children would never be bewildered or ignored. For years I have been running into new ideas that become, when I have lived with them for a time, recognizable as echoes of ideas that resonated in my childhood. For years, too, I have been trying to sort out how much of this heritage was special and how much was shared by everyone growing up in that period, the first generation to live with the commonplace that man could destroy this planet and all of the intricate relations of life on it almost as easily as that community in New Hampshire could be destroyed by anger feeding anger or my aquarium could be destroyed by my attempts to change it.

Life lived on the edge of a perpetual conference and in the wash of speculation and good humor that continued in the recesses of the adult sessions alternated with trips to visit my father in California. During the fifties, he was doing research on problems of communication and organization in schizophrenia, looking at the family as a system and discovering that the peculiarities of thought in schizophrenic children, often taking the form of logical and symbolic errors, could be related to distortions in the communication patterns of the family. My father and I used to go camping in the California State Parks and, in between efforts to get me to master the multiplication tables, he would respond to my demand, "Teach me something," with an account of how amoebae divide or Mendel's experiments with peas, Möbius strips or an explanation of the dark symbolisms of William Blake, or he would translate for me ideas he was working on. Over the years he has published a series of fictionalized father-daughter conversations, some of which took place and some did not, to express ideas that were perhaps only communicable as dialogue and only with a mixture of art and play.[4]

*Daughter:* Daddy, what is an instinct?
*Father:* An instinct, my dear, is an explanatory principle.
*Daughter:* But what does it explain?
*Father:* Anything—almost anything at all. Anything you want it to explain.
*Daughter:* Don't be silly. It doesn't explain gravity.
*Father:* No. But that is because nobody wants "instinct" to explain gravity. If they did, it would explain it. We could simply say that the moon has an instinct whose strength varies inversely as the square of the distance——
*Daughter:* But that's nonsense, Daddy.
*Father:* Yes, surely. But it was you who mentioned "instinct," not I.
*Daughter:* All right—but then what does explain gravity?
*Father:* Nothing, my dear, because gravity is an explanatory principle.
*Daughter:* Oh.

.     .     .

*Daughter:* Could we do without the idea of "instinct"?
*Father:* How would you explain things then?
*Daughter:* Well, I'd just look at the little things: When something goes "pop," the dog jumps. When the ground is not under his feet, he wiggles. And so on.
*Father:* Well. There are scientists who try to talk that way and it's becoming quite fashionable. They say it is more *objective*.
*Daughter:* And is it?
*Father:* Oh, yes.

.     .     .

*Daughter:* What does "objective" mean?

*Father:*      Well. It means that you look very hard at those things which you choose to look at.

*Daughter:*  That sounds right. But how do the objective people choose which things they will be objective about? . . . Which are the things they avoid?

*Father:*      Well, you mentioned earlier something called "practice." That's a difficult thing to be objective about. And there are other things that are difficult in the same sort of way. *Play*, for example. And *exploration*. It's difficult to be objective about whether a rat is *really* exploring or *really* playing. So they don't investigate those things. And then there's love. And, of course, hate.

*Daughter:*  I see. Those are the sorts of things that I wanted to invent separate instincts for.

*Father:*      Yes—those things. And don't forget humor.

       ·     ·     ·

*Daughter:*  Daddy—are animals objective?

*Father:*      I don't know—probably not. I don't think they are subjective either. I don't think they are split that way.

       ·     ·     ·

*Daughter:*  What are the really big differences between people and animals?

*Father:*      Well—intellect, language, tools. Things like that.

*Daughter:*  And it is easy for people to be intellectually objective in language and about tools?

*Father:*      That's right.

*Daughter:*  But that must mean that in people there is a whole set of ideas or whatnot which are all tied together. A sort of second creature within the whole person; and that second creature must have a quite different way of thinking about everything. An objective way.

*Father:*      Yes. The royal road to consciousness and objectivity is through language and tools.

*Daughter:*  But what happens when this creature looks at all those parts of the person about which it is difficult for people to be objective? Does it just look? Or does it meddle?

*Father:*      It meddles.

*Daughter:*  And what happens?

*Father:*      That's a very terrible question.

*Daughter:* Go on. If we are going to study animals, we must face that question.

*Father:* Well . . . The poets and artists know the answer better than the scientists. Let me read you a piece:

*Thought* chang'd the infinite to a serpent, that which pitieth
To a devouring flame; and man fled from its face and hid
In forests of night: then all the eternal forests were divided
Into earths rolling in circles of space, that like an ocean rush'd
And overwhelmed all except this finite wall of flesh.
Then was the serpent temple form'd, image of infinite
Shut up in finite revolutions; and man became an Angel,
Heaven a mighty circle turning, God a tyrant crown'd.[5]

*Daughter:* I don't understand it. It sounds terrible but what does it mean?

*Father:* Well. It's not an objective statement, because it is talking about the *effect of* objectivity—what the poet calls here "thought"—upon the whole person or the whole of life. "Thought" should remain a part of the whole but instead spreads itself and meddles with the rest.

*Daughter:* Go on.

*Father:* Well. It slices everything to bits.

*Daughter:* I don't understand.

*Father:* Well, the first slice is between the objective thing and the rest. And then *inside* the creature that's made in the model of intellect, language and tools, it is natural that *purpose* will evolve. Tools are for purposes and anything which blocks purpose is a hindrance. The world of the objective creature gets split into "helpful" things and "hindering" things.

*Daughter:* Yes, I see that.

*Father:*  All right. Then the creature applies that split to the world of the whole person, and "helpful" and "hindering" become Good and Evil, and the world is then split between God and the Serpent. And after that, more and more splits follow because the intellect is always classifying and dividing things up.

*Daughter:*  Multiplying explanatory principles beyond necessity?

*Father:*  That's right.

*Daughter:*  So, inevitably, when the objective creature looks at animals, it splits things up and makes the animals look like human beings *after* their intellects have invaded their souls.

*Father:*  Exactly. It's a sort of inhuman anthropomorphism.

*Daughter:*  And that is why the objective people study all the little [things] instead of the larger things?

*Father:*  Yes. It's called S-R psychology. It's easy to be objective about sex but not about love.

When I was in school, I spent a part of every summer with my father, but I saw him less frequently in college and then, after I was married and in graduate school, where the fascination of trying to communicate with people from other cultures had led me into linguistics, our visits were spaced further and further apart. So when I accepted an invitation from him to come to a conference in Austria, I was looking forward to our first intellectual collaboration. As an adolescent, I had berated my father for his cynically stated reluctance to become involved, his sense that the universities and the political and economic structures of the world were irremediably steeped in folly. Now, in the emerging awareness of ecological crisis, he had decided to care again, so this would be our first collaboration in commitment as well.

His invitation to the conference came with a Memorandum detailing the question of whether human consciousness, perhaps especially as it is shaped in modern western culture, "might contain systematic distortions of view which, when implemented by modern technology, become destructive of the balances between individual man, human society, and the ecosystem of the planet":

---

*Effects of Conscious Purpose on Human Adaptation*[6]
"Progress," "learning," "evolution," the similarities and differences between phylogenetic and cultural evolution, and so on, have been subjects for discussion for many years. These matters become newly investigable in the light of cybernetics and systems theory.

In this conference, a particular aspect of this wide subject matter will be examined, namely the role of *consciousness* in the ongoing process of human adaptation.

Three cybernetic or homeostatic systems will be considered: the individual human organism, the human society, and the larger ecosystem. Consciousness will be considered as an important component in the *coupling* of these systems.

A question of great scientific interest and perhaps grave importance is whether the information processed through consciousness is adequate and appropriate for the task of human adaptation.

To introduce this question the following considerations are offered:

1. All biological and evolving systems (i.e., individual organisms, animal and human societies, ecosystems and the like) consist of complex cybernetic networks and all such systems share certain formal characteristics. Each system contains subsystems which are potentially regenerative, i.e., which would go into exponential "runaway" if uncorrected. (Examples of such regenerative components are: Malthusian characteristics of population, schismogenic changes of personal interaction, armaments races, etc.) The regenerative potentialities of such subsystems are typically kept in check by various sorts of governing loops to achieve "steady state." Such systems are "conservative" in the sense that they tend to conserve the truth of propositions about the values of their component variables—especially they conserve the values of those variables which otherwise would show exponential change. Such systems are homeostatic, i.e., the effects of

small changes of input will be negated and the steady state maintained by *reversible* adjustment.

2. But *"plus c'est la même chose, plus ça change."* This converse of the French aphorism seems to be the more exact description of biological and ecological systems. A constancy of some variable is maintained by changing other variables. This is characteristic of the engine with a governor: the constancy of rate of rotation is maintained by altering the fuel supply. *Mutatis mutandis*, the same logic underlies evolutionary progress: those mutational changes will be perpetuated which contribute to the constancy of that complex variable which we call "survival." The same logic also applies to learning, social change, etc. The ongoing truth of certain descriptive propositions is maintained by altering other propositions.

3. In systems containing many interconnected homeostatic loops, the changes brought about by an external impact may slowly spread through the system. To maintain a given variable ($V_1$) at a given value, the values of $V_2$, $V_3$, etc., undergo change. But $V_2$ and $V_3$ may themselves be subject to homeostatic control or may be linked to variables ($V_4$, $V_5$, etc.) which are subject to control. This second-order homeostasis may lead to change in $V_6$, $V_7$, etc. And so on.

4. This phenomenon of spreading change is in the widest sense a sort of *learning*. Acclimation and addiction are special cases of this process. Over time, the system becomes dependent upon the continued presence of that original external impact whose immediate effects were neutralized by the first-order homeostasis.

Example: Under impact of Prohibition, the American social system reacted homeostatically to maintain the constancy of the supply of alcohol. A new profession, the bootlegger, was generated. To control this profession, changes occurred in the police system. When the question of repeal was raised, it was expectable that certainly the bootleggers and possibly the police would be in favor of maintaining Prohibition.

In this ultimate sense, all biological change is conservative.

5. In extreme cases, change will precipitate or permit some runaway or slippage along the potentially exponential curves

of the underlying regenerative circuits. This may occur without total destruction of the system. The slippage along exponential curves will, of course, always be limited, in extreme cases, by breakdown of the system. Short of this disaster, other factors may limit the slippage.

6. It is important, however, to note that there is a danger of reaching levels at which the limit is imposed by factors which are in themselves deleterious. Wynne-Edwards has pointed out that—as every farmer knows—a population of healthy individuals cannot be directly limited by the available food supply. If starvation is the method of getting rid of the excess population, then the survivors will suffer if not death, at least severe dietary deficiency, while the food supply itself will be reduced, perhaps irreversibly, by overgrazing. In principle, the homeostatic controls of biological systems must be activated by variables which are not in themselves harmful. The reflexes of respiration are activated not by oxygen deficiency but by relatively harmless $CO_2$ excess. The diver who learns to ignore the signals of $CO_2$ excess and continues his dive to approach oxygen deficiency runs serious risks.

7. The problem of coupling self-corrective systems together is central in the adaptation of man to the societies and ecosystems in which he lives. Lewis Carroll long ago joked about the nature and order of *randomness* created by the inappropriate coupling of biological systems. In Carroll's famous game of croquet, Alice is coupled with a flamingo, and the "ball" is a hedgehog. The "purposes" (if we may use the term) of these contrasting biological systems are so discrepant that the randomness of play can no longer be delimited with finite sets of alternatives, known to the players.

Alice's difficulty arises from the fact that she does not "understand" the flamingo, i.e., she does not have systemic information about the "system" which confronts her. Similarly, the flamingo does not understand Alice. They are at "cross purposes." The problem of coupling man through consciousness with his biological environment is comparable. If consciousness lacks information about the nature of man and the environment, or if the information is distorted and inappropriately selected, then the coupling is likely to generate meta-random sequences of events.

8. It is surely true that the content of consciousness is no random sample of reports on events occurring in the remainder of mind. Rather, the content of the screen of consciousness is systematically selected from the enormously great plethora of mental events. But of the rules and preferences of this selection, very little is known. The matter requires investigation. Similarly, the limitations of verbal language require consideration.

9. It appears, however, that the system of selection of information for the screen of consciousness is importantly related to "purpose," "attention," and similar phenomena which are also in need of definition, elucidation, etc.

10. If consciousness has feedback upon the remainder of mind and if consciousness deals only with a skewed sample of the events of the total mind, then there must exist a systematic (i.e., non-random) difference between the conscious views of self and the world and the true nature of self and the world. Such a difference must distort the processes of adaptation.

11. It is suggested that the specific nature of this distortion is such that the *cybernetic nature of self and the world tends to be imperceptible to consciousness,* insofar as the contents of the "screen" of consciousness are determined by considerations of purpose. The argument of purpose tends to take the form "D is desirable; B leads to C; C leads to D; so D can be achieved by way of B and C." But, if the total mind and the outer world do not, in general, have this lineal structure, then by forcing this structure upon them, we become blind to the cybernetic circularities of the self and the external world. Our conscious sampling of data will not disclose whole circuits but only arcs of circuits, cut off from their matrix by our selective attention. Specifically, the attempt to achieve a change in a given variable, located either in self or environment, is likely to be undertaken without comprehension of the homeostatic network surrounding that variable. The considerations outlined in paragraphs 1 to 7 of this essay will then be ignored. It may be essential for *wisdom,* that the narrow purposive view be somehow corrected.

To conclude, let us remember that Job's narrow piety, his purposiveness, his common sense and his worldly success are

finally stigmatized, in a marvelous totemic poem, by the Voice
out of the Whirlwind:
> Who is this that darkeneth counsel by words
> without understanding . . .
> Dost thou know when the wild goats of the
> rock bring forth?
> Or canst thou tell when the hinds do calve?

---

As the time of the conference approached, I began to receive details from the Wenner-Gren Foundation (which was
sponsoring it) about transportation to Burg Wartenstein, their
European Conference Center in Austria, and about the format
of our meetings; there would be fourteen of us meeting for
seven days, intensively together and isolated from all outside
ties. We would be trying, by our combined efforts, to understand something of the nature of that "wisdom" that would
allow man to act in human society and in the natural world,
with all the complex interactions or "couplings" between these
systems, without precipitating changes that would in the end
be deleterious or fatal to himself. The aspect of wisdom which
my father had emphasized in the Memorandum was the limited
awareness of complexity imposed by purposive consciousness,
and against this he set the insight of cybernetics into the nature
of stability and change, namely that all change can be understood as the effort to maintain some constancy and all constancy
as maintained through change.

When I received the instructions about preparing papers, I
began to muse on the way in which language might enforce
lineal thinking in general, and variations on this in particular
cultures. I looked forward to the conference with some trepida-
tion mixed with my excitement. I had taken no biology in college and almost no mathematics, and I was sure I would be far
out of my depth in technical discussions. What I brought from
my childhood was a willingness to think in systemic terms—
but not a skilled use of the terminology. I remembered sitting
and listening to hours and hours of adult talk which drifted in
and out of the range of my understanding, constantly working

to find a way of listening that would be meaningful for me. Often the children of intellectual parents simply block out such talk. I suppose that what made it possible for me to listen was that I could hear the emotion in the voices: the vivid concern about the problems that were being discussed and the delight at the interweaving of the ideas. Now I could go to Austria with the conviction that the problems we would be discussing were urgent and that new understanding would have to be developed to meet them, not just concern and a willingness to work hard.

During all of this preparation, I was in Manila, where my husband had been working on a project from Harvard Business School and I was teaching and doing field work. We were coming to the end of our stay in the Philippines and planned to reach Europe on our slow trip home just in time for the conference but, in the middle of this planning, I discovered that I was pregnant and began writing to the Wenner-Gren office about travel plans and doctors in Vienna. In March I went on a retreat, spending four days as the guest of gentle Filipina nuns, wandering between the garden and the chapel, luminously happy. Indeed, I may have spent more time in the garden, my thought centered by looking carefully at a snail or a beetle at least as well as by a spoken prayer. The tropical fauna of the Philippines was elegant and extravagant and I spent many hours looking at different creatures, without knowing their names or habits. I was quietly very much amused at this unexpected pregnancy in disregard of my planning and conscious purposes, and in meditation I had a sense of wonder at the beauty and intricacy of the human body. For me, very intellectual and professional and responsible, it seemed amazing that the foetus lived and grew regardless of whether I was paying attention at any particular moment of time. The pregnancy did not go well, however, and in May a son was born prematurely. We called him Martin and he lived for an afternoon and then died.

Grief is too familiar a part of all of our experience to need describing. But to explain the state of mind in which I went to the conference, it needs saying that at the deepest level I tried to meet my grief by weaving a wonder at death into a wonder about life that included the human body and birth and even the smallest creatures in the grass. Nevertheless, I arrived at the conference believing that I could now put these feelings aside and engage with an intellectual problem, and this, I suppose, is what many of us believed. The conference ritual, with its trappings of papers and tape recorders, resulting in a partial meeting of minds and perhaps a volume for publication, was familiar to us all, and I was off to show my mettle and do my job as rapporteur and linguist-anthropologist. The list of participants included a few strangers, a few casual acquaintances, and, in addition to my father, a few people beloved from my childhood, but I went to meet them in the chosen estrangement that is perhaps an immediate result of the separation of thought and emotion. Indeed, it is out of our separation of ourselves from nature and the separation of our minds from our bodies that all of our estrangements are forged. If we had no notion of transcendent mind, no mind-body problem, we would not be lonely.

This was essentially the problem that all of us brought as we gathered at Burg Wartenstein, a problem that was slowly resolved as we used our intellectual discussions in taking soundings for a deeper knowledge of each other.

# IN PREPARATION
# FOR THE ADVENT
# OF AWARENESS

*[The First Three Days]*

# · C H A P T E R  1 ·

# Around the Circle

THE CONFERENCE WAS HELD in a castle, the fortress of Wartenstein which stands on a peak above the town of Gloggnitz, guarding the Semmering Pass. We had arrived in the afternoon, meeting and greeting, and then the following morning we gathered around a great round table in an upstairs conference room.

Most of that first morning was spent in self-introductions, our first groping efforts to get to know one another. Each of us, a few feet apart, dominated an arc of the table and each of us brought some special background so that as our knowledge was combined we would be able to talk about the circular patterns in nature.

First was Warren McCulloch, my father's earliest colleague in the group. He had been chairman of the Macy Foundation Conference on Cybernetics and before that they had met at the Conference on Cerebral Inhibition in 1942. Warren was studying such problems as how it is possible to reach out for something and had discovered that what appears to be a straight course is actually composed of oscillations, where coordination is continually being corrected for small errors of aim. It was to the study of such self-corrective feedback processes that Norbert Wiener eventually applied the name cybernetics.

Warren had bright, fierce eyes and held his head dropped

23

low between thin shoulders. He had white hair and a white beard and a curious blend of glee and grief, of belligerence and gentleness. The night before, those of us who were not too tired had sat around the fire after dinner, all rather bewildered by the new place and too many cocktails, and talked briefly about the form which a record of our proceedings might take. Warren sat down in the lotus position and interrupted with anecdotes about the mistakes of recorders. "I talked about a Turing machine, the editor turned it into an automobile. I talked about taking a woman under a tree while a mocking-bird was singing, the editor turned it into a nightingale." He looked at me belligerently, with the fire snapping in the fireplace behind him. "My telephone is always tapped. I'm always on these Presidential committees; they'd be crazy if they didn't bug it. I let my friends talk on the telephones; they're always planning with someone, say in Washington, how to go to bed. I just send any message I care. No one can tap and get anything; no one bothers to listen. There is a bug against a bug, but I don't bother. They say to me, 'do you solemnly swear . . . ?' and I say I'm interested in other things. In everything people say I see a kind of mishmash and I intend to fight like hell to get the concepts sharper than hell."

As we went around the table with introductions, Warren said, "Well, I'm an old man. I was born in '98. I expected to be a theologian. I got seduced by mathematics. I got interested in the epistemic problems of all science, particularly mathematics. I majored in philosophy, minored in psychology, went to medical school in order to get the workings of a machine called a brain. I've been at it ever since. I have lived among brilliant youngsters who keep turning up new ideas all the time. I am very happy, very puzzled, very hopeful."

Beyond Warren was Barry Commoner, whom I had met just once before, at lunch with my mother, when both were working on the beginnings in St. Louis of what has come to be called the "Information Movement"—the effort by scientists to make technical facts available to the public, so that moral decisions on policies affecting the environment could be made

by an informed citizenry. I find in my booklet of data about
participants that he is the author of numerous papers on
"tobacco mosaic virus biosynthesis, fast kinetics of unpaired
electrons in photosynthetic systems, electron spin resonance
spectrometry, deoxyribonucleic acid, and the molecular basis
of self-duplication," but he is above all a political animal, a
warm, enthusiastic New Yorker whose comments tend to grow
into speeches. After years of research on phenomena at the
borderline between living and nonliving things, Barry inveighs
against the reductionist assumption that the way to study complex wholes is by fragmenting them and studying their parts,
instead of looking for emergent properties which exist only in
the whole. This is the philosophical position he brings to an
involvement in the question of environmental pollution.

Next to Barry was Will Jones, a historian of philosophy
whom I had not met before, and beyond him was Fred Attneave, a psychologist specializing in problems of perception, a
tall man with a goatee and a careful Southern pronunciation.
Both Will and Fred commented as they introduced themselves
that they were not sure why they had been invited, or what
contribution they would have to make to the conference.

Beyond them was Gordon Pask, a British cyberneticist
perched and grinning in his chair like a leprechaun. He and
my father had never met, but each had recently begun to read
the other's work, intrigued and hungry for more. In deference
to his Britishness, we vacillated between calling him Pask and
Gordon. Gordon had submitted a long and difficult paper attempting to give cybernetic precision to the notions "goal,"
"purpose," and "individual."

Bernie Raxlen, who had been invited to join the conference
at the last moment, sat beyond Gordon, and next to him was
Horst Mittelstaedt, a German scientist. He was trained as a
zoologist and then self-trained as a cyberneticist and physicist.
"My scientific history is practically isomorphic to Barry Com-
moner's," he said. "I went to study under Erich von Holst and
I got my thesis on the equilibrium of dragonflies. Since von
Holst, we could see that the system was the important thing,

but at that time the atomistic approach was overwhelming. Reflex theory dominated the thing. So in order to make myself understood to the atomists, I invented the setting of the reaference value of feedback loops, and I thought it was a new discovery. Then we got the Macy papers and von Holst came in and whispered, 'They know it already, they have it.' Well, we found quite a lot of work still to be done, particularly the . . . this . . . mathematicians, as precise and sharp as they seem to be sometimes, have this curious . . . thinking seems difficult for them, actually. So we tried to clear up, *ja*, what cybernetics really is. Then, because we studied equilibrium in dragonflies and fish, perceptual systems, how our environment seems to be stable and so on, I have an interest in the mind-body problem . . ."

"Would you mind telling me what you mean by the mind-body problem?" Warren interrupted darkly.

Horst blinked. "Well, if you assume the Cartesian view, Cartesian dualism, then you have it immediately, one word, 'body,' which is sort of objective, and another one that seems to be totally unrelated, some sort of epiphenomenon that we call 'mind.' It's artificial. It comes into play only if you've assumed a Cartesian partition."

Will Jones in his paper had explored the history of the mind-body problem in his careful, scholarly way:

---

The basic formula was worked out by Descartes. There are, he held, two fundamentally different kinds of substance—*res cogitans* and *res extensa*. *Res extensa* has just those properties that the new physics was interested in. It is extended; it is inert, but in motion, being propelled by "outside" forces; its motion is completely determined by antecedent events in time. *Res extensa*, it will be noted, lacks all those properties (color, taste, smell, life) which physics felt incapable of handling. These other properties are assigned by Descartes to *res cogitans*. How does thinking substance come to know the motions that are occurring in extended substance? Descartes' answer was that changes in *res extensa* are communicated through the intervening medium to our sense organs (which are of course a part of *res extensa*) and so to our brains (also a part of *res extensa*). Changes in brain state occasion ideas, and these ideas correspond precisely to those changes out there in *res extensa* which are their ultimate causes.

The most important element in this whole scheme was the notion that mind and matter are substances, for a substance is, by definition, independent; it is something that stands alone. Accordingly, mind would be just exactly what it is, if there were no physical world; and so would matter, if there were no minds. Of course, if there were no minds, matter would remain unknown. But when we come to know something, the mind enters into the presence of the object that it contemplates in much the same way that a ship maneuvers up to a dock. Neither mind nor matter is fundamentally altered by the knowledge relationship; each remains itself, just as, when the ship moves away from the dock, ship and dock will be intact. If this were not the case—if either mind or matter were altered in any fundamental way as a result of cognition —then minds could never know the "true nature" of self and of world. In the Cartesian world view, *res extensa* was perceived as a completely self-enclosed, encapsulated territory; none of the "truths" that physicists were discovering about *res extensa* could have any bearing on the truths established in theology, nor could the truths established in theology have any bearing on the truths established in physics. Hence the theological establishment ought to leave the physicists alone to get on with their business.

---

Next to Horst in the circle was Peter Klopfer. The last time my father and Peter had met, Peter had been studying goats, and now he had shifted to galagos, a kind of proto-primate, sometimes called bush babies. Not only were his expressions and movements subtly changed, but he had grown a beard for the creatures to hang from, so that when we gathered for cocktails, after arriving, my father had failed to recognize him. When he described his background, he said: "I suppose my major activities have been in the question of what determines the number of co-existing species in a particular area. Then secondly, I've looked at questions of what causes an infant to stay with its mother and why some mothers are good mothers and some aren't—problems which involve studies of perception, self-awareness, play, all of which I think bear some relation to the problems of consciousness."

Beyond Peter was Tolly Holt. Tolly was another member of the group whom I had known since my childhood, when he visited the house as an adolescent and later as a graduate student, talking passionately of his work and teaching me miscellaneous bits of mathematics. Tolly was forty-two, but you would have to look carefully for the marks of years and grief or you would think he was twenty-five. He sat in the sessions broad-shouldered in an old turtle-necked shirt, curly black hair standing on end or falling forward on his brow, his emotions— glee, exasperation, rage—playing freely across his face.

He described a long journey from field to field: first psychology, then physics and chemistry, then mathematics and linguistics, and finally work with computers. "It took me about fifteen years, from the time that my intellectual life began, to notice that I did not want to be a scientist. It's clear to everyone, I would think, that what one sees is a function of the glasses one looks through, as well as of what's out there to be seen. What I do is to fashion glasses that you look through—I build conceptual toys which make it possible to see things in interesting and useful ways.

"I had a terrible time writing a paper. I'd like to read a couple of opening paragraphs of one that I started in a burst of anger and never finished:

---

The title of our conference, "The Effects of Conscious Purpose on Human Adaptation," has the *form* of a scientific question but the substance of a warning cry. Bateson observes that we (humankind), riding on our technology, seem to be on the steepest incline of a toboggan run, accelerating with all our might toward the void of total destruction. "Stop this insanity!" he cries with the sentence: "It may well be that consciousness contains systematic distortions of view, which, when implemented by modern technology, become destructive of the balances between man and his society and his ecosystem"; and "Wake up before it's too late!" with the sentence: "It is suggested that the specific nature of this distortion is such that the cybernetic nature of self and the world tends to be imperceptible to consciousness." He rightly observes that this has the form of a system failure—i.e., cybernetic failure. Given our monstrous capacities to amplify and distribute information and power, it has become possible for a very small number of human decisions to create effects which alter the fundamental conditions of existence for very large segments of the human population.

I passionately endorse the cry of warning and the fitness of the forthcoming conference as a means to amplify it.

I reject the implication that we are to be convened as scientists to consider what can be hypothesized, objectively observed, tested and measured, etc., about human consciousness in relation to human adaptation.

I also reject the broader cultural climate which lends such especial prestige to the so-called "objective truth" as revealed to science. An attack upon this climate, even if detrimental to scientists, may do as much toward blocking the race to destruction as any cybernetic truths which our conference may uncover."

---

When he finished reading, Tolly looked up. "I decided not to write that paper, so what I did was to try and sing my own song. I tried to describe without mathematics what I've done about trying to clarify the notion 'system.' "

Beyond Tolly was Gertrude Hendrix, who is a teacher of mathematics and a teacher of teachers, from Indiana, where an avocation of training and raising horses has informed her studies of teaching and learning. We had met five years before at a conference on how people communicate with one another outside of language. Next to her was Bert Kaplan, who described himself as a psychologist who had spent most of his career trying to get outside of psychology. "I have taken up the strange subject of psychology as a humanistic discipline, building on the traditions of eighteenth- and nineteenth-century German philosophy, and I am interested in the phenomenon of consciousness as identical with the phenomenon of humanness, something changing and moving. I suspect that I'm at the fuzzy end of the continuum of clearness on this," he said awkwardly. "The only clear thought that I have or that I'm able to hold in mind is Cartesian dualism. When I leave that, I find that whatever clarity I have disappears."

"I was amazed; your paper was most unfuzzy. I thought it is not quite Cartesian at all," said Horst helpfully.

Ted Schwartz introduced himself as bringing a special concern for the cybernetic understanding of the development of goals in social movements. He described himself as an anthropologist interested in linguistics, and I described myself as a linguist interested in anthropology.

Finally we completed the circle and came to my father, Gregory Bateson, the organizer of the conference. I will call him Gregory, as the others did. He is a very tall man and gives himself a massive look by hunching great shoulders as if to conceal his height. He sat at the conference table alternately quizzical and hollow-eyed, chain smoking with fingers stained dark with nicotine. "I grew up thirty years obsolete on pre-Mendelian genetics," he began. "My father had been a geneticist before Mendel was rediscovered. Genetics was then the problem of how an organism becomes internally organized and patterned: why, for instance, if you have monstrously two hands on the end of a single arm, those two hands have to be one right and one left, disposed as mirror images of each other, and similar problems of biological regularity. I left zoology and pursued the same problems in New Guinea: how regularity is maintained in a culture, how the internal morphology of a culture is kept in order by the internal dynamics of the relations between persons, and how persons are, in a sense, patterned in their ways of thought and action to fit in with this cultural or social morphology."

As Gregory went on to talk about the origins of this conference and some of the correspondence which had taken place during the planning period, I looked around the table at the curious group he had gathered. More than half of us were people who had shifted fields at least once in our lives and even those who continued to bear the same labels had been deeply involved in interdisciplinary work. The ages ranged from Warren's seventy years to Bernie and myself in our late twenties. Three, perhaps four intellectual generations sat at that table: Warren was the senior who had introduced Gregory to some of the ideas that would be crucial; Gregory in turn had passed his ideas on to Tolly fifteen years before; and Bernie was even now his student.

There was also a great variation in what each of us experienced as science and in the texture of our normal working hours. Tolly fiddling with a pencil, Ted sitting and talking with a New Guinea native, Peter holding a galago or a kid in his arms, Barry in a biochemical laboratory, Gertrude in a high school classroom—each one brought an experience of search that would contribute differently to the attempt to move toward discovery in this context of discussion. I felt in the fresh morning a warm anticipation of hearing what these different people would have to say, although I had been little touched by the prepared papers I had received in the mail during the preceding weeks. More than anything else, I was delighted at the idea of a thesis on the equilibrium of dragonflies.

"What I'm mainly interested in," said Gregory, "is a formal description of the ways in which human planning and applied science tend to generate pathology in the society or in the ecosystem or in the individual. Tolly raised the question of whether screaming a warning is a scientific act; it is not, until you're able to express that warning in rather formal terms. What I think we're here to construct, really, is a sort of meta-applied-science. Applied science is something about which you can ask scientific questions, moving up a level of abstraction, and I think this is a reasonable subject for us to be investigating. I rather doubt whether we shall come up with much clarity on the subject of consciousness and I think on the whole we would do well for the moment to use this as a rather vague heuristic term.

"I find I've been giving a great deal of thought lately to mind-body problems. Horst mentioned the 'mind-body problem,' and McCulloch said: 'What is it?' Well, McCulloch has recently published his collected essays under the title *Embodiments of Mind*,[1] in which he substantially follows a biological position which, I believe, was first taken by Lamarck at the very beginning of the nineteenth century. Lamarck, of course, was not majorly interested in evolution, but in the nature of mind; only about a third of his *Philosophie zoologique*[2] is devoted to evolution."

Lamarck's work followed on centuries in which forms of life were classified as creations and partial reflections of the Divine Mind at the apex of the taxonomy, with man just below, "a little lower than the angels." "He took the whole taxonomy of the animals, the Great Chain of Being, and looked at it upside down, saying that it starts not with mind at the top, but with the protozoa at the bottom, the infusoria, and goes *upward* by evolutionary change. Then it became logical for him to see mind not as the *explanation* of the whole chain, but as the *explanandum*, that which is to be explained by it. He reached the point of saying that mind is immanent in whatever complexity might be appropriate for its generation, rather than transcendent. We, today, can look at the orders of complexity among material things which will exhibit mental-type behaviors, self-corrective behaviors, and so on. To this extent, up to consciousness but not including it, there is, in a sense, no 'mind-body' problem.

"On the other hand, man over the last two thousand years has always and necessarily had his solutions to the mind-body problem. As Blake puts it:

> All Bibles or sacred codes, have been the causes of the following errors: 1. That man has two real existing principles, viz: a Body & a Soul . . . but the following Contraries to these are True. 1. Man has no Body distinct from his Soul for that call'd Body is a portion of Soul discern'd by the five Senses, the chief inlets of Soul in this age.[3]

'*A portion of Soul discern'd by the five Senses.*' All our ideas of responsibility, our social forms, our ideas of will, the whole supernaturalism of religion, and so forth—these are all expressions of folk solutions to the mind-body problem. I suspect that, in addition to the sort of false coupling that I tried to talk about in my Memorandum, a part of our disturbance today in social matters, on the campuses or in the cities, is related to the fact that our folk theory of mind-body relations, which has on the whole been predicated on the notion of transcendent mind, has undergone really profound change and that our social structures no longer fit our current folk ideas about mind-body. The new wine does not sit very well in the old bottles."

There was general agreement that it would be necessary to spend some time talking about popular attitudes, as well as about the rigorous cybernetic or mathematical aspect of problems. Warren said, "We have folkways in our country that . . . In the Armed Services Committee of the Senate of the United States, it's not merely that the men are senile, that would be bad enough. But there is a tradition so fixed with them, from so far back, that it is going to be more difficult to contain them than it will be to contain the 'Roman Holidays' in our cities. I think the world goes through periods in which it generates religions and I think it's hit one of those again."

"A time for a rephrasing of the mind-body problem, in fact," Gregory added. Warren nodded.

"I think that a lot of very ancient human habits have become maladaptive," said Tolly, "especially the kinds of habits that interest me most, which are the symbolizing and conceptualizing habits. For example, if one man comes to another and says he can do something cheaper, then there are, generally speaking, no arguments, right? And letting him then go ahead has been okay under the conditions that have prevailed for a long time in the human world and is well on its way toward being not okay. Similarly, when people say they want to undertake some enterprise, this is an initial step toward organizing activity on behalf of getting it done, and that, too, is no longer quite so safe as it once was. What's changed is the order of magnitude of effect which can be created by 'undertaking something or other,' both because we are able to produce fantastic physical power and because it is now possible to communicate to an extent that was previously unheard of. As soon as you have the Joint Chiefs of Staff, who dispose of a certain kind of power, the context has changed to such an extent that it's no longer clear, right? that they can proceed with their purposes without destroying what you hold dear." What Gregory once referred to as the "power-ratio" between purposive consciousness and the environment has shifted massively in the last century and continues to shift at an accelerating rate. "Anyhow," said Tolly, "you know, I talk like I guess most of us do, from a kind of prejudiced, human point of view. I mean *me* and *us* to survive."

As we continued groping toward a definition of our agenda, I was amazed to find that the word "consciousness" itself was for some the subject of the conference, rather than a landmark used in tracing out the more general theme of Gregory's Memorandum. We were going to feel two different pulls, one from those who wanted to explore abstractions, such as "consciousness," and work toward precise definitions, and one from those who would want to go directly into planning ways of bringing about change, what we came to call the "political problem."

Gregory had explained in a letter, some weeks before we gathered, that his concern with consciousness was related to its apparent etymology—the possibility of sharing information. We would be concerned with "the distortions of group planning which result from the sharing of only a skewed sample of total available information, where language and various sorts of needs to conform act as filters to limit what can be shared and act to determine goals and plans which can be commonly envisaged." Coming from our different backgrounds, we too were confronted with the challenge of developing a common, non-lineal consciousness, a shared and mutual knowing.

And yet, difficult as the task seemed, there probably would have been no way of bringing together all the different strands that would be important in our thinking except by gathering such a group, with the special, twisted career lines of each person. Issues in the history of science, which have long since merged into familiar common-sense categories—the belief that wholes are best studied by reducing them to their parts, that the objective and the subjective can be separated in the effort to analyze and manipulate a physical world "out there" contrasted with the internal world of experience and perception—these would have to be combined with an examination of the actual effects of technology. We would have to think at once of man's creative consciousness and individuality and the sheer mass of human bodies on this globe. Gregory had posed for us the problem of the coupling of individual organisms (including persons), societies, and the ecosystem, so that inevitably we needed expert knowledge of each, but even more urgently we needed the mathematical and cybernetic knowledge to trace the ways in which each system acted in order to maintain continuity—certain crucial constancies—producing changes to which other systems responded. Even though it was an effort to work my way through the more formal, abstract papers, I was prepared to believe this approach was central.

Gregory had proposed that we start by asking Barry Commoner to give us a picture of the crisis in the environment, which we could then examine in terms of the abstract structure of the errors that had been made. "I don't think we can plan action until we've gone through the intellectual phase, but I think the rather structured documentation of the urgency, not just a scream but a formal statement of the sort of thing that happens, will be very important here. I suggest we now drink our coffee and then ask Barry to start us off."

When we broke for coffee we had spent almost two hours in the initial attempt to get to know each other and set a direction for our talk.

· C H A P T E R   2 ·

# The Substance of

# a Warning Cry

IT WAS BARRY WHO kindled the concern of the group, making
the danger to our world immediate to all of us, so that our
search for understanding could become a vivid and impassioned
quest. Even though each of us knew some of the story and all
of us knew in principle that we were in a time of "ecological
crisis," we were quickly caught up in this analysis of the slow
unraveling of the texture of our lives. It was like the story of a
nation gradually slipping into open war: attack and foray and
threat are followed fast by open conflicts, each one promising
to restore harmony, and we end with the harmony of dusty
fields and lifeless ponds.

Barry emphasized how strange our acts, committed again
and again without a knowledge of their consequences, seem if
we try to think of man as conscious of what he does, acting out
of understanding. For example, we used to be told that radiation from the fallout produced in nuclear tests was harmless;
the danger from Strontium-90 was first mentioned in a government publication as arising only in the unlikely event of someone eating a sliver of bone! Only now, long after the damage
has been done, we know differently. The bombs were exploded
before we had even a partial understanding that they would
increase the incidence of harmful mutations, leukemia, and

36

birth defects. Smog was another effect of technology that should have been predicted, and yet the chemical nature of smog was not known until it had been massively produced—the first analysis was made simply by piping Los Angeles air into a laboratory. Barry shook his head. "You see, don't you, science is simply acting backwards."

Barry continued the appalling roster of recent technological mistakes in the environment: lead additives in automobile fuels reaching toxic levels in the air; insecticides unexpectedly killing birds and fish, as well as insects, and even accumulating in the human body, permeating the environment to the point where there may soon be no insect-eating birds left, no earthworms to turn and aerate the soil of our fields and forests, and the carnivorous fish of the ocean become too dangerous for man to eat. We have non-degradable detergents in our rivers, herbicides in Vietnam, alterations in the temperature and gases in the atmosphere—and the possibility of nuclear war. Barry went on to give a detailed description of the nitrogen cycle and man's interference with it, both because it shows so well the circular character of natural processes and because it shows how interventions at different points combine to increase the seriousness of the situation. The convergences in the skein of disasters made the story an epic of destruction.

Nitrogen, with carbon, hydrogen, and oxygen, is one of the four chemical elements that make up the bulk of living matter. These elements move in great interwoven circles through the biosphere: now a component of the air, now a constituent of a living organism, now part of some waste product in water, after a time perhaps built into mineral deposits or fossil remains. Barry first described the nitrogen cycle as it occurs in the water, drawing on the board a circular diagram familiar from high school biology, a diagram as applicable to my tiny aquarium when it was in balance as to huge lakes and rivers. As we saw, nitrogen passes through a variety of compounds with carbon and hydrogen, and there is, in the natural cycle, a narrow stage when it is in an oxidized inorganic form: after waste has been converted by the bacteria of decay into $NO_3$ and before the

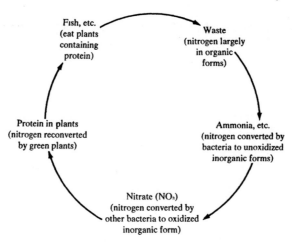

green plants nourished by it have reconverted it. In general, the scarcity of nitrogen in chemical combination with oxygen is conspicuous throughout nature. Life originated in an environment from which free oxygen was absent, and it is in its unoxidized form that nitrogen appears in thousands of organic compounds. By contrast, there are very few organic compounds containing oxidized nitrogen and these are rare and toxic.

The cycle Barry illustrated is the normal one, continually occurring in natural bodies of water so long as the equilibrium is not destroyed by human interference. In a balanced natural system, the amounts of organic nitrogen and nitrate dissolved in the water remain low, the population of algae and fish is correspondingly small, and the water is clear and pure. This was recognized by man, who discovered that water repurified itself and saw this as a solution to the problem of sewage disposal. This worked well as long as the quantities of additional waste were not too great to be assimilated into the cycle, but sometime in the mid-nineteenth century it was discovered that the natural cycle could break down when there was not enough oxygen dissolved in the water to sustain bacterial activity; when the oxygen becomes depleted the bacteria die and the body of water goes anaerobic. Thus, a limitation in the oxygen supply creates a bottleneck in the degree to which traffic can be increased in this natural cycle.

The modern sewage plant is a way of domesticating the microbial activities that degrade organic wastes in natural streams and lakes, meeting the oxygen demand by bubbling air into the treatment pools. If the system works well, the resulting water is a clear dilute solution of the inorganic products of sewage treatment, of which nitrate is most important for this story. The inorganic products of sewage treatment, which are free of immediate oxygen demand, can then be released to rivers and lakes without causing an immediate drain on the oxygen available in the natural waters, and presumably flow in the end to the sea.

Barry went on to describe the sewage treatment complex around Lake Erie, serving approximately ten million people. "This was the pride of technology. And do you know, just a few years ago, they discovered the whole thing was wrong! It just doesn't work. The nitrate hadn't been flowing out, most of it simply never left the lake." The effect of eliminating the bottleneck at one stage in the cycle has simply been to shift it to a later stage. Most of the inorganic products released into the lake are reconverted into organic matter in the form of algal protein. When the algae die, their organic matter creates such a huge demand for oxygen that in recent summers most of the central portion of the lake has gone to zero oxygen.[1] One of the symptoms of the sickness of Lake Erie has been the appearance each summer of huge algal "blooms"—vast areas of the lake where, under the impact of excessive fertilization, algal growths give the lake the appearance and consistency of pea soup. Algal blooms grow quickly; they die off equally fast and, sinking into the lake, foul it with decaying organic matter, so that the bottom of the lake has become a huge underwater cesspool. This has so far been contained through most of the year by a layer of iron oxide which forms a skin over this mass during cold weather, but in the summer the "skin" breaks, and the lake begins to asphyxiate from the oxygen demand of the newly released bottom materials. So far, the process has not completely depleted the oxygen before the return of cool weather, but the whole of Lake Erie is likely to go anaerobic quite suddenly. Barry predicted that by the summer of 1980 every river system in the United States could go to zero oxygen in the summer months and thousands of beautifully balanced ecological communities be transformed into rank, muddy sinks and gutters. Such a disaster is hastened, of course, by untreated sewage and industrial wastes poisoning the rivers, but even when these sources of "pollution" are controlled, the process continues. Because nitrate does occur as part of the natural system and because it is not directly offensive to man, it is not usually considered a pollutant and yet by its excess the natural system will be destroyed.

Then Barry went on to talk about the related problems of the nitrogen cycle in the soil. Here the cycle is similar, with the same need for sustaining an oxygen supply: nitrogen compounds are released into the soil by the slow operation of bacteria on decaying organic wastes; for the plants to absorb these and convert them into protein, their roots must be able to breathe. The oxygen supply in the soil depends on its porosity—which is maintained by humus, a complex and poorly understood organic substance which normally contains at least 80 per cent of the soil's nitrogen, in a relatively stable form. Thus, the soil's porosity, its oxygen content, and the efficiency of nutrient absorption are closely related to the organic nitrogen content of the soil.

Now when man begins to farm the land, he harvests the crops, much of which end up as wastes overfertilizing the rivers instead of returning as organic nitrogen to the soil. The technological solution to this has been to supply nitrogen in an inorganic form in chemical fertilizers, which have come into greater and greater use in the United States, encouraged by the Department of Agriculture. In 1942, half a million tons of chemical fertilizer were used; by 1967 the annual figure was six million tons. This makes it possible to maintain or raise productivity, but brings about drastic changes in the soil. Nitrogenous fertilizers do only one of the jobs naturally done by organic nitrogen compounds; they supply nutrients, but they do not support soil porosity to allow oxygen to reach the roots for efficient absorption of those nutrients. Aeration becomes difficult and the soil becomes less able to absorb and store water, so that the overall process decreases in efficiency.[2] Nitrate fertilizer not absorbed by the plants is leached out of the soil and drained—into the lakes and rivers. What man has done is to take a cyclic process and convert it into a lineal one: we cut into the system at the point where nitrogen synthesized into proteins in plants would normally decay into the soil, continuing the cycle; the crops are removed and when they decay the wastes go into the rivers. We treat the severed cycle by a transfusion of inorganic nitrogen at one end and at the other end let it bleed into our surface waters, with terrible consequences at both ends. The split between good—resources—and evil—wastes—is here produced precisely by cutting into circuitry to produce lineality.

Barry predicted a tremendous conflict about whether the cities or the farms are destroying the water. Then he went on to add skein after skein to the tangle of disasters combining to increase nitrate levels. For instance: car engines about a decade ago reached the temperature at which oxygen and nitrogen react, so they now synthesize nitrate from the air, and weed killers inhibit the conversion of nitrate to protein in plants, so that nitrate accumulates in the leaves. Already, excess nitrates, which simply accumulate in plants instead of being converted, present direct threats to consumers.[3] Cottonseed meal used as livestock feed has poisoned animals and within the last ten years infants have been poisoned in Germany, where vegetables are very intensively cultivated, by nitrites to which nitrates in spinach are converted in the digestive process.

Barry summed up with an evaluation of the technological intrusion on the environment: "This has reached a magnitude that matches the scale of the natural processes themselves. Currently about six million tons of inorganic nitrogen fertilizer is added to U.S. soil annually and, at a conservative estimate, perhaps 15 per cent of the annual input of inorganic nitrogen to the soil is lost to surface waters and an equal fraction is lost to the air.[4] From urban waste, agriculture, industry, and transport, together, we intrude roughly five million tons of inorganic nitrogen per year into the U.S. water system. The magnitude of this effect can be visualized by comparing it with the total nitrogen content of the food eaten by the U.S. population, which is, so to speak, a measure of the nitrogen which we extract from our ecosystem annually to support our population. Based on nutritive requirements, this amounts, again very roughly, to about seven million tons of nitrogen per year. Thus the overall magnitude of our technological intrusion into the nitrogen cycle in the U.S. is roughly equivalent to the amount of nitrogen which we withdraw from it as food each year, but it attacks the cycle itself because we introduce it at the wrong points in the cycle and in inappropriate forms. These numbers indicate how large a part of the annual turnover has escaped from the primeval soil-to-food-to-organic-waste cycle. What we take out as organic nitrogen is returned in exactly the wrong form, as inorganic nitrogen, thus creating a tremendous strain at the most sensitive point in the natural cycle.

"I have one other thing to say," Barry concluded. "This description that I've just given you and the comparison of the size of the intrusion was, I guess, unique to me as of 1967. I ran into this and I started to worry and just began digging into it, and there it is. This is childish in terms of science. Here is a fantastic situation in which the fundamental facts have really been known for a long time, but we're somehow totally blind to the consequences, and one reason, I think, is the failure to understand the cybernetic aspects of the situation. Technology has failed us in understanding the way we are relating to natural systems. One can take almost any one of the modern pollution problems—smog, radiation, insecticides, detergents, chemical and biological warfare—and the same kind of appalling saga of disasters can be delineated.

"Take, for example, the business of biological or germ warfare. Presumably this is about setting off artificial epidemics. Now an epidemic is a very complicated thing of feedback and amplification and so on. We know very little about natural epidemics and certainly very little about unnatural ones, because so far as I know, no one has ever tried to start one. There is no way of converting this into a weapon the consequences of which can be even crudely predicted, without testing it on yourself, on a real population, with old people and children and so on . . ."

"We've plenty of generals," Gregory muttered. "They have children."

"Well. All I'm trying to do is get across a sense of the appalling contradiction of this to everything that is involved in the notion of consciousness, or science, if you will—the notion of *human* interactions with the environment. We create these massive effects without knowing what we're doing."

Ted picked Barry up on his assertion that our failure is a failure of cybernetic understanding. "It seems to me that you're not putting your finger on the right place. We do understand it; you have explained it beautifully. Science includes us; we're not talking about 'them.' "

"Right, well, the understanding is not embedded in our technology."

"Not embedded in our technologists, you mean," said Gregory.

"Yes, that's clear. For example, the engineers did not know what the outcome of . . ."

"More important, didn't care," Tolly interpolated.

". . . of non-degradable detergents would be. We now have a flat statement from the chemical engineers who were involved in developing the non-degradable detergents that, in the research and development on this product, no one stopped to ask what happens after the detergents go down the drain.[5] They studied the process of synthesizing them, their washing ability, how easy they are on the hands, how long they'll last on the shelf, their consumer acceptability, and so on, but no one realized that the ultimate consumer is the bacteria."

"The bacteria simply couldn't consume them," said Gregory.

"That's right."

After listening to Barry's presentation, I tried to sort out how much of what he had said I had known myself. The problem seemed to move in and out of focus in my mind. On a simple factual level, I had certainly been familiar with the dangers of soil depletion due to overcultivation and of water pollution due to sewage and industrial waste, even though I would have been hard put to give details on the biological processes involved. In fact, I had been thinking of the depletion problem almost in terms of a simple loss or removal into foodstuffs of something from the soil, which would then not be available for subsequent crops, and thinking of the pollution problem as consisting of additions, additions of noxious fluids and wastes in such bulk that they could not be diluted or washed away. On reflection, however, I knew I had been aware that the richness of the soil was based on the accumulation of decaying organic matter over long periods of time, and my own aquarium had shown me how small quantities of waste could simply disappear. In a curious sense, although I knew of the natural cycles, I had tended to think of the human intrusions as intrusions into a static system, rather than seeing them as entering into an existing and continuing natural cycle at certain points and straining that total cycle. In a sense, biological "resources" and "wastes" exist only as artifacts of the cognitive or actual severing of natural cycles by man.

On the other hand, cyclical models were familiar enough so that once I was shown this set of facts in this particular way, it was not difficult to follow the processes described. I could try and visualize them as in balance or homeostasis, with all of the stages progressing simultaneously at mutually adjusted rates. It was easy to imagine, however, that lacking the model or the language to talk about it, one might look at Barry's diagrams and try to concentrate on small portions of them, not wanting to be distracted by talk about fish in discussing problems of algae or by talk about soil aeration in discussions of nutrients. Looking at short causal chains rather than systems, one might just suppose that an increase at a particular stage would lead to an increase down the line, without wondering what system properties would be affected by such a change.

Now that I had listened to Barry I could repeat the story,

but I knew in another sense as well. I knew in grief and anger, as well as in my intellect, that the continuation of the natural cycles is, for a river or a field, what my own continuing metabolism is in me—life—and that Barry was speaking of the death of rivers and fields.

Later in the day, Will Jones began to develop a typology of ignorance: ignorance of the facts; ignorance resulting from the lack of particular theories or constructs to interpret them; and ignorance resulting from limitations in world views. It was as an example of such a limited world view that he had described for us the Cartesian way of knowing, a world view that affects the interpretations not just of one theory but of whole masses of theories and is still with us today. Finally, he mentioned affective ignorance—the not caring about something that one knows. Only if changes occur at *all* of these levels can the race toward ecological disaster be averted.

Corresponding to Will's analysis of types of ignorance was an array of types of knowledge, which we never listed, and an array of types of learning that we experienced in those days. As we heard about fertilizers or sewage or some of the specific topics that came up later—from DNA to the Manus Islanders of the South Pacific, or how a horse and rider come into harmony or the first hours in the lives of ducklings—a certain kind of factual ignorance was being replaced by doses of vivid information. We were learning models and theories for thinking about these things and, as we became aware of their intricate circularity, we were learning to care in new ways. At the same time, we were learning to know each other at all of these different levels, often coming into conflict as we tried to express our different levels of awareness, by demonstrating either concern or objectivity, an interest in detail or an interest in abstraction.

Gordon said, "It seems to me that all these sorts of ignorance occur in dealing with the environment and each is perpetuated because they interact."

Barry was nodding. "Every one of these types of ignorance can be illustrated from the events of the last twenty-five years."

"And many of the classes of ignorance," Gregory said,

"are themselves homeostatically supported in the society . . ."

"Surely."

". . . by all sorts of economic and professional factors. We have to remember, when we start to make plans for altering the way people think about the nitrogen cycle, that we are butting into other cyclic systems and trying to change them and we are going to turn some of them into positive feedback systems where formerly they were equilibrated."

Barry began to describe the vicious reactions of professionals in agriculture and public health when some of his material had been quoted in the newspapers. "It's obvious that this impinges on a very tightly organized social structure. I think the issue here is not simply ignorance, but *unperceived* ignorance. These are examples of the intensely complicated situations into which we are intruding without having an adequate understanding of the consequences of our intrusion."

"We don't know that we don't know," Tolly agreed. "We have never thought of these as intensely complicated situations in the first place."

Gordon cocked an eyebrow at Tolly. "People are not simply perverse when they refuse to take the cybernetic point of view. They look at it, they say yes, that's a cybernetic system, but for heaven's sake, I cannot bound the variables. It's not a neat case, I can't publish papers on it. Since all of these systems share this characteristic of not being neat, closed systems, there is obviously a need for a limited language for talking about them. Then there is a certain sense in which a current model becomes acceptable just insofar as it is possible to prescribe something to do about a situation. The cybernetic model that we have here allows us to make certain descriptions, but I'm still not sure whether we could make prescriptions about what actually ought to be done with the sewage. We have a pragmatic or operational ignorance. I mean, can you prescribe an ideal procedure or a good procedure, Barry?"

"Oh yes, it's been used for a long time. Recycle. Just put it back on the soil."

"This will solve all our dilemmas?" Gordon asked skeptically. "Are you sure we can't get into some kind of funny trapping stage this way?" Barry said that would be the natural way and it was that kind of naturalism we had destroyed. Gordon continued, "You have to make a distinction now between a linguistic type of control system and a basic homeostatic type. Christopher Alexander makes this distinction in terms of architecture, which after all is very similar. He talks about self-conscious and un-self-conscious societies, saying that an un-self-conscious society makes housing by an essentially homeostatic procedure, which is continually being tested as adaptive in the environment. This is a naturalistic system— dump it back on the soil. Now you're pointing out very rightly that the self-conscious society is liable to all sorts of defective control procedures, but, unfortunately, it is also the only thing efficient enough to handle the variety which is perpetually increasing, so that, indeed, one has got to come to terms with self-conscious societies. I think I would require that our model provide a prescription within the terms of the self-conscious society, not one borrowed directly from the un-self-conscious society."

"Going back to your question about where the system ends, Gordon, I think there is another question of whose business it's going to be to think about these things," Fred Attneave said. "Ten, twenty years ago, when the detergents were being developed, within what agency or discipline or profession, as these are traditionally structured, did this problem lie? I think the answer is nobody's. This is a matter that has been nobody's business within the current structuring of interests and responsibilities."

"Nobody makes any money out of it," said Barry bitterly.

"That's not unalterable," Fred replied. "If it becomes a respectable discipline with a name and a journal, then you can publish papers in it, and get promoted and so on, and it's all right." Already when we met, hundreds of people, from college professors to ad men, were learning how to make money and reputation by mobilizing concern about the environment. It appears all too easy to shape fresh good will and commitment into existing molds, with the possible danger of actually accelerating the system.

"Why, people can be crucified because of trying to take a stand on this," Gertrude declared, flushed. "It's because of Barry's freedom from the restraints of belonging to an organization whose domain this is, that he can *slam away* without bringing down a whole world on top of his head. We don't *dare* depend upon dispelling ignorance as being sufficient. What good would it have done for Billy Sol Estes to know about the nitrogen cycle? There are lots of people now who, if they see a chance to make one million or ten within the next five or six years, are going to drive *right on ahead* hoping that somehow or other things can be corrected after that, even when they have some kind of feeling of ethical responsibility for the rest of the human race. The pressures of society to become financially successful are going to make them. Dispelling ignorance is necessary, but we don't dare dream that it's going to be sufficient. At some point there has to be a way of making people *not able to stand* not doing anything about it. Now, I don't know whether this is dispelling ignorance or acquiring faith, but there has to be a conviction instilled in the whole generation that something be done about these things."

"Well, yes," said Gordon dryly. "We could make it aversive to behave in this manner. You could build in some sign which occurred and which people didn't like."

In the correspondence that preceded the conference, Gregory had referred to the kind of spreading change by which a system adapts itself in order to maintain internal constancies as a sort of learning:

---

The conventionally drawn distinction between "reward" and "punishment" depends upon a more or less arbitrary line which we draw to delimit that subsystem which we call the individual. The rat who is rewarded with food accepts that reward to neutralize the changes which hunger is beginning to induce; thus we call an external event "reward" if its occurrence corrects an internal change which would be punishing. And so on. In this ultimate sense, all learning is aversive.

Consciousness and the "self" are closely related ideas (possibly related to genotypically determined premises of territory), crystallized by that more or less arbitrary line which delimits the individual and defines a logical difference between "reward" and "punishment." When we view the individual as a servosystem coupled with its environment, or as a part of the larger system which is individual plus environment, the whole appearance of adaptation and purpose changes.

---

From this point of view, we have to think rather carefully about proposals to punish people who behave in ways that damage the environment. Punishment depends on a search for those constancies in the self-definition of members of the society for the sake of which they would alter their economic behavior, but a change in self-definition would make environmental change inherently punishing. The ultimate goal, whatever sanctions are put on environmental damage and whatever changes in awareness occur, is a change in the individual's own boundaries.

"Another way to consider the problem, of course," Gordon continued, "is to make predictions of what people will do and take it into account. You don't just prescribe dumping sewage back on the soil, you prescribe something which is a social and symbolic act taking into account the gentlemen of the type Mr. Billy Sol Estes, or whoever else."

Meanwhile, Gregory was exploring the idea of classifying the possible ways of disrupting systems, so that technologists could be taught the appropriate kinds of caution. "There is error due to ignorance of the most sensitive point. The $NO_3$ spot, for instance, is a critical spot in the circuit structure of the nitrogen cycle. It's obviously very important in all future applied science to know where the sensitive spots are in the circuit structure and this is a question people could be trained to ask.

"Then there is error due to ignorance of the set of possible interventions whereby a self-corrective circuit system changes to regenerative feedback—positive feedback. I don't know how much can be said about the characteristics of that sort of pathology." This was the kind of intervention Iago made so fatally between Othello and Desdemona: he so undermined the trust between them that any effort to repair their relationship made it worse.

Such a change, from self-correcting steady state to runaway, is even more complex when many different parts are linked together. As the days passed, I could see this in our group: our ability to work together depended on holding in check a dozen potential conflicts with a mixture of tact and conciliation, so that disruption in one part of the group could not proceed so far as to cripple the whole conference. So tense was the balance sometimes, however, that when Gregory tried to intervene and redirect the group along some new path, the strain on the overall balance was reflected at once in some single relationship. In an ecosystem, many different species are in balance, with each species ready to run off on an exploding population curve and the whole aggregate interlinked in a steady-state system. We need to know which interventions in the whole can trigger slippage along one of these curves, instead of being taken by surprise by some sudden runaway seemingly far from the point of our interference, a plague of rats or a mushrooming growth of algae. "The classification of 'errors' and 'forms of ignorance' is a hot spot for the applied-science business and it ought to be a great deal more formal and worked out," Gregory concluded.

I had wondered at a phrase that Barry used earlier, when he had said that the scale of our intervention matched the scale of the natural phenomena, and asked him during a break whether he had a formed theory of scale-matching. "No," he said, "in this case it's just that simple, nothing subtle—just the number of tons involved." When we gathered again, Ted Schwartz had worked out a list of detailed questions, including one on scale-matching. "Barry has pointed out that we're approaching a critical point just because the scale of intervention is approaching the scale of the phenomena. As I was thinking about this, things occurred to me that seemed to be exceptional but might have to do with what you were saying, Gregory, about critical points. If you measure an intervention in terms of the amount of system accommodation necessary, you can get a very drastic intervention from minute amounts of highly toxic substances. I wanted to ask whether McCulloch or Commoner could possibly answer what toxicity is. I suspect that very small masses of highly toxic substances interact not with the total mass of the system but with key components of the systems that are themselves of small mass."

"The one that is best known in the whole world is KCN," said Warren, "ordinary cyanide. It tightens out your brain from above down. Up to 1.1 milligrams per kilo of body weight, it just hits your respiratory mechanism, your brain stem will keep going." He gasped loudly to illustrate. "You're out for three minutes and you come back. I've given it to sixty-five human beings ten times each and all to break them out of a psychosis. Now, it is absolutely lethal at 1.4. At 1.3 milligrams per kilo body weight, you're going to kill half of them whether it's a mouse or an elephant. The German war gases, for example, are toxic in much smaller quantities . . . Now always, whenever you find something like this, you can say there must be a target reaction in the human being which is going to be blocked or which is going to explode, and under certain circumstances it will be due to very small quantities. Okay?"

LSD was another example Warren cited, where the molecular structure of the drug locks into neurological processes so that a tiny quantity can have a drastic effect.

"I took a look at the German war gases," Barry added. "Such toxic agents are powerful because they hit critical feedback mechanisms. The way in which we get energy out of food and oxygen involves not a direct interaction between the food and the oxygen, but a series of intermediate oxidation-reduction cycles with very tiny amounts of cyclically turned-over substances, which are all water-soluble vitamins." These are first oxidized and then food is oxidized in interaction with them, while they in turn are freed to repeat the cycle. Because they are reused in this way, only small quantities need be present. "Now any poison, anything that blocks one of these, will operate at very low concentrations. In other words, to put it in the most general sense, such biological systems are amplifiers."

Horst asked, "Can one say, generally, that if you have a feedback loop and you divide it, one part with high amplification and one part low, if you act before the high amplification, then you have an enormous effect?"

"This is a bottleneck problem," Gregory agreed.

For the first time now we were dealing directly with formal analogies between minute systems and very large ones, in this case single brain cells and large ecosystems like Lake Erie. Part of the excitement of a discussion like this for me was that the similarities became visible even with next to no knowledge of the subject matter. I knew what was being talked about, even though I had to guess at the spelling of every technical term used as Barry and Warren alternated in their examples drawn from biochemistry. "I don't know if you've seen these charts that biochemistry graduate students have on their walls," Barry went on. "They have several hundred interconnected substances on them, with wheels within wheels, cycles and so on, and any intrusion in one place is going to spread throughout the whole thing, with amplification and so on. The kind of cycle I talked about with nitrogen is typical of metabolic process."

Gregory went on to put what we had been saying about systems into computer terms. My understanding is that computer specialists generally divide computers into two main types: analog and digital. Digital computers manipulate discrete and arbitrary signals, whereas analog computers manipulate quantities, as a slide rule computes by manipulating lengths or a woman measures a quarter cup of butter by adding chunks of butter to a measuring cup already containing a quarter cup of water until it reaches the halfway mark. The kind of errors made in an analog computer are the kind of errors that are likely to occur in the manipulation of real quantities: if you use a slide rule for multiplication it is difficult to be precise about the last digits of a large number. On the other hand, when a person adds up a row of figures, he is just as likely to make an error in the left-hand column as in the right: the error is not a small but inescapable error of more-or-less, but can change the result completely, because his calculation is digital.

"Barry's ecosystems are really like analog computers," Gregory commented. "The cycles depend upon real quantities of nitrogen and other elements which must be handled by the system. When the quantities are much too great or too small the system may go off the tracks, change its essential structure. But the moment you get to systems which operate digitally, of course, as language does, you've got quite a different position and, as Omar remarked, a tiny *alif*, being just a single vertical stroke in Arabic script, may mark the difference between yes and no, between life and death." He grimaced. "There was a pesticide manufacturer who wrote an infamous piece the other day in which he argued that parts per million is terribly little and doesn't matter in pesticides. On the other hand, obviously one pesticide manufacturer per two hundred million of population can be lethal—because he communicates digitally, he's an *alif*."

Peter was delighted to discover an analogy with his goats. "Very comparable things happen at a much more molar level, in the interactions between a mother goat and a kid, for example. We have almost identical kinds of circular systems where an intrusion that will last just a few seconds will be amplified and lead to very gross disturbances in the mother–young relationship." Certainly it is true of human interactions that events that are very brief or involve very little energy can distort interactions between human beings forever.

Ted resumed his questioning. "Now on this business of scale-matching, observation is also a form of intervention, and questions of epistemological indeterminacy are largely questions of scale and scale-matching; if the thing you're observing and the scale of the means of observation are fairly closely matched, observer effect is enhanced and you get large-scale indeterminacy."

"Right," said Barry, "and much of what I've said could be put into that context, namely, that what's happening is that the degree of determinacy which we always associate with science and technological intervention has now been lost, because we are operating with an almost one-to-one correspondence between the scale of intrusion and the scale of the system intruded upon. As far as I can tell, there is a basic premise in modern physics that, if you want to make precise observations, you have to use an observing system which is far more complex than that which is being intruded upon. This raises all kinds of interesting questions about what happens between two people or between one ecosystem and another, both of which may be equally complex." All of the imagery of man against nature seemed to be evoked and questioned in the discussion—a tiny creature tinkering massively with his world, with the possibility of knowing what he is doing precluded by the very disparity in complexity, since his own complexity is part of the complexity of what he seeks to understand, joined in a single system.

When the time came to stop for lunch we were still very much shaken by Barry's presentation. Through all of our analogies with other types of systems, we were extending our horror, noting that mistakes made with drugs and mistakes made in human relationships could be the same kind of mistakes as those made in the disruption of the nitrogen cycle. As we started to file out of the conference room to go downstairs to the cheerful dining room overlooking the mountains, Bernie tried to lighten the mood. "Is there anything you'd suggest that we eat?" he asked gaily. "I mean, we can't have milk because of Strontium-90, and how about the vegetables? Don't they have nitrates in them, and . . ." Barry stopped and began speaking to the meeting again, from a sort of figurative podium. "I should make one point that's just a personal point. I find it impossible to live with this thing in a personal way. I simply ignore it. My wife says I'm interested in people if they come in hundreds of millions and that's all." Ted said that this might be one of the roots of the problem—the way that each of us finds to live with the horror. Barry nodded and we went on down to our meal. In the academic enterprise, as long as you can remain separate from your subject matter, there are some forms of knowledge you are spared.

· C H A P T E R  3 ·

# Of Parts and Wholes

AFTER LUNCH, Barry contrasted our relationship with the natural environment to that of the Bushmen of the Kalahari Desert.[1] These people in their harsh environment seem to us to be almost totally lacking in technology and yet their survival depends on an extremely intimate knowledge of nature: the possibility of finding food or moisture in every plant or animal is known, and extreme care is taken not to waste or disrupt the balances that allow them to survive—not to pick the wild gourd before it is fully ripe, or tear it up in such a way that it will fail to grow again. Looking around the room, I was amazed at how many of us seemed ready to accept Barry's indictments, a continuation of the indictment in the Memorandum. We were agreeing with Barry as he attacked the whole technological and economic basis of our society. Finally he remarked himself on this implication: "I think we have to recognize that we are living in a society which believes it has an enormously powerful command of nature. The story I'm telling is that this is a false idea, that behind the façade of scientific and technological competence lies a very rotten structure, which is headed for collapse. Now, it seems to me that the first step is to break down the confidence in technology. But also, our technology is in many ways the product of the peculiar kind of science that we

have created in the last three hundred years and what is called
for is a very sweeping change in the structure and nature of
science itself. We have to become aware that despite what it
says on television and so on, we actually are much less well off
than the Kalahari Bushmen in relationship to our environment
and this relationship will determine our survival."

"Didn't you want to develop another example?" Gregory
asked.

"I wanted to close the door on an escape. You see, I assert
that, in the systems we're dealing with here, the properties of
the system are decisive, rather than the properties of the
isolated parts." Barry went on to try to demonstrate that our
basic ignorance was a world-view ignorance of the type Will
had mentioned, involving the generalization of an approach to
problem solving that was overwhelmingly successful in the
development of science. In this tradition, we have tried to understand complex questions by reducing them to simple ones.
Assuming that the complex religious belief of the adult is accounted for by the residues of childhood experience is a form
of reductionism, and so is the belief that all questions involving
whole organisms can ultimately be answered in terms of biochemical properties of their parts—cells, molecules, or even
atoms. Barry used the two terms, reductionism and atomism,
almost interchangeably, to anathematize an intellectual tradition
that discounted properties which emerge only in complex
wholes. "I think it can be shown that many of our difficulties
come about from the atomistic concept, where the engineers
thought they really understood something when they were looking at some small part.

"Well, there is a defense against this claim. If I were arguing for my opponent, I would say: all right, we realize that so
far we're getting into trouble by the fact that we haven't understood how to deal with these natural systems, but if we hurry
up and collect a lot of atomistic data, eventually we will come
to a revolutionary point at which everything will become clear
and we can reconstruct the whole, and if we do it in time we
will save ourselves. Now, I think this won't work. I think proof

of it is that in just the last five years the validity of the atomistic approach to biology has been disproved."

Barry looked around the room. "Do you want me to just sail into this? You know, I'm a little embarrassed at standing up here and doing all the talking, but this has some interesting abstract things about it and it's a lot of fun." We nodded and he went on, repeating an argument given in his paper, where he used an attack on DNA theory as his principal example, supplementing it with examples from perception, endocrinology, and other fields of research where atomistic approaches are losing ground and where Barry maintained that holistic approaches were needed.

DNA theory has been one of the most exciting areas of science in recent years, firing the imagination of laymen as well as specialists, and the molecular biologists are often spoken of as having cracked the genetic code and discovered the secret of life. Crick and Watson, who succeeded in describing the molecular structure of DNA, or deoxyribonucleic acid, laid the foundation for a very rapid development. Much of the excitement is because self-duplication appears as a key property of living things and the DNA molecule is known to be able both to replicate itself and to initiate the chemical processes in the cells from which the rich specificity of the whole organism flows.

The properties of cells can be traced to the action and interaction of different proteins within them; these are all composed of some twenty different amino-acid building blocks, which are differently arranged for each type of protein, producing a vast number of different combinations. The specificity of nucleic acids, such as DNA, depends similarly on the arrangement of thousands of the four or more possible nucleotide subunits. Thus, just as biological specificity can be seen in those features that distinguish a particular living thing from other forms of life, biochemical specificity is the property that distinguishes a given protein or nucleic acid molecule from others. The DNA hypothesis is that the biological specificity of DNA alone determines the sequence of amino acids in proteins, including the enzymes that govern much of the internal chemistry of the cell. DNA also determines the nucleotide sequence in the next generation of nucleic-acid molecules synthesized by it. DNA is thus sometimes referred to as a "self-duplicating molecule." Crick's "Central Dogma" asserts that DNA is the *sole* source of genetic specificity, and in particular that DNA governs the specificity of proteins, while protein has no corresponding effect on DNA.

The Central Dogma was formulated in 1958. In 1962 Barry pointed out the essential role of the enzyme DNA polymerase in the synthesis of new DNA, declaring that it too probably plays a role in determining the nucleotide sequence (and therefore the genetic specificity) of the DNA which it synthesizes, and that this role is not fully determined by the DNA of the preceding generation. Since then he has been collecting evidence to call the Central Dogma into question.[2] He has been swimming upstream, since much of the evidence he cites to disprove the DNA hypothesis is culled from parenthetical mention in experiments written up to support it. In general, biological self-duplication can occur only in highly specific environments: amoebae can divide only when air and water and nutrients are available and the temperature is right, roses seed new roses only within a climate and environment that would take volumes to specify, and adult human beings are succeeded by adult offspring only after many years, when thousands of contextual factors are appropriate. Thus, by any hypothesis, DNA governs the synthesis of the chemicals active within the cell only under highly specific contextual conditions, some of which are necessary for the process to occur at all, while others may contribute information. Barry looked for evidence of the fallibility of DNA in cases of partial self-replication. For instance, when mutations of the bacterium *E. coli* alter its DNA polymerase, this causes a high frequency of mutation in *other* genes.[3] The altered enzyme produces a DNA unlike the DNA in the presence of which it was produced.

Barry went on to cite examples of other experiments which, by his interpretation, show that a number of other cell constituents contribute to the specificity of inheritance. Specificity can be altered by changes at several points in the sequence and the line separating context is blurred. Barry maintained that the process must be seen as a cybernetic one. He cited the phrasing of many experimenters,[4] who write up their equivocal results in terms of "ambiguity," "infidelity of information transfer," and "duplicity." A picture of inheritance emerged in which the specificity of a number of different kinds of molecules was mutually regulated, rather than all dependent on the DNA. Barry asserted that, to describe self-duplication, it would be necessary to describe an interaction, rather than simply specify the static structure of a particular molecule. As I tried to follow Barry's argument, I found I had difficulty defining to myself just what there was about the DNA hypothesis that was non-systemic. I found a part of the answer in the introduction of Tolly's paper, where he prefaced his attempt to describe process: "The principal objects of description are systems of repeatable events. The repeatable events constitute a system because their occurrences are mutually constrained." In all the cyclic chemical process that is the life of the cell, it was this mutuality within whole systems that Barry felt was denied by the Central Dogma. If DNA is affected in its turn by proteins, as Barry argued, then biological specificity is not accounted for by reference to DNA only, a part of the cell. Instead, a holistic approach, one which looks at the whole system, is needed—the opposite of atomistic reductionism.

Barry gave ominous point to his attack on reductionist biology by suggesting that scientists working on reductionist assumptions are especially ready to propose faulty forms of human engineering, such as the "control" of human inheritance by the chemical manipulation of DNA. If the biological specificity transferred in inheritance is due to mutually dependent properties of numerous substances, it cannot be controlled by a chemical transformation of any single substance. He finished his presentation with a burst of vehemence. "Do you know how one of the experiments I've cited as disproving Crick's Central Dogma was concluded? Having shown that the Dogma sometimes failed, the author concluded that he had demonstrated its '*essential* universality'![5] What I'm doing here is saying that the king is wearing no clothes. The question of differences in approach such as atomism and holism is ludicrously important, and yet there is a total lack of concern about this kind of question among practicing biochemists and molecular biologists—it's really a peculiar sort of cultural situation: the rigidity of the establishment extends to censorship, condemnation, inhibiting grants, and so on. There's a vast cultural superstructure here and I think it's important to keep in mind."

"The state of mind of the genetical establishment." Gregory shook his head. "A very peculiar establishment. Always has been."

Barry continued. "Another parameter that I just want to mention is the assertion that this whole atomistic approach has worked in atomic physics, the one area of science which has really succeeded, and the answer is that it certainly has, but only in the sense that, by looking at the properties of the electron and the proton and so on, it is possible through quantum mechanics to arrive at the expected properties of the hydrogen atom and I think possibly the hydrogen molecule, but not beyond that. That's a fact. Most biochemists and molecular biologists assume that atomic physics has provided a predictive foundation for all the rest of matter, but this is simply not true. Most physicists and chemists, modern ones, now regard the atom as being the one narrow segment in the spectrum of material structures that happens to be explicable by an atomistic approach. For example, the nucleus of the atom has now become biological, as in the 'boot-strap theory' of the nucleus, which says that the particles that you can get out of the nucleus have no self-sufficient existence inside the nucleus, where their properties are determined by their neighbors and vice versa. As soon as you get beyond the hydrogen molecule, the situation is holistic—the properties of the molecules are emergent and not predictable from the properties of the constituent parts.

"One of the fairy tales that my generation of biologists was brought up with was that we ought to emulate physics and learn how to take a complex system apart and find the crucial basic parts that will explicate what is happening in the whole. There's a very peculiar thing, culturally, that's been happening: while the biologists have been driving toward this atomistic approach to emulate the physicists, the physicists and most physical chemists have given it up and are concerned with holistic problems." A fairy tale we all live with, I thought, especially since we give physics such great prestige without really knowing the details of what is going on. I had been aware that the claims of genetic engineering were inimical to some of the values I hold and that the effect on society of such meddling was likely to be disastrous, but after a Nobel Prize I had taken it for granted that the claims of the DNA theorists could not be denied on biological grounds. So often in our society, things are done simply because they appear technologically possible.

As Barry went on to nail the final plank in his platform, Gregory was trying hard to interrupt: "Is there a supplementary statement to what you've just said—that from subatomic particles up to human societies there is a sort of alternation of atomism and holism? You can in fact handle atoms atomistically, but you cannot handle their nuclei atomistically; you must handle the interior of molecules holistically, but as between them you can handle them atomistically to some degree; you can handle human beings individually, but then they make up societies which are holistic. Is there some sort of alternation?" This was a question that seemed important as an analogy with the human nervous system, in which analogical processes, that can deal with continuous and patterned wholes, are connected by digital processes, the firing of discrete nerve impulses. Thus, if human perception works by such an alternation, this was a first place to look for similarities or contrasts between the way information is handled by human beings and the properties of systems to which they are responding.

"No," said Barry firmly. "My position is this: If we consider all the forms of matter that we know about, only in regard to a narrow spectrum is there a possibility of what might be called the 'atomistic approximation' succeeding. Everything else is necessarily holistic, so that what has appeared to be a universal basic approach to science since the Greeks—atomism —is really a special case, which only worked where it has worked and is not going to work anywhere else, up or down. It's a narrow window, a special case; but, because of the enormous consequences of understanding the atom, it has misled everyone into believing that atomism is synonymous with science. I think this is the great evil in Western science today."

"It would seem to me that the problem is not atomism or holism, but the dichotomy," said Ted. "The trouble with atomism is that it's part of this dichotomy. A holism that does not imply an analysis into components of systems and systems which are themselves components of larger systems is also useless. Rather than adopt the slogan that you've put forward, it would be much better to drop the dichotomy and take up some kind of 'relational materialism.' If we move, let's say, from saying there is one specifier in the genetic system to saying that there are three, we haven't really made an enormous difference."

Gregory and Tolly instantly denied that this was what Barry was doing.

"He's saying that they can be related circularly in a cybernetic system, yes. But nevertheless, this system is also analyzable," Ted protested.

"No, at this point, so far as I know, no one knows how to analyze such a system," said Barry.

The question of holism has taken different forms in different disciplines, so we responded to Barry's discussion in a variety of ways. Some of the notepads around the table even had the word spelled "wholism"—which would indeed seem more appropriate except for an accident of etymology. Anthropology and linguistics moved into their modern development through the recognition that the significance of any trait or artifact or linguistic item is the way it fits into a whole grammar or a whole culture, so that scrap-bag listings of curious facts gave way to descriptions of a unified way of life. At that level, I had joined in many conversations about method, emphasizing studies of system rather than collections of items to be listed or analyzed statistically; in human behavior, when you start by looking for something you can count, it is often the least interesting thing going on. Even in anthropology, however, the effort to deal holistically is sometimes mocked as a sort of mysticism. I kept remembering something Warren had said on the first day: on the one hand, systems with only one or two parts cannot be made a basis for the analysis of more complex systems; on the other hand, no analytical tools are available yet for being really rigorous about even a triad. Put the problem of the observer effect next to the problem of describing wholes, and it becomes unclear what we can know at all—especially since the properties of the things we try to describe are always related to some whole of which we too are a part. At best, our knowing is a condition of a larger system.

Tolly said, "I think the issue is more . . . the way I would state it is related to a sign that I'm hoping to print up as a sticker for my car, which will say HELP STAMP OUT NOUNS. What has to change is our fascination with nouns, to be replaced by a fascination with process, which does not depend on a prior conception of a set of entities. Let me leave that as a teaser for what I hope to say in a more organized fashion when I have the opportunity." Then Tolly went on and read out loud from a paperback he was carrying around with him that week, Alan Watts's *The Book*.[6] What he read was a description of the set of ideas that make up the traditional belief of the relationship between mind and body, with mind conceived as a controlling officer, informed by the senses, who governs the movements of the body from deep within. "Few people seem to use the word ['I'] for their whole physical organism. 'I have a body' is more common than 'I am a body.' . . . We seem to use 'I' for something *in* the body but not really *of* the body, for much of what goes on in the body seems to happen to 'I' in the same way as external events . . . [Memory] gives the impression of oneself, the officer, as something that remains while life goes by—as if the conscious self were a stable mirror reflecting a passing procession. This further exaggerates the feeling of separateness, of oneself changing at a pace so much slower than outside events and inside thoughts that you seem to stand aside from them as an independent observer."

"I'll stop there," he said. "But I read this because it rings in my head as strangely related to what Barry was talking about and to the theme of this conference. It's one strand of the whole knot of conceptual prejudices, okay?—which stand behind the DNA story." In a sense, it was to be our task for the remainder of the conference to explore the relationship. DNA is seen as standing apart from the flux within the cell, influencing without itself being influenced, and this notion is analogous to our alienation from ourselves, the body-mind dichotomy Watts was exploring, the alienation of man from nature, and the mistaken effort to think of nature or our bodies as explainable in atomistic terms. These were words that echoed constantly in my thinking in the days that followed, perhaps because pregnancy, with the changes it brings in both thought and feeling, calls on a woman to be committed to her physical being. She cannot continue to think of her "self" as separate from and ruling her body; if she continues to think in terms of a separation she begins to feel like a prisoner, smothering in a vast house of flesh.

"Right," said Barry to Tolly. "I think the same kind of reductionist bias has its grip on physiology, on psychology generally, on sociology . . . even history is beginning to be 'scientific.' In a way, we can thank the molecular biologists for having reduced the consequences of this bias to its final absurdity, at least in the case of life. I have the feeling that there is a widespread running-out of the usefulness of atomism in all of the sciences and that the moment has come for a kind of grand alliance around a holistic approach."

Warren inserted a fierce staccato of specificity. "One remark. Let me put it simply. Suppose I look at the eddies forming downstream from a post in a river. Ultimately, they have to come off right-handed and left-handed; there can be no halfway in between. These are discrete affairs, but they can all be computed from a perfectly continuous hydrodynamical theory, okay? And it doesn't take a very complicated one. The most beautiful one of those I've seen recently is an analysis of turbulent flow by Iberall. The equations are continuous, but by putting in the volume coefficient of elasticity, the equations become eighth order and highly non-linear, and if you look at them in the time domain there are singularities everywhere. Now, every one of these singularities will be, so to speak, a little whirlpool on its own. Am I clear? You attack it from a continuous theory and you end up with discrete entities. Now I don't know whether you could possibly, by going from the little whirlpools themselves, ever come back to the equations of the stream, but the other way around works."

More than anyone else present, Warren tended to use an uncompromisingly technical vocabulary, referring to scientists I knew nothing of and calling on unfamiliar mathematics and neurophysiology. As I listened I kept checking to see whether I was sorting out what each example was about, what kind of thing he was trying to say in this interdisciplinary context where not more than two or three people could follow the substance of most of his examples. He went on to give more explicitly technical examples of the problems of holistic description. In describing the human brain, there has been an effort to assign particular functions to particular regions in the brain. "If you ask about the relation between the structure you're looking at and the function you're interested in, in one case you get something that's supposed to be atomistic by way of an answer, but in other cases that's a nonsensical question. Sam Winograd, who's a marvelous mathematician, and Jack Cowan, who is not only a good mathematician and a good physicist, but also a fine logician, came up with a theory that for the first time makes sense of the reliability of a brain made out of unreliable components. The theory requires that you scatter each function over a large number of components which will be involved now in one activity, now in another. If you ask me concerning a particular cell what its function is, you've asked a question like what's the function of the second letter of every word in the English language.

"Now, if I approach something from the analysis of the large affair, treating it as a continuum of some sort, I will inevitably turn up things that are going to behave somewhat atomistically. But if I approach it from the atomistic point of view, I'm never going to get the continuum out of it, it just doesn't come out. You're very likely to find yourself dealing with probabilities and things equally silly, instead of with facts, and then having nothing to count, and if you can't count, probabilities are meaningless.

"Let me make one more remark and I quit—been talking too long. Ted suggested before that we need a relational materialism, but I don't like the notion of a materialism here, at all. What we need for our problems is a logic of relations and such a logic looks to be pretty well underway. There are two boys in the Cambridge area who are doing beautiful work. When I get back, I'll be with them.

"Now, the exciting thing that turns up when you look at the logic of relations is that triadic relations are the crucial ones. Let me make it very clear: The moment you give me triads, all I've got to do is stick two of them together and I've got four arms hanging out, I've got a tetrad. You can't build with dyads; you can make rings and strings like oxygen, but there it ends.

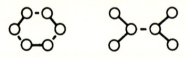

If you want to build in three dimensions, you want something like carbon. Now I know of no relation yet that cannot be broken down to triads, but there are lots of triads that can't be broken up any further. The notion 'between' is such a one— '*b* is between *a* and *c*.' So is '*a* means *b* to *c*.' So are all the typical problems of communications inherently triadic. Yep. The most exciting thing is this: when you look at these things, the great problem is the context. We've all tried to handle context as though it were a general background, but when you look at a calculator it appears in the form of an operator. It will be another few years before we make sense out of it, but I believe this is the first great breakthrough in handling real languages. Noam Chomsky handles phrase-structure grammars that are context-free beautifully. We cannot handle natural languages because they're context-determined. But if we can handle the context properly as an operator in our logic, I think we're going to go places. And that's my only remark."

Warren stopped abruptly. "Does anybody want to ask some clarifying questions?" said Gregory tentatively.

"Now you say the context appears in the form of an operator," Gertrude ventured cautiously after a pause, "but . . . is there an example of that? I can't think of one."

"Yep, there's a very famous one," said Warren. "A man meets a girl and he asks her to take off her clothes. If it's a cocktail party, it's a dare; if it's a boudoir, it's the right thing; if it's in a streetcar, he's a pervert. The moment you take the context in, it decides how you deal with the rest of it. It behaves as an operator in a strictly formal sense. It doesn't come in as a vague background."

"Going back to atomism and holism," said Barry, "my feeling is that the whole system is the operator on the behavior of the parts . . ."

"Has to be," said Warren.

". . . and that the feature of a part that is important is determined by the character of the system as a whole. I think that's a useful way to get back to that dichotomy."

Gregory asked Warren, "If I give a signal 'this is play,' and now under the general rubric of that signal I do such and such, the thing inside the rubric is, so to speak, multiplicatively changed by the thing outside that bracket. That's the idea, isn't it, of the notion 'operator'?"

"Very definitely," said Barry. "If I say to Gregory, 'You son of a bitch,' and I don't smile, he might get angry . . ."

"I just write it down in my notes," Gregory mocked.

". . . but in the context of a smile it's a term of endearment."

Gertrude suggested that perhaps even the phenomena of the hydrogen atom would be better explained holistically. "It would be so nice if this was not the exception it seemed to be, if we needed only one principle of explanation."

"I could live with it as an exception," Barry muttered, "but keep it caged."

"We're still trying to take sides in the universe," Ted declared. "No atomism is absolute and neither is any holism. If it were, you couldn't do scientific work on it."

Barry agreed. "I don't know any hard operational way to deal with holism. It's hard to explain how to even go about thinking about it, without getting caught up in mysticism, yin and yang, the whole oriental business. We need to understand the relationship between the parts and the whole, so obviously I'm interested in the atomistic data. The problem is selecting, among properties of parts, those that are crucial in understanding the whole."

"I can't help thinking about the state that educational psychology was in in the late thirties and early forties when what was called an 'eclectic' view was the one that was supposed to save everybody from everything," Gertrude put in. "We had books in which we taught prospective teachers some conditioning theory and some field theory and a bit of everything else and gave them examples that were explained by each. We never once indicated that there were inconsistencies, that this theory over here implied a contradiction to something that you could adduce from this one. We were building a tolerance of inconsistency into these young people that produced a *mind crust* against sensitivity to things that they ought to have been able to notice later on."

"And they've all turned into molecular biologists," said Barry bitterly. "I think that's a very good description of exactly what's wrong with molecular biology, the insensitivity to inconsistencies such as the inconsistency between 'essential' and 'universal.' "

"That's it!" she affirmed. "I think that's the most crippling thing that can be done to a human being. I always have the feeling that when there's something like the atomistic theory that has produced modern physics, seemingly inconsistent with the holism that is necessary to explain another field, there's some overall explanation that will convert one into a special case of the more general thing. And I believe we ought not to relinquish the search for such a theory. We don't have to tolerate a contradiction. Contradictions ought to be a *challenge* to look for resolution."

Gregory suggested the need for two different spheres of explanation, with a need to keep them carefully distinct. "There is a point at which there is a sort of Rubicon crossing-over. In explanations related to billiard balls and atoms, that which happens has to have a preceding cause. In the world that we deal with, of communication, organization, representation, self-duplication, and so forth, this is not necessarily so. The letter which I do *not* write to my aunt can evoke an angry reply. Now this is because all communicational phenomena and all information (in the information-theory sense of the word "information") are based on difference. Now, without difference there is no information. And since zero differs from one, zero can give you information and can be a cause of your behavior.

"This is quite a different world from the world of the atoms that have to push each other around and are supposed not to move spontaneously. It's the biological world, what the Gnostics called Creatura, which is based on distinction, not the world of Pleroma. This is a dualism I am familiar with not through Gnostic writings but through a little book that Jung wrote in three days during a period of psychosis and to which he attributes such insights as he later had, *Septem Sermones ad Mortuos.*[7] He felt this was really the beginning of his being able to think clearly. The notion approximately is that there is—I'm putting it my way rather than his now—a world of explanation in which the analogue of 'cause,' call it that for the moment, is distinction, difference—Creatura, because after all the whole thing starts with God's dividing the land from the sea, the light from the darkness, etc. God's establishment of order is always a 'distinguishing between' and difference becomes the causation of response. Now, the moment *difference* is the causation of response, then you do not look for an energy input from the stimulus. The stimulus exists as stimulus only by virtue of being different from non-stimulus. Difference, of course, cannot be localized: the difference between these two matchboxes is clearly not in either matchbox, or in the space between them, and I can't pinch it. It is a phenomenon existing in a total circuit structure involving the two matchboxes, a lot of light, and a lot of gunk in my head that is so set that it will respond to differences. One of the criteria, then, for mindlike properties immanent in the complexities of matter would be the storage of energy that makes it possible to respond to the negative.

"The Pleroma, on the other hand, is that world of explanation in which causation is associated with energy exchange and messages as such do not exist, although our description of that world of course involves distinction all the way down the line. This is a sort of rephrasing of the problem of the bishop in the woods and does the tree make a noise when it falls. There is no denying that the tree falls, but by taking the bishop out of the woods, you separate a world of explanation of this kind from a world of explanation of that kind. There is no description in the woods, except insofar as the beetles and red deer make descriptions, which of course they do."

Warren quoted:

> "Did the drink we dreamt we swallowed
> Make us dream of all that followed?"

And we adjourned for the day.

· C H A P T E R   4 ·

# Small Societies in Crisis

BARRY'S PRESENTATION had given us a sense of the structure of
human misunderstanding of natural processes and of the type
of spreading disaster that could overtake such natural systems
as Lake Erie when coupled with a modern industrial society
committed to accelerating change. After this, it made sense to
look at pathologies of human societies and, as is often the case,
this could best be done by looking away from urban America
at a small and preliterate group of people trying to find their
way through conditions of stress and contradiction, through the
disruption of the ancient balances in their way of life. For such
an example, we turned to Ted Schwartz and asked him to report
on his field work in New Guinea.

The idea we were pursuing came close to the assertion in
the Memorandum, "*plus c'est la même chose, plus ça change.*"
Under pressure from outside, the self-corrective mechanisms in
a system make those internal changes that allow the maintenance of crucial constancies, and yet these changes may be so
extensive as ultimately to change the nature of the system or
threaten its survival. Running along under our discussions, of
course, was the awareness that many such changes can be seen
happening today in the United States, changes that must be
recognized as attempts to correct for the type of pathologies

that Barry had described, sometimes hopeful and sometimes ominous. It was with this point that Gregory opened the day's discussions.

"We've been talking as it we are now at a high point of the intellectual and value-pursuing vices that Barry's been describing—scientific 'reductionism,' 'atomism,' whatever you want to call it—as if the damage that we've done to Lake Erie, to mother-child relationships, to all sorts of things in the civilization, through this atomism, were at its maximum, and we had only to correct the atomism. But the efforts to correct that atomism are already underway. We already have a vast number of people building up anti-intellectual, anti-thoughtful, anti-manipulative cults and groups, perhaps most conspicuously on campuses, but also in many other parts of the civilization, the hippie movement and so on. We have not only the problem of correcting the etiology of the disease, but also a problem of trying to deal with those symptoms which are themselves attempts at correction, but not always wise ones—the by-products of the previously existing disease. It's not clear that we can win that race. I thought a way of looking at this paradox that we have on our hands would be to start with Schwartz, talking about cargo cults, as events in individuals and societies attempting to correct for certain sorts of pathogenic or communicationally contradictory circumstances."

"I have sometimes thought that hippies are an intellectual cargo cult," Ted acknowledged, smiling faintly, "so we might as well get into that."

I met Ted Schwartz for the first time in 1953, when he was a graduate student accompanying my mother to New Guinea, and later I visited him when he was doing field work in Mexico, but I hadn't seen him for several years. Ted is handsome in a spare, ascetic way; his features are precisely chiseled beneath a high, pale forehead. He moves economically, his face quiet and his back straight, and often his eyes, behind thick lenses, seem concealed.

There is a story—which Ted denies—that when he first traveled up the Sepik River into the interior of New Guinea, he awakened in the middle of the night, sure that mosquitoes were biting him. On consideration, he concluded that this was impossible since he was sleeping under a brand-new mosquito net and therefore, reassured by his logic, he went back to sleep. Later he awoke again to find he really was severely bitten, his hands and face swollen, and when he shone his flashlight around, his net was in tatters. Voracious cockroaches had chewed through the new, starched fibers, leaving him unprotected. Whatever the story, he has always seemed to me to be a very cerebral person. Because Ted is concerned with combining field work with the theoretical development of anthropology, there was a continual tension during the morning between his wish to elaborate a theoretical position and our fascination with the vivid detail of his data.

Ted had been studying cargo cults in Melanesia. Cargo cults are examples of a kind of religious revival that has taken place in many parts of the world where primitive peoples have had the pattern of their lives disrupted by contact with Europeans. These so-called nativistic cults vary from place to place, but generally involve an interweaving of old ideas with borrowed notions and promise a restoration or vindication of the native culture. At a time of apathy and confusion, when all the purposes of the old way are undone, prophets arise; whatever the details of their promises, they mean above all that the world will once again make sense—and they make immediate demands on their followers, giving them a direction and a purpose. In North America, the Indians believed that the religion of the Ghost Dance would restore the wide grazing lands and herds of buffalo. By contrast to this emphasis on restoration, the cults of New Guinea have imagined not a return, but the sudden achievement of all the benefits of European civilization—symbolized by the cargo of goods which would arrive, this time for them rather than for the white man.

A primitive culture depends on the consistency of a set of intricately interwoven ideas. Beliefs about the origin and nature of the world and the rights and duties of people in relation to one another are closely tied to the details of daily life: the planting of crops or the gathering of food, marriage and the begetting of children, and the acceptance of death. Among some peoples with very homogeneous cultures, this fabric is so closely woven that even brief contact with an alien culture or the sight of a plane overhead can start an unraveling in which first a cosmology is shaken and finally all of life is in shreds. In Melanesia, however, cultural variation is a familiar aspect of life. Each small group speaks its own language, has different crafts and ceremonies, and whispers different esoterica about the universe. Within this diversity, a strange form of basket weaving or a dance or even a piece of myth can be bartered from a neighboring tribe. European incursions have been gradual, so that, although the first record of cargo cults in New Guinea goes back to 1890, there are still tiny warlike groups in the interior which are only now being pacified and exposed to Western pressures and influence, and cults can be studied at every stage of development.

Ted first described his field work among the Manus people of the Admiralties, about 150 miles north of the New Guinea coast.[1] Their old culture was highly entrepreneurial, everyone trying to get ahead and to pay the debts incurred at the time of marriage. In addition to their currency, wealth was stored in the form of obligations, which required skillful manipulation and exploitation. Thus, when the Manus had their first contact with Europeans, they were confident that they would be able eventually to acquire the wealth the Europeans possessed, wealth on a scale they had never dreamed of, and they immediately set out to find the appropriate techniques, following a reasoning which combined what little they could see of European civilization with their traditional ideas. They made all sorts of assumptions—for instance, that each European represented the whole civilization. They abandoned their own religion and invited missionaries in, hoping that this would be a key to the Europeans' wealth. They were very devout—the Manus were regarded as the best Catholics in the area—but they stayed poor and did not stop dying.

Throughout Melanesia, under the impact of European culture, this kind of magical thinking was applied in the belief that any detail of European life might be the key. Artistic traditions were abandoned in favor of European artifacts, since even a tin can or an oil drum had come to seem beautiful. This logic was eventually carried to its extreme in the rituals of the cults, when natives in various parts of New Guinea tried marching in drill formation or setting up perfect replicas of European dinner tables, telephone poles to talk to God, or committee meetings with the dead. One group in New Britain locked a missionary in the smoke house to be smoked in place of copra, the principal export of the area.

Up until World War II, although cults had appeared in other areas, the Manus were living very close to their traditional way of life, except that some young men would go away to work on the copra plantations or in the police and return with a little capital and a little knowledge of the outside world. They came into intense contact with Europeans during the war, when the Japanese drove out the Australians and then two years later the Americans bombed and drove out the Japanese; suddenly the Manus Islands became a base with a million Americans and hundreds of ships and planes, displaying a terrific scale of wealth—leveling mountains, building roads and Quonset cities and a Coca-Cola factory.

At that time, there was a young man named Paliau working as a sergeant-major in the police, which was the highest position a native could aspire to. When he came home after the war, he sent word before him that he had a plan and the Manus expected him to bring the revelation of a cult. Since he was an original and basically secular thinker, he instead brought ideas for reorganizing Manus on the model of European society. However, shortly after he began to hold meetings calling on people to unify and start work on reforms, a cult prophet did arise in a nearby village, prophesying the millennium for the second Sunday and calling on his followers to destroy all their property, including their canoes and sails, as a token of their expectation. This doctrine spread to the villages where Paliau's meetings were being held and everyone scattered homeward, carrying it with them. There were visions and prophecies, speaking in tongues and convulsive seizures, and the cult spread like a fire, the excitement and the promise of immediate fulfillment infinitely more attractive than the hard work and reform demanded by Paliau.

The Manus were already somewhat disillusioned with the mission, which had failed to bring them long lives and wealth, in spite of their docility, and had begun to suspect that the missionaries made a profit on each convert—Paliau said, "The natives are the copra of the missionary." Now in the excitement of the cult they broke with the mission. Concluding that the missionaries had been lying to them and had given them a false Bible, they set out to discover the truth by a reinterpretation of what they had been told, retaining and stressing such ideas as the Apocalypse and the Resurrection. The new Apocalypse of the cult promised that Jesus would come with the ghosts of their own dead, bringing the cargo with them: key ideas were lifted out of the context of mission Christianity and these were joined with elements of the native tradition. The circumstance of a drastic change in life style, due to outsiders, set the stage for a general anticipation of drastic change—a new world and a new life. Ted described the relationship as a resonance between primitive Melanesian themes and survivals from our own religious history.

In the early stages of a cult, ordinary activity is suspended and there is an urgent demand for ways to maintain fervor in the period of waiting, a new way of praying or some new vision. The first stage of high excitement, accompanied by behaviors resembling pathological seizures and hallucinations, Ted termed the meta-stable state of the cult. It is a state which people would like to maintain, but because of its inherent instability it can be maintained only by *increased* intensity. The idea of the cult at this stage seems to be to force the hand of the supernatural by making it unthinkable that the promise will not come true, but with a secret uncertainty, a profound ambivalence underlying the cultists' assurance. The Manus, for instance, commanded to destroy their possessions, put all the

American money they had accumulated in a box and threw it into the sea. Without acknowledging to themselves that they were doing so, however, they threw it on the reef where they would be able to fish it out later.

When the promised day arrived, the Manus villagers were at the very peak of excitement, having thrown away all that they owned and destroyed their canoes—the means of their livelihood—in a desperate attempt to convince themselves and the ghosts of their sincerity. Nothing happened; the cargo failed to come. After this, the cult might have been expected to go through a series of revivals, alternating with periods of apathy, effectively keeping the people from making real changes in their lives, but at this point Paliau came forward again, pulling them out of their despair and using the aura of the cult for his secular Reform Movement. The ground had been cleared. So much had been destroyed that there was room for a great deal of innovation. Paliau succeeded in persuading the Manus to leave their houses on stilts over the sea and move into European-style buildings, side by side with the bush people. They put on Western dress, re-established a local form of Christianity, held endless meetings, reorganized family and economic life, and opened a school, moving rapidly and enthusiastically into the twentieth century. Since that time there have been periodic revivals of the cult, each one somewhat muted as compared to the last, and each one more compatible with an ongoing society; and Ted has studied their development in a series of field trips. "The hard core are still sitting around trying to regenerate these intense feelings—it's an addiction. And the other people are out doing everything under the sun."

Barry wanted to know whether the secular Movement had succeeded in making inroads in the poverty of the Manus. Said Tolly, "They weren't 'poor' before the Europeans got there!"

This paradox seemed to be related to a shift from a stable culture, where the future was regarded as an extension of the present, to what Ted called a "vehicular culture," one in which you are not where you want to stay. In the cult, a goal state is visualized, radically different from the unsatisfactory present; in a secular movement for modernization, like Paliau's, the future is also visualized in terms of change, but change through a sequence of steps, based on more realistic expectations. In neither, however, is the present seen as something to be perpetuated. Thus, although the Movement has brought about very real changes, people are still occupied with visions of further change, and the Movement has inevitably failed to satisfy these visions. Although it did a good deal to reorganize life, using native materials, the Movement stalled at a certain point for lack of capital.

Ted had entitled his paper for the conference "Beyond Cybernetics," and he had already raised several questions about how to account for the setting of parameters for a system. Although cybernetics describes the way in which a thermostat, for example, maintains a set temperature, it does not account for a new setting on that thermostat. Similarly, Ted's position was that the cybernetic model might be adequate to account for a stable society, such as the Manus were before contact, but that human communities also have the property of being able to readjust their parameters and orient themselves to new goals. The Manus, having left the state of equilibrium, have entered a new state in which the equivalent of stability is a constant rate of change; this new state is analogous to the American economic system, in which it has become fashionable to regard constant expansion as the appropriate stability. Gregory nodded dourly and described the alcoholic who is only comfortable when the level of alcohol in his blood stream is gradually increasing: for two days, perhaps even for three, he can maintain this slow increase, but eventually he ends in the gutter.

In recent years, the danger of commitment to a constant rate of change, putting increasing strain on the environment, has become more and more apparent, and a nostalgia for stable and primitive ways of life goes hand in hand with the new Romanticism. Nevertheless, I had to remember as I listened to Ted that there is no way back for the Manus to the kind of stability that existed before contact, and few of them, perhaps only some of the very old, would choose to go back. The old culture was an ancient and stable pattern for human life within a particular environment, but it was a harsh and competitive one. Today, in spite of the frustrations of exclusion from the material wealth of the West, the Manus feel enriched by the values they have borrowed from outside and by the widened range of identity and imagination this has given them.

There is no way for Western civilization to move backwards, either, returning to an ancient stability. Even if we manage to escape our addiction to economic growth and a continually rising material standard of living, the search for knowledge is embedded in our civilization, and systems of knowledge grow exponentially as each new fragment interlocks with the whole. Recurrent and accelerating changes in our understanding will continue, and few would advocate giving them up. Nevertheless, we need to examine stable systems, such as the precontact Manus, and the kinds of things that can happen when change in one part of the system breaks loose from change in some other part or threatens to uncouple the system either from the sanity and sense of meaning of individuals or from the environment. I believe we are going to have to slow down in those areas where our behavior is directly coupled to constants in the ecosystem or to variables that change much more slowly: we must stop population growth because of the many substances necessary for human life whose quantity is fixed. Change in knowledge and communication is not subject to limitations of this sort, but even here we need to work for balance so that, for instance, our value systems and religion may continually grow in depth and flexibility in the same way as our technology, effectively controlling it. We urgently need knowledge about how a society can adjust itself to different kinds or rates of change.

Ted's further interest was in the relationship between changes in the whole society and the goals and expectations, the "orientational constructs," of individuals. "I wanted to know what is happening when a culture is metaphorically 'on the move.' Obviously, in a cult, temporal orientation is radically different from that of the movement. Part of the meta-stable state is that they want immediate realization and so they behave very differently from people who have accepted the fact that Christ is not going to come in their lifetimes. If you thought he was coming next week and bringing everything you wanted, you might destroy food crops or discontinue maintenance activities. By acting *as if* they don't think there will be a future, they are magically helping to ensure the future they hope for. The understanding of magical thinking is . . ."

"That moment!" Barry broke in, "the moment when the anticipated fails to materialize, that's the one that's important to us here. That's because the modern technological society in which we're living is just now in the process of failing to deliver the goods, and people know it."

"Please let me go on. In a sense, the nonfulfillment of the prophecy is built into the thing from the beginning," Ted objected. "You can see it in the behavior of the people, and very possibly with us too. It's not just when that cargo doesn't come that counts."

"If they were really sure the ship was coming, they wouldn't need to destroy property," said Gregory.

Ted agreed. "Much of what they're doing, including the convulsive behavior and all the rest of it, is predicated on this disparity and on the fact that you're working for something that is not by any means a certainty. By the way, in Manus in 1946, when the cargo didn't come on the second Sunday, the prophet said, 'Kill me and I'll go see what's holding up the cargo,' so they did. Now they are holding seances with his ghost.

"This is one place where I disagree with Leon Festinger and his notion of cognitive dissonance.[2] In his analysis of a flying saucer cult, whose members expected a certain lake to overflow and flying saucers to carry them away, he says that disparity in belief, which he called a dissonance, arises at the point where the lake doesn't overflow. I think it started long before that and it's been operating all along. Obviously, one of the things you could do to terminate such a dissonance is to give up the belief, but that's not what people do; they go out and recruit all the harder.

"Festinger sees this as an effort to dispel and get rid of dissonance, but I can show how people both do this and at the same time work to maintain dissonance, which is one of the things that makes life seem worth living. Every single one of the cargo cults that I'm talking about, as it is set up, generates an opposition. They not only recruit and proselytize, they exclude. They generate the opposition as they do the dissonance, because the state of feeling and the hostility has value for them. Then there's ritual skepticism—everybody who comes in has to profess profound skepticism and have this overcome. It's part of the entrance procedure and it actually enhances and maintains the dissonance. We're probably caught up in this too: if you want to see why people don't react to smog in California, in an area where there are more health nuts per square mile than any other place I know of, or why people don't give up smoking, you have to assume there is something valuable to them in the dissonance between the destructive fact and their continuing coexistence with it. One thing I came to realize as I studied the non-cultists—they are also being enlivened and are given a state of feeling and hope considerably beyond their real prospects. Nobody on either side wants to see the utter eclipse of the cult."

In a divided society, I thought, where much of the drama of life comes from the polarization, each individual embodies a little of the conflict in himself. Thinking of our own society, I wondered whether even those most rigidly committed to an American style of life, to extending the worst waste and ethnocentrism of the present, might not secretly share in and be excited by the thought of revolution, even as it terrified them. I am sure that most of the revolutionaries, putting their own future in jeopardy on the basis of a belief in revolution, must know that the revolution they prophesy will not come. Half of our society expects a continuation and amplification of the present; half of it holds the goal of abrupt change to a simpler and more loving age; and between the two we may find the courage for the necessary thoughtful change.

Ted went on to talk about some of the new forms that cults

are taking in other areas. "They just keep going on. So far, some of the most educated people that a contact culture has produced are still in it and the things take on more and more sophisticated forms. In 1964, in New Hanover, they were asked to vote in an election for House of Assembly members and they refused and said, 'No, we want to be governed by the Americans instead of the Australians. The Americans are better and richer and they're going to develop us faster; therefore, we vote for Lyndon Johnson.' They even raised a sum of money to try to induce him to come over. I read about this, described as a thoroughly secular thing, based on justifiable grievances, so I went over there and almost immediately I could see that it was a cargo cult in the classical sense. There were all kinds of elements that people hadn't seen; they're building special cemeteries and the dead are going to be returning with the Americans. One of the main reasons why it looked secular is that we believe in the existence of the Americans, whereas in reality they are the supernatural beings of this particular cult, and the believers are profoundly uninterested in Americans like me and any others around—we who don't come bearing cargo, but make apologies and say that it doesn't seem very likely that a flotilla loaded with cargo is about to arrive from America. They are being visited by Americans at night; they are building helicopter pads out in remote parts of the bush; there are phantom helicopters that call on them; the cult leaders have been taken to America repeatedly on submarines that call at night; things of this sort. Here again we have a cargo cult. People would read off a list of concrete grievances and then the government would say okay, you want more agricultural extension, we'll give you more agricultural extension. It always puzzled them that people were so indifferent to this promise of meeting their grievances. But that would deprive them of this really exciting and vivifying meta-stable state of existence. People become addicted to it in the sense that they keep wanting to revive and go back into the cult state."

"That's like the modern anarchists who are upset when a grievance is met by the administration because it then destroys the confrontation and what they want is perpetual confrontation," said Barry.

"Some of the anarchists are aware of this though. I don't think the people in cargo cults are at that level of awareness. But we're aware of what we are doing with things like cigarette smoking. These have always been self-destructive acts. Every night we see very clever ads on TV, telling us we're going to get lung cancer, and we still smoke. The more they keep telling us, the more consciously self-destructive the act becomes, and the dissonance itself has value. It persists because there's a pay-off in it."

Ted went on to compare what he had seen during the three years he had lived in Mexico. "They have a grim life, vastly worse in many ways than that of the Manus where, for example, there's never been a food shortage. These people tend to suppress goals and to have a very heightened sense of expectations, which they set so low that virtually any calamity is better than expected. I call this a deflationary society. One of the functions that I see in casting expectations very low and suppressing goals is as a kind of counterdepressant. Anything that happens, no matter how bad, is still better than you expected, or at least you have the satisfaction of having your direst expectations confirmed, and much conversation is occupied with this. But at the same time, I think it is an institutionalized depression that is a substitute for real individual depression, and has a counterdepressive effect.

"In Melanesia you have a kind of antithesis of this, what I call an inflationary society, and this also affects people's adaptation. In Manus, for instance, Paliau had some really good ideas on how they could actually begin to earn more money and yet this part of his program failed. The people could start plantations that are much larger than those that Europeans own, and they know every aspect of copra technology, having worked in it for fifty years. Over and over, everybody has tried to persuade them to plant those damn coconuts and earn some real money and yet they sit and don't do it. In Manus in '53, I sat through endless meetings about this; I come back fifteen years later and

I sit through endless meetings about the same plantations that nobody's planted."

"Like housing in New York?" said Barry.

"Yes, but I'm not sure the reason is the same. It doesn't puzzle me because I know what's on their minds. It's still that compared to the goals that they have projected, all of this is so paltry, a lot of hard work to achieve a kind of intermediate goal culture that is not very interesting to them. What they do is to set their goals as far ahead as they 'can. In fact, they go one better than European society; they have taken our technology and fused it with magical ideas, so that one has only to think, 'I will be in a car, I will go to such and such a place,' and you're there."

"Could you describe again the pay-off of not quite believing what you're believing," Barry asked, "this hedging, or interpenetration of belief and disbelief?"

Ted was beginning to expand on the way in which a previous skepticism enhanced the value of a conversion, when Gregory interrupted, cocking his pencil at Barry. "I'm becoming very uncomfortable about your use of the word 'pay-off.' You are applying to the homeostatic maintenance of dissonance a term which belongs essentially to a lineal argument, the pay-off for a sequence of events, or reinforcement. Now I think this is epistemologically very, very bad. I mean, granted the metaphor, and granted that perhaps you didn't really want the metaphor to be used . . ."

"No, I agree. Ted used the word before."

"I know, I know, I sort of formulated what I said at the moment he used it. It's one of the words that's around. We keep taking the very gross oversimplifications of stimulus-response and reinforcement psychology, for example, which are little sequential bits, and then looking at a very complex homeostatic maintenance of a schismogenesis or dissonance and talking as though that were to be dissected onto an epistemology of stimulus-response psychology or the economic theories of manufacturers and financiers."

"I see what you're saying," said Ted, "and I would agree

with it. The important thing to me is how the system gets set to the parameters that are being maintained. I do think that the hostility and the dissonance, the states of excitation and heightened feeling, become the real point of the thing after a while. It's a kind of an addiction. The hope for the cargo, which would be a kind of instrumentative relation whether magical or not, is gradually replaced by the state of expectation."

Gertrude said, "To me, the tolerance of diversity is not the same thing as tolerance of inconsistency. I hold the tolerance of diversity of belief, for instance, or even of behavior, as a value concept. I must not expect everyone else to enjoy the same things that I enjoy or believe the same things that I believe, nor must he expect me to conform to his beliefs and all of his patterns of behavior. But tolerance of inconsistency is an internal thing that I believe to be very destructive for the individual. If I try to hold a pair of contradictory principles, I'm in danger of coming out with *anything*. One pair of contradictories within my system, on a dynamic subverbal level, can, it seems to me, produce complete insanity. I can come out with just any old thing—the moon's made of green cheese! Furthermore, I think that I have examples of it producing complete paralysis in an animal. There was no outlet whatever; the animal didn't have recourse to language so he could say, 'I believe this and I believe this, but those can't operate at the same time,' so the organism is completely paralyzed, can't even move.

"Now, this dissonance business—is that like what we used to call 'suspended judgment'? The Manus are trying to believe that the Judgment Day is near, and so on, but all the time there's a suspended judgment? It may not happen and in that case I'd better put the money on the coral reefs where I can go out and get it again. Now if that's a sort of suspended judgment, that isn't necessarily destructive."

"No, I don't think that's the way it works," Ted said slowly. "That would be just covering the other possibility—it sounds as if you're seeing it as a kind of conscious calculus. There were some individuals, on the other side, who tried to cover their bets. But the people in the cult who threw out the money couldn't admit that the cargo might not come; that would be the end of everything. In fact, one of their prevalent explanations as to why the cargo doesn't come is that people are not believing with sufficient intensity."

"That's the way out," Barry nodded. "In order to save the cult, you've got to build into it this loophole. Even table tapping works that way, or dianetics."

Ted was preparing to elaborate further on a theory of the role of orientational constructs in culture, when Tolly interrupted: "You said that the Manus were tremendously interested in wealth before, right? But then the whole scale is upset and what before simply served the functions of creating invidious distinctions between individuals within a society now becomes translated into a goal for the society as a whole?"

"That's right. You have a certain scale on which people are competing for distinction, for validation of themselves, and suddenly the scale of wealth is tremendously upset and you have a notion that colossal wealth exists in the world, so your exchanges of pigs and dogs' teeth are suddenly very paltry. The problem of converting to another scale is one of the problems that we're dealing with."

"Yes. The business of scale is extremely critical for this conference in several different respects," Tolly agreed. "There's also the pathology of the conversion of economic wealth, as a method of becoming better than your fellow man inside of society, to a goal for society as a whole. Such things, for example, as generalizing from the rational man to the 'rational society,' whatever that might mean, or from the efficient enterprise, you know, one steel mill, to the 'efficient society'—these large-scale translations of concepts."

"With a jump of logical typing when you translate," Gregory added.

And a jump in values, I thought, as when we disrupt the lives of individuals in the city in pursuit of the illusion that we are making the city a more human and livable place.

"It's an aspect of reductionism," Barry commented.

# The Vision
# of the Apocalypse

ALTHOUGH I HAD KNOWN the Manus story before, with an emphasis on how successful the Paliau Movement had been in bridging the gap from disruption to the beginning of membership in the modern world, as compared to other primitive societies, I found a great deal of newly disturbing meaning in the story in the context of the conference. Like Barry, Ted was giving an account of the way in which Westerners, carelessly wielding their technologies, had broken into and destroyed ongoing patterns of life, without appreciating their internal structure or the fact that they could never be reconstructed. Warren mentioned, in an aside on the irreversibility of loss, that an average of two animal species had become extinct every year since 1900, each a unique solution to the problem of survival. Whatever the accuracy of this figure, no one can specify the number of human cultures that have been irrevocably disrupted since then, or throughout the history of imperial expansion, but each of these is an equally irreversible loss. Even where large numbers of individuals survive and are assimilated into other cultural systems, we are the poorer for a pattern of possible human life, tuned and balanced over thousands of years of developing the internal stability that Western cultural systems have forsaken.

The Manus story underlined our awareness that our problems were cybernetic because, drastic as the alien interference was, it was less drastic than what the Manus themselves did during the cult in order to maintain a continuing sense of competence. It was the homeostatic search for one crucial constancy that caused them to destroy, of their own property, as much as Japanese and American bombers ever destroyed. It also underlined the communicational nature of the disruption of systems: a society is as effectively disabled by distortions in its pattern of meaning and authority as by epidemics, massacres, and deportations—in fact, when these physical attacks finally overthrow the system, it is by destroying the channels of communication.

Ted's material was especially disturbing, however, because it threw light on the systemic effects of ideas about the future, which he called orientational constructs. Here we were, thinking about the future and trying to imagine a type of planning that would not be as disruptive as sewage engineering. We had identified a certain type of purpose as dangerous; now we were looking at hope and expectation as causal in human behavior. Bert Kaplan was especially moved because he responded sympathetically to the cargo cults and immediately recognized, through the unfamiliar and even grotesque details, an echo of the most exalted hopes of the West: the coming of the Kingdom, the coming of a just society after the revolution, the end of yearning and waste and grief.

During lunch he and Ted sat together, Ted cautious and reserved, and when we came back for our afternoon session Bert began to draw the lines connecting Ted's material to our concern.

Bert is a tall, gentle man with a slight stammer and an ardent and diffident manner. His large moist eyes protrude slightly behind his glasses and he has a bald, domed forehead. "I found what Ted had to say extraordinarily moving. He feels I should be on my guard, but I think social scientists are so used to having their work make very little difference that the possibility of something generally important in what they're doing is almost a danger to their being social scientists.

"I would like to say what the cargo cults mean to me. As I understand it, Marxist theory, Christianity, a great many of our important religions and intellectual endeavors, seem to me to have exactly this form. This morning I began to see lots of things as cargo cults. All of these start from an interpretation of the present life under the aspect of deprivation. Marx called scarcity the main fact of life for us, and the socialist order was to be an order of abundance, a different kind of life, without need and without goals. This is the same as the Christian notion of the apocalypse as a move out of the needful life into the life of abundance. Now, I just think that kind of change is a stirring notion. I compare that to the cybernetic notion of the pre-European Manus in which the goal would seem to be just the maintenance of the system. What's contemplated here, really, is the final opening of a flowering universe; God appears, instead of being hidden from us, and there is no more deprivation.

"Now, Ted says that it's kind of exciting when you're waiting for God, but it seems to me the issue must be something other than making life a little more interesting. My thoughts keep turning back to this notion of life as deprivation. Then there's the notion of the end of history, so if you take history as a kind of march, you ask, toward what? And the answer is given in the cargo cult: the ship comes in and there's no place further to go."

Ted said, "If the cargo comes, then they leave this long ride on a vehicular culture and they're once again in a situation that is perpetuable, only now they'll be living like Europeans, perhaps a bit better."

"That seems very strange to me. Their apocalypse is precisely what we have. We have the technology, we have the stuff that they feel would be a final event, the end to their religion. I think there's a lesson in it, that this isn't such a hot apocalypse. The cargo of things that technology brought us doesn't really end history. It leaves us still with a kind of emptiness that just isn't filled by any technological event that produces goods more abundantly."

"One needs a movable apocalypse," Ted commented.

"Well, it can't be an apocalypse if there's . . . if there's any notion that it can be moved," said Bert.

Tolly said very forcefully, "It's the idea of the conceivable existence of *anything* which is independent of process. It's the confusion that what I strive for is what I strive for, which is nonsense. Pardon the queer way that I've said it, but I don't know of any concise way of expressing what I mean: *What I strive for cannot be what I strive for.*"

"Quite," said Gregory. "It doesn't exist." Listening, I had a sudden sharp sense of loss. So many things seem to become more vividly real as we long for them and yet the vividness belongs to the longing; static attainment is a withering counterfeit. The Manus were deluded not only because the committees of the dead did not exist—they were deluded because the cargo of happiness that they thought they saw day after day on the docks and landing strips, consigned to the whites, did not exist. The boxes contain only goods and supplies, ornaments and machinery, not the end of desire. I sat and grieved.

Bert was bewildered. "Why not exist? I don't understand."

"I don't know whether I ought to try to explain. I chose that form of expression because . . . I mean . . . that's despair. For me to try to explain to you . . . well, I don't know how to say why that's such nonsense."

"May I try and say it?" Gregory offered. "If I do not write a letter to my aunt and she writes me an angry letter in reply, what is the 'cause' of her angry letter? The 'cause' of her angry letter is the difference between the letter which I might have written and the letter which I didn't write. These are both fictitious; they are not nouns and the difference is not a real object. The moment you start talking about *that*, over in the future, as the cause of *this*, in the present, you are passing through this whole fictional structure."

"It's also the illusion that if strawberry shortcake is a good thing, then more strawberry shortcake is a better thing," Tolly added.

"That's the vulgarization of thinking that what you strive for is what you strive for."

"Look," said Bert, "the best understanding we have of striving, goals, needs, purposes, and all the rest, can be assimilated to the same structure, based on deprivation. Within your own reality there is an absence . . ."

"Absences are causes," Gregory amended, "the cause being the difference between what you have and what you desire, not the object of your longing."

". . . and the human being is a being who can feel such absences. We are able to project possibilities which are different from what we have, what we are, and we live with this disparity. That's the structure of striving."

"Now the actualization of removing that disparity is the death of you," Tolly said.

"Well, you see," Bert explained, "that's the Faustian notion, that the reality of life is striving or yearning. Now these apocalyptic religions have in some way the idea of a life that isn't a life of endless striving."

Tolly was disgusted and Horst said, "You don't feel Faustian? It's an interpretation of you from the outside, yes?"

"There's a chasm as big as the universe!"

"Well, I thought I could reconcile . . . see, many now agree with Bert. If we said that filling the gap is the goal, the gap is not the goal? But maybe I'm at odds with both of you?" Horst's bright eyes flicked back and forth between Tolly and Bert.

Bert continued, "The main alternative to life dominated by deprivation that's been conceived, I think, is the Nietzschean notion of life lived out of one's real powers . . . that is, the conception that a human being is . . . has real possibilities to live out . . . he's not simply emptiness of something else. Nietzsche criticized Christianity for being the religion of a weak person living with his weakness, moving toward something he didn't have. The conception of the movement from deprivation to power is another idea that has stirred Europe in our time."

Still trying to resolve the disagreement, Horst turned to Tolly again. "It's not too far away. I mean, I do understand correctly? A translation problem?"

Tolly was not playing. "I see little chance of being more explicit about what I've said than I've already been."

"Wait," Gregory said, adding another element to his description of the Creatura. "It is in the nature of living things that their energy expenditure is an inverse function of their energy input: Amoebae get hungry and they move faster when they're hungry than when they're not hungry. This is what it's about. Correspondingly with plants, which grow faster on the dark side: their energy input is related to light, the light hits the plant on one side, so they grow faster on the other and of course bend over toward the light, their equivalent of locomotion. Now this is so. This means that we deal essentially with signals rather than with quantities. The whole dream of plenty is built upon the fallacy that life is not constructed that way, but is constructed some totally other way. That's what you're objecting to really, isn't it, Tolly?"

"It is this dream of plenty as expressed in the Christian apocalypse and the cargo cults in thousands of cultural forms which, combined with our technological cleverness, is about to put us out of business altogether, in a way which is much more fundamental than the nitrogen cycle even, if that can be. We're about to put my hands out of business, and my eyes. We've already very nearly put my legs out of business."

"Right," Gregory continued. "As to the question of why there are apocalyptic cults under situations of cultural disruption, I think the point is this: in a self-maintaining system, with its complex homeostatic loops and all the rest of it, it is reasonably easy to see what you should do next and you can create a value structure which will deal with a large number of judgments of different sorts of alternatives. Once you really smash that steady-state maintenance, by introducing all sorts of other premises into your system, then it is not at all easy to see what to do next. We live in a culture that—I mean, we're here around this table saying, oh my God, what are we going to do next with this civilization? and we haven't the slightest idea. If you don't have a preference scale on which you can judge what to do next, the easiest solution is self-maximization of some kind, or maximization of some single identifiable variable. And there are various ways you can reconstruct the world, albeit illusory, to give you a value structure which will at least tell you what to do next. One of the ways is to go to war—if you go to war, then you know that guns are better than butter. In peacetime, it's very hard to judge the value of guns as compared with butter, but in war, by God, it's easy. The great relief about going into war is that you know more or less what to do next. You can set up preference scales which make sense because there is one variable in the center of the picture that you want to maximize."

"And there's something to weep about," Tolly added.

"Yes, but the way we are at present, as far as I can see, there are nothing but sort of old-fashioned reasons to indicate clearly whether it's a bad thing to shoot Bobby Kennedy or a good thing to shoot Bobby Kennedy. I mean, so what? Where are we going? What do you want? It's not clear that there's anything we want to maintain in our present state and it's not clear that there's a direction in which we want to go. We don't have a value structure. Now these apocalyptic cults and so forth fill that sort of a need, I suspect. Does that make sense, Tolly, with what you are trying to say?"

"Yeah, it makes sense. It's just kind of not as straightforward as I'd like it. I mean, we're in the midst of destroying my uses of me, or in other words, just me."

"Not only me, but us."

"But of course, please understand."

"Do you mean to say that a cult or a war effort provides a goal by oversimplifying what is real?" Barry asked.

"It oversimplifies, which is the same as vulgarizing, really, and within the falsified frame created by that vulgarity, it's pretty easy to know what to do—produce more shoes or, you know, increase the G.N.P."

Tolly sat very quietly, while Ted went further into the theoretical background of his presentation, and then he drew us back again from the Pacific to our own dilemmas. "I would like to put forward the idea that there is a strict analogy, I mean a really strict analogy, between the people who kill off their livestock, destroy their canoes and, in general, destroy what they had to sustain their life with, under a certain set of cultural expectations, and our own situation, with the destruction of the nitrogen cycle and the general exhaustion of other resources, also under a certain set of cultural expectations. Now most of you, I think, ought to feel revolt at my suggesting that's a really strict analogy."

"I *do*," said Gertrude, appalled.

"Most of you ought to feel that that's just somehow very wrongheaded. For example, the Bushmen and all these other people manage to get along with nature without having had professors and chairs and departments of this and that, but I would think most of you would maintain that they do this only insofar as they are consistent with scientific fact. I'm probably the only one here who would deny that this is so. I will insist that the system which we call science is nothing more than a cultural transactional system complete with its microscopes and electron smashers, long corridors and glass doors with professors' names on them, and all the other paraphernalia which goes with it. I'm thinking of the enterprise of science as indistinguishable from its dictates. I would say that the Bushman who gets along with the environment shares none of this and does not depend on it. What we call scientific fact is only an excrescence or a secretion of our scientific transactional system. That in turn constitutes a set of beliefs, having something to do with our ability to get along with nature, and what we call the mythology of other peoples has something to do with their ability to get along with nature and is a part of their total transactional system. It is along lines such as these that I would argue that we are facing a situation which is not different in principle from the cargo cultists and others who have destroyed their means of existence, as a result of maladaptive transactional systems."

Will Jones had picked up the word "illusory" early in the debate and now he came in to disinfect it. "At one point, Tolly was saying in effect that the apocalyptic value system, which I thought Bert was in a way defending, was illusory. Now I don't think that's at all a clear or straightforward notion. What makes a value system illusory? Well, you might be tempted to say it doesn't get the people who have the value system what they want. Well, then, you are judging this value system in the light of some meta-value system, so you're still inside a value system. As a footnote to that, I'd be disposed to say what you probably mean is that it doesn't give them what *you* want." Will continued fastidiously, "I do feel, I confess, that a good deal of this discussion has been culture-bound."

"So *WHAT!*" Tolly shouted.

Will bridled. "Well! Well, why shouldn't there be a what to my so? But the next thing one might say about an illusory value system was that it conflicted with the facts. Now that's where I think what Tolly was saying before is relevant, because I suspect that what we take to be the procedures for ascertaining the facts, which are science, are themselves deeply infiltrated with elements of the value system. It might well turn out that, inside of a certain system, you had various self-corrective features, including your science, to reassure you about the truth of your values. It's very *easy* to talk about illusory value systems, but it's very difficult to find ways of telling unambiguously whether value system$_1$ is more or less illusory than value system$_2$."

"Would it be fair to notice that they gave up their art when their culture cracked and they went into all this nonsense? Giving up their art is perhaps as good an indication of their having engaged in an illusory operation as any other," Gregory said.

"But then, if I remember what Ted actually said, they got another art of tin cans . . ." Will persisted.

"So have we," said Gregory dourly.

"Aren't you assuming, from a different value system, that . . ."

"That one is better than the other, right," said Tolly.

Ted had given us, in his description of the Manus, the beginnings of a picture of the integration of a single society, but he interwove so much detail from other and highly different cultures in New Guinea, as well as from other parts of the world, that it was easy for the non-anthropologists in the group simply to lump all of his examples together. We used the phrase "cargo cult" to refer to any apocalyptic cult and referred to the Manus as the supreme example of a people whose culture had been disrupted, ignoring the fact that the cult had been a relatively transient episode for the Manus. The Manus before contact were a pragmatic, competitive people, with virtually no art except what they purchased from their neighbors, but they had to stand in our discussion for hundreds of other groups who really had given up their art under Western contact. What we were concerned with was the loss of a complex, stable way of life, exchanged for a simplified commitment to change on the Western model, usually change that was meant to maximize one or two values. The paroxysms of the cult expressed one extreme of that commitment to change. Bert had connected the cult idea with the pervasive modern notion of moving away from deprivation, and the cyberneticists among us were aware of the formal similarity between the cults, the Paliau Movement in Manus, and the Western dream of progress, in spite of the difference in pace.

"I think some things are better than others. I think life is better than death," Gregory finished.

"We'd better make politics here," Tolly said in exasperation, "and not, you know, try to find the foundation for the foundation for the foundation."

"I'll make the following assertion," Barry declared, "that perhaps the most serious consequence of modern science and technology is that it is serving as a way of blocking the development of value judgments. Take, for example, what I think would be a very serious value judgment—that it would be okay to wipe out all people on the surface of the earth. I would assume that this would require some very profound examination of morality, the most serious value judgment the human race has ever faced. Now, why haven't we faced it? Because the situation is couched in a priestly language which only the priests understand, namely, science. People all over the world have no sense that this is upon them, because they don't understand about 'mega-deaths.' This can go right down the line. The people who live around Lake Erie are faced on a smaller scale with the same kind of value judgment. In order to understand it, they have to know all about the nitrogen cycle and phosphates and detergents and so on. What is science if not, in this sense, a way of blocking value judgments?

"My feeling is that the cargo cult is the science of the Manus. You know, a lot of what you've described, Ted, sounded very reasonable. After all, somebody comes with a helicopter, and it's clear that one of the reasons why the helicopter is there is that there was a place for it to land. That's what happens in Vietnam; you make a little place and then, by God, the helicopters come. I agree with Tolly that the lesson has to be applied very directly to our cultural situation. That's what this conference is about."

Ted was deeply disturbed at the kinds of things his material was being compared to. Gregory was trying to get as much mileage as possible from the little anthropological data we would have time for, and he was letting the non-anthropologists ride roughshod over the specific ethnography in pursuit of a set of abstractions he thought important, while Ted was being prevented from developing his own theoretical system and frustrated by our easy talk about the Manus he knew so well. I was reminded of an incident I had heard about Gregory in Bali, when he became so fascinated by photographing the intricate postures and interactions of a group of people watching a cock fight that he never photographed the fighting birds themselves. Gregory had insisted that Ted leave interpretation to the group and Ted was increasingly impatient at the way Barry was pressing the material into illustrating his concerns. Now he spoke, sitting straight and pale, glaring at the table.

"We're in very grave danger of failing as a conference. We could, if we wished, go around and each make a value declaration, and we could greatly oversimplify all of the material that is presented. I think Barry has done just that with the cargo cult. I think if we come out of this with great oversimplifications of every single subject that we broach, it will really be a disgrace. We would all go home comforted, having made our self-righteous and moral statements, but I think we're just . . ."

"We are concerned with the dynamics of this business," said Gregory sharply, "with analyzing it, rather than regretting it and shouting about it. The dynamics are not easy and we keep funking the dynamics for reasons which perhaps we should also go into."

"But I agree with Ted, believe it or not," Will drawled, his eyebrows slightly raised. "It seems to me that we're tending to make far too many value commitments which merely express our own feelings. It isn't necessarily the case that cargo cults are bad for the Manus, as we think they are. It is, indeed, extremely difficult, I think, to find out ways of insuring they're bad for the Manus."

"As I hear the tone of remarks being made," Ted continued, "I think we are just making ourselves feel good rather than doing anything that is creditable to our supposed experience and research. I don't think there's a person in this room that deviates from a general humanistic concern with the survival and welfare of the human race, and a more human life, and all the rest of it, and we shouldn't occupy our time with showing that we're the right kind of person."

"I grant," said Gregory, slumped heavily in his seat and choosing his words carefully, "that we are not always talking strictly to the point. I grant that our language is often ambiguous and can often be suspected of representing the epistemologies which are likely to destroy us. On the other hand, I don't see what we can do exeept go on working, as best we can, and every now and then, we are going to shout about things we don't like. I'm prepared to give 10 per cent of the conference time to shouting about the things we don't like. We're human too, you know."

We searched briefly for a rephrasing of the difference of views between Tolly, Bert, and Will on apocalyptic value systems, and Gregory continued, "I think there are many more interesting things than our personal dislike of apocalyptic systems. It is interesting to know what their dynamics are. How did the Manus get there? As far as I can see, they got there by a fragmentation of what was previously an elaborately interlocking value system."

"If you want to do that, I don't think it's helpful to denounce apocalyptic value systems, which we tend to do," said Will.

"Are you willing to denounce the fragmentation of a culture?"

"Are we here for that?" Ted asked. "If so, let's have a resolution and have everyone sign it."

The room exploded in angry argument.

"Wait a minute," said Gregory above the medley. "Wait a minute. We are here because we are worried. It is suggested that that which we are worried about is related to the fragmentation of our value system. It is therefore reasonable to ask how value systems get fragmented. What are the symptoms of fragmentation, and how does it all work? There is a much more difficult question which faces us of how, when fragmented, you get back again to an unfragmented system. That I don't know."

Barry said, "I take the view that the signs of our potential success are exactly the things that Ted worries about—namely, that there appear to be threads which tie his very elegant, scientific considerations of the Manus to the immediate motivation of the conference as Gregory just expressed it. Now, it's understandable that you will wince at the necessary oversimplifications that occur as these threads are drawn. Obviously we don't know beans about the Manus. But the fact that you are wincing, Ted, tells me that we are trying to make the links between what you have studied and what we are concerned with. I think that the conference could easily fail by doing a very lovely, detailed, scientific job on what each of us has to say about the Manus, or DNA, or teaching, which would be sound, unambiguous by our own lights, and totally unrelated to the burning issues of today, which are why we're here."

"I have also been trying to make such links," Ted retorted. "I have been trying to do it not simply by telling you what I believe in, though any of you are entitled to such a declaration any time you want it. I have been trying to do it as I've been trying for the last fifteen years, that is, really struggling to understand just what happened. If we are here simply to register agreements and disagreements on values . . ."

"No, we're not, we are here to discuss systems of thought."

"That's right," Tolly agreed, "but then if we switch to an entirely different mode of thinking, in which we're really not very much more qualified than anybody else . . ."

Gregory was exasperated. "I haven't switched," he said vehemently. "I don't know that anybody's switched. I mean, I'm just waiting impatiently to get around to the next presentation when this nonsense stops. Peter has a question."

"Can someone give me an example of a culture that lacks apocalyptic elements or phases?" Peter asked.

"Balinese. Not the slightest interest in the future," Gregory snapped.

Peter continued in a gentle, tentative voice. "I wondered whether it would be possible to come to some kind of judgment as to the relative viability or stability of cultures that are comparable in most respects but this one. Can a comparative study of groups help us to derive value judgments? I'm sort of flip-flopping here, taking first one view and then another. For example, a look at modern technology as equivalent to the cargo cult makes sense. Many times I've given lectures on the population problem, for example, and the response has often been, 'Oh, we don't have to worry about it; when the problem gets acute, technology will solve it, as it has solved everything else.' This is the cargo cult aspect of science. At the same time, I have to recognize that many of these people will also take the position that technology isn't always going to solve all our problems and it would be a very dull world if it would. There's a fundamental premise that, as we solve one problem, we generate another, so the apocalyptic vision is not tied to the notion of paradise gained. I wondered, Ted, whether you would comment on either the usefulness or the feasibility of a comparative approach?"

Ted was not prepared to play. "Not at the moment."

"Part of the question is whether it is dangerous for cultures to be directed toward change at all," I said in a hard, brittle voice that startled me. "It's not the fact that there is an apocalyptic notion that makes people meddle with the environment. It's the fact that they want to bring about major change. The apocalyptic notion is one extreme of a continuum within which people have decided that they're no longer going to live in a balanced system; they're going to look toward change. Operationally, the specific technical effort to implement short-term goals may be much more dangerous to the environment than waiting for an apocalypse you can't do anything about. The Manus that belong to the Movement look much more rational, much 'nicer,' than the ones that dance around speaking in tongues, but that's not at all clear. It's the people in the Movement that will be bringing in the chemical fertilizers and pesticides and so on."

"Right," said Gregory.

Bernie said, "You spoke of being surprised, Ted, by the self-corrective mechanisms that had appeared within a system that had looked as if it was going to destroy itself. I was wondering if it was fair sometime to try and look at some of the elements in our society that are beginning to be self-corrective mechanisms—if we can, in a way, draw parallels and begin to maximize these elements. Gregory spoke, for example, of maximizing values in ways so that we know guns are better than butter. Well, the attempt, for example, to maximize war in Vietnam isn't working. When you take the child out of a schizophrenic family and you try and get it well by itself, as it were, the family kind of closes back and makes somebody else sick, and if you put the person that you've helped in the hospital back in the family, he gets sick again. You have to put someone into this system who can demaximize certain things and maximize others." Bernie gave several different examples that did not work out quite analogously, and then pulled himself back. "I'm not making myself as clear as I can. I just want to ask you, Ted, what self-correcting mechanisms can you see now that have a parallel in the cargo-cult system?"

"Well, I think one of the things that I get out of this cargo cult that is relative to our own society is an increase in my understanding of human systems in their dis-analogy, their lack of analogy. . . . What word would you use?" Gregory suggested catalogy. "Good. Their catalogy, with the kind of things we're trying to carry over from more primitive cybernetic systems. The kind of focus that I personally thought I would bring was to get back into the discussion of systems. Unlike some other kinds of systems, these are systems of people: they have internalized representations of the system and they are self-excitatory and generate or reformulate the goals of the system in response to a complex set of needs. This is something that I cannot handle completely in the cybernetic sense, because the cybernetic model accounts for goal-seeking, but it doesn't account for goals or for the way goals are generated. So I see this as a kind of extremely dynamic system that we could take as a model for other human systems, in order to find out what happens when we play around with goals, and what the dangers are in the very flexibility that we have in the motivated construction of our expectation, reconstructing both our present and our past in such a way as either to maximize our sense of accomplishment or to minimize it. I think we do this often, when we are trying to construct a world in such a way that it is a projection of our values. I think that sort of thing has been happening with what I've offered with the cargo cult. All of us have been projecting like mad onto it. Sometimes I don't recognize what we're talking about!

"I think anthropologists have made maybe 90 per cent of their work worthless, because we use our field experience as our muse—we'll make anything of it that we want to make of it. If our problem today is, let's say, environmental pollution, then we will make our work a paradigm for talking about environmental pollution. It registers to me as an intellectual hodge-podge that has made any of us unable, I think, to strive for a sensible understanding of the world. Instead, I have the feeling we simply want to stand around and produce statements. I'm disturbed at the moment, I apologize for it."

"Excuse me," said Bernie, "That's just the kind of answer that I didn't want. I thought my question was reasonably specific and then you went off and gave another value judgment about science and the ways of anthropology . . ."

"Your question was about ten minutes long and I really didn't understand it. For the last hour, I've been understanding very little of what anyone is saying!"

"If you didn't, you could have told me to clarify! Maybe this is what's happening a little bit, too. I don't want to misuse your system, and I don't want to jump into the stratosphere and do things that I shouldn't do with it. That's what I'm asking you."

"Well. Let's have some coffee," Ted whispered.

Getting up from the table, I fled from the conference room, as much puzzled by my own cold fury as we moved toward the end of the session as I was distressed by Ted's. It was a conversation in which I had felt driven by each person's comment away from an understanding of the previous comment which had seemed acceptable—Bert with his reminder of the magnificence of the apocalyptic hope, Tolly with his attack on its assumptions, Will reminding us that we were talking within our culture, and Tolly's resounding "So what!" Finally I had to break in, saying don't use common sense on the Movement either, look at it in this same radical way for the dust and ashes it will produce, and let us admit that for the moment we are attacking all purpose, all action to bring about change, all the modes in which our thought finds optimism and improvement. It seemed to me that if we turned away from such a discussion with the excuse of a search for rigor, it would be because we were afraid. And I myself was certainly frightened, as my sense of our conflict among ourselves resonated with my sense of man's conflict with the balance of nature.

# Learning: An Entry into Pattern

AMONG THE MANY ATTEMPTS to correct for the decay of our value system, one important strand is a rejection of rationality and science. This very rejection can be seen as a symptom of the way in which contemporary styles of thinking and knowing seem to provoke alienation rather than insight, so that those who seek wisdom turn to oriental religion, to drugs and meditation, for the wholeness that these may offer. Will Jones pointed out one day that there has been a continual fluctuation in Western history in the value placed upon rational consciousness. Classical Greek thought valued it highly, with Aristotle making it the touchstone of reality and constructing a hierarchical universe ascending toward increasing consciousness. During post-Classical times, with Neo-Platonism, Skepticism, and above all Gnosticism, the pendulum swung in the opposite direction, only to reverse again during the Middle Ages. The most drastic swing against rational consciousness took place at the end of the eighteenth century, with the beginning of the Romantic era. This was partly triggered by a reaction to the claims of science, since by that time Descartes's program had essentially been fulfilled in the work of Isaac Newton and science could promise a complete and true description of the natural world.

It seemed to me that the possibility of a new Romanticism was very much a part of the intellectual context of the conference, judging by the ease with which we had accepted Barry's indictment of science and technology. However, the group gathered at Burg Wartenstein would hardly represent a flight to Romanticism if we could get our position articulated clearly. The opposition the Romantics felt to the science of their time was echoed in some of our discussions of atomism and reductionism, but the Romantic poets feared that the rainbow was unwoven by Newton's analysis of the prism, that nature's beauty was destroyed by a knowledge of its structure; we were in fear of a more drastic and direct unraveling of the texture of life, where nature's loveliness was threatened by man's actions based on incomplete understanding, not by knowledge. Then too, although our conversation at times came near the elusiveness of poetry by the interweaving of our ideas, most of us were trained in science or mathematics and brought with their precision a sense of a new loveliness they could reveal. Barry inveighed against atomism out of a certainty that the time for atomism had passed and Gregory condemned consciousness only because of its incompleteness. In effect, the group demanded better science to meet the crisis, rather than a rejection of science. The problem was how to know with one's whole being, and how to mesh such knowledge with language and the traditional disciplines of mathematics and the sciences. To lead us further toward an understanding of this question, Gregory called on Gertrude, the teacher in our number. Wisely, he called on her after Ted, at a moment when the tension was high and we needed to listen quietly for a time or we would be at each other's throats. Although her presentation was tangential to the immediately preceding discussion, it was an essential part of the synthesis, and in the meantime soothed jangling nerves and tempers. So we turned from vehemence and argument to watch Gertrude, graceful and girlish at the board, speaking in a sweet, sane voice, telling her story from the beginning.

Gertrude's report was about a discovery she had made thirty years ago, which she still recounted with delight. Her description of the process by which she made her discovery was important to us, too, because it involved the kind of sudden transfer of insight from one area of experience to another that was needed in such a conference as ours, where the subject matter of the presentations was so widely separated. Then, too, because she was speaking of the possibility of knowing something without being able to put it into words, she was making us aware of our slowly growing sense that there was order in our discussions, that we were indeed beginning to have a new understanding of the relationship of conscious purpose and human adaptation which we could not yet articulate, as we moved through a series of examples in preparation for the advent of awareness.

In 1937, Gertrude was working as a young teacher of demonstration math classes, in which she was developing and teaching an inductive approach. Instead of giving the students a rule on the basis of authority, they were asked to discover their own rule by being led carefully through a series of examples and then asked to put their discovery into words.[1] At the same time, she was working to retrain a horse, and here her teaching was based on a conditioning theory of learning. The horse had been bred and trained for the show ring, but he had become unreliable and dangerous, growing frantic under the saddle and trotting faster and faster until he broke over into a runaway gallop. Gertrude had followed a long and tedious sequence of exercises with him, and that spring she set out to try and condition him to associate relaxation, slow speed, and a light mouth with the foot-order and rhythm which make up the gait called "canter." Each day she gave the horse a workout, cantering in an enclosed ring, so small that when the impulse to plunge and run came on him he regained his poise before trouble developed.

---

By the first week in May, I decided it might be safe to test the new learning. I planned a six-mile ride on country roads, along the second and third miles of which were four level stretches with a steep hill at the far end of each stretch. I planned to canter along the level stretch and to bring the horse back to a walk on the incline, trusting the hill to help me get him under control if he lost his head. I was also depending upon the fact that the animal would be headed *away* from home at the time.

The first stretch of canter was negotiated with complete success. The second was equally successful. Intervals of walk, then trot, then walk were inserted between each two places to canter. Everything went perfectly until we walked around a curve where the third level stretch with a steep hill beyond came into sight. Suddenly, my nice, quiet, well-poised horse began to snort and dance. He positioned himself for the canter signal which he had been taught, a signal from which the horse lifts into a collected canter from a halt, and he was so bursting with excitement and eagerness to do it that I knew I did not dare to let him try. Excited as he was, he would have lost his head and would have tried to run—and all that I had accomplished in two months of "conditioning" would have been lost.

But my load of discouragement and defeat was pierced by a shaft of wonder: What kind of thing was this new learning about appropriate places to canter? And so on that morning ride in May, heartsick with the failure of the long, tedious sequence of horse-training lessons, even as I faced with dread the more than three miles of struggle ahead of me to keep my nervous horse from "running away" home, I became excited at the thought of what had happened. Had not the horse generalized from the sameness in the first two examples? If verbalized, what the horse had discerned would be something like this: "When we come to a level stretch of road with a hill at the far end of it, then I am permitted to canter."

In the canter the feet come down in the same order as in the gallop. To a powerful, healthy, highly animated, hot-blooded horse on a cool May morning, the desire to run must have been very strong. It seemed to me that with this kind of motivation, the horse had generalized by the time he came to the third appropriate stretch of road. The highly motivated generalizing had cut through and taken precedence over eight weeks of careful but unmotivated training based on the conditioned-learning hypothesis.

In the ensuing weeks I changed all my training tactics to

conform to my new hypothetical interpretation of the learning I was trying to promote. I thought of each thing that I
wished the horse to learn as a universal generalization, a universal if-then, if you please. I was careful to preserve a consistent temporal sequence for "if" events and "then" events.
The horse would reveal by his behavior the instant he became
aware of the relation between an "if" set of events and the
related "then" set of events. It seemed to me that the first
such instance was always accompanied by a half-hesitant,
questioning motion, and the immediate acceptance and ap-
proval on my part seemed to produce a ripple of something
like satisfaction, or even elation, in the horse.

The horse progressed rapidly in his training from that
morning on. He became delightful to ride and drive, and on
show he paraded as though his heart would burst; his mouth
stayed light; and he "kept his head" every step of the way.

I am sure that to a casual observer, many of the things
done during the schooling sessions following that Saturday
morning ride would not have been distinguishable from
things done in the earlier sessions which had been planned
with a conditioning hypothesis in mind. Just how doing almost
the same things but for different reasons could produce such
different outcomes is a question worthy of contemplation.
Certainly, the trainer's regarding each new thing learned as
awareness of a generalization elevated the equine learner to
a position of higher respect in the trainer's regard. There was
a kind of pervasive dignity between trainer and horse which
had not been there before, a kind of empathy which generated a greater respect in trainer for horse, and, very soon, a
seemingly greater respect of horse for trainer.

---

Over the years, Gertrude has met a tremendous resistance
to her assertion that an animal trained in this way is aware of a
principle. The very dignity and sense of shared excitement that
she found in her method seem to be repugnant, when associated
with a horse, to many people concerned with teaching and
learning, and such dignity and shared excitement are equally
absent from much of our training of children and even of college students. Gertrude's years of arguing with people unwilling

to concede dignity to any kind of knowing not already dignified by words were apparent in her tenacious concern about terminology, to which she kept returning, picking her way between the terms knowledge, understanding, awareness, and others. Here Warren came in with a key distinction: "If I take a cat and hold it up by its legs four feet from the floor and let it fall, it lands right side up, but it can't tell me a single thing about conserving angular momentum. If I take the professor of physics and hold him head down, four feet from the floor, and let him go, he'll go down on his head, but he can tell me exactly how he should have straightened himself out. Now. The cat was aware of what? The professor was aware of what?"

"I'd say the cat was 'aware' of whatever it was that was put into practice in righting itself to land on its feet."

"Would you agree with me that most living systems solve problems without knowing how they solve them and that most of the time they solve problems without even knowing they're problems?" Warren asked.

"The shark never knew that hydrodynamics was a problem," said Gregory.

"And it is entirely possible that our effort to know that which no other living thing bothers knowing will lead to mistaken notions of what we don't know," Barry said ominously.

Gregory forestalled a further debate about terms. "Gertrude," he said, "would it help if we dropped the word awareness for the moment and said the creature behaves as if it had use of such and such information? Now, it depends a great deal in what form that individual organism has the information inside himself. Take the shark. The shark is nicely streamlined to fit the water, but it is nonsense to say that the genome of the shark, which determines the shape it grows into, has hydrodynamics pickled in it. What it has pickled in it is how to cope with hydrodynamics. This is a sort of coding that records the operation of adaptation, not the thing you're adapting to, what Don McKay calls 'transcoding.' This is a very different kind of coding from what we do when we abstract a principle of some kind."

Gregory had once remarked to me that of all the people he invited to the conference, Gertrude was the one he was most certain of, the one whose work seemed to dovetail most precisely with his own concerns. In the Memorandum, he had asserted that only a portion of experience is brought into consciousness and that men then make decisions of terrible adaptive import on the basis of that fragment. The abstraction of a principle is a process that throws considerable light on the relationship between conscious and unconscious mind, and this became clear as Gertrude went on to describe her work on human learning.

During the same period as her experience with the horse, Gertrude in her demonstration algebra class set out one day to teach the students how to clear an equation of fractions. The class moved through a series of examples where, in the beginning, they had to try number after number as possible multipliers, and in the end were able to race through a list of problems, recognizing immediately that an equation such as $\frac{2x}{3} + \frac{x}{5} = 2$ could be cleared of fractions by multiplying by 15.

---

It was only after the dismissal bell for that class hour had rung and the usual conference with my observers was under way, that I realized that I had omitted calling for a verbalization of the newly-discovered rule. I had instead enthusiastically accepted behavioral evidence of *awareness* of the rule, just as if I had been working with the horse! I apologized to my observers for having omitted what was probably the most important step in the inductive lesson, and promised to finish the job the next day.

At the next meeting of that algebra class it was evident that the class had been quite successful with the problems assigned. The students were tested with some more new examples before I called for a statement of the rule for clearing an equation of fractions. The classroom atmosphere immediately changed from one of animated success to an atmosphere of laborious effort. By the time a sentence acceptable to the teacher (i.e., to me) had been achieved, all the excitement of learning was gone and nobody wanted to work that kind of problem any more. Although the student teachers and I discussed this effect in our next seminar meeting, it still did not occur to any of us that verbalizing the discovery might not add anything to the learner's power to apply the discovery in the solving of new problems. What I *thought* I had acquired was a procedure for being sure whether a learner had arrived at a stage at which it was *fair* to request him to verbalize.

---

Gertrude went on developing the technique of allowing students to reach generalizations inductively and then verbalize them for the next nine years, and then in 1946–47 took a leave of absence and set out to test how the way in which a generalization was learned, by authority or by induction, affected the capacity to apply that generalization to new kinds of material. She used three groups of students in her experiment. One group was taught how to solve a certain type of problem by being given a rule; one group was led through a series of examples until the behavior of each showed that they had become aware of a generalization that made quick solutions possible and then were dismissed; and one group was made to stay on after they learned to solve the problems until each had arrived, often after several attempts, at an accurate verbal generalization of their insight. A few days later, all the subjects were given a test which included a scattering of examples that could be solved by a short cut if the student could transfer the principle used in the experimental sessions. As expected, those in the conscious generalization group did more than twice as well as those who had learned by authority, but no one was more startled than Gertrude to discover that the unverbalized awareness group did even better. The difference was small but statistically significant.[2] Gertrude felt that she had hooked a much bigger fish than she could play, a startling contradiction to the old adage, "If you can't tell it, you don't know it."

As Gertrude explained it, the group of students who learned by being given a rule learned at only a superficial level, except for a few, those whom Robert Maynard Hutchins once referred to as "the people who can learn from books," those given to testing generalizations against examples they themselves construct and thus experiencing their truth at a deeper level instead of accepting it on authority. The other groups arrived at the generalization through experience, generalizing at levels of their minds outside of consciousness. The difficulty in verbalizing, plus the slight edge that the students who did not verbalize their generalizations had, are evidence of the incomplete match between things brought into consciousness and the mental processes that underlie them. Gertrude argued that the very nature of language creates a necessary distortion when the instantaneous "aha" flash of insight is strung out along the time axis in sentences.

It would have been easy to take Gertrude's evidence as one more element in the new Romanticism, with its emphasis on direct experience as superior to verbalization, except that here again we were asked to go one step beyond the Romantic position. Unverbalized discoveries may be abstract and powerful generalizations and they may indeed be somewhat weakened by the experience of verbalization, but Gertrude went on to assert that such detachment is necessary if one is to test his own discoveries for truth and reliability.

---

There is another and more fearsome angle to the possible detachment effect which accompanies successful verbalization of discoveries. When one has "discovered" something false, as long as the discovery remains unverbalized, the person cannot prevent himself from applying the false generalization. If a teacher is on hand to confront the student with a counterexample to his unverbalized learning whenever his behavior reveals possession of a "false" awareness, the false "thing" learned can be obliterated. But if a person is working alone, the only way he can free himself from the consequences of such "learning" is to bring it to the conscious generalization stage. Then he can examine his own discovery as if it were proposed by someone else. The value of this power of detachment through use of language is, in my opinion, on a par with its value for communication. It is the great safeguard against transfer of *unsound* learning. It is a procedure by which a person can free himself from prejudices and other false impressions. As long as an organism holds a generalization on the unverbalized awareness level only, the organism cannot stop himself from applying what he has learned. The dynamic effect of the awareness "turns on" whenever the organism is in a situation to which the unverbalized generalization applies. A person "aware" of two contradictory generalizations is paralyzed by a situation in which both generalizations "try to turn on" at the same time. Such states have been produced over and over in animal behavior studies to reveal results that could have been predicted a priori from the hypotheses reviewed in this paper. It is a bit of the irony in the nature of things that language, the very instrument which enables man to detach himself from unsound learning instead of blundering on as a slave to it, is also the instrument by which he may detach himself from sound and valuable learning to the point of losing a tendency to apply what he knows.

I have proposed a hypothesis[3] which I believe partially explains some of the losses of transfer power through verbalization of insights. If the nature of language is what I suspect it to be, the person who writes or utters in his mother tongue an incorrect verbalization of a new awareness involuntarily experiences a literal interpretation of the sentence he has composed. When this interpretation contradicts the original discovery, the awareness itself may be mutilated.

---

Gertrude used her approach to teach the members of the conference who were not mathematicians the "distributive principle for multiplication" and, when she had finished, each of us had some kind of opinion of what it was that we had learned, without being able to identify the process. Gertrude's term was that we had awareness of the principle, but Ted maintained that he had merely an awareness of a procedure that would work, without any awareness of an underlying principle.

"I'm trying to understand how this differs from the way I

learned math, which was of course the worst possible way," he said. "I learned by the old math, which is to say I learned to compute. It seems to me that one of the differences here is that the kind of procedures your kids are learning resemble the structure of the principles. The kind that I learned also had these principles implicit in them, but it was far less obvious. I never learned them until late in college."

"There's a very interesting point here, Ted," said Gregory. "The way you learned, as you've described it, does communicate a principle to you, that is, 'you find a trick and you use it.' "

Learning to "find a trick and use it" or to accept a rule on authority and use it without hoping to understand are far more general and wide-reaching lessons than particular mathematical procedures, and yet these lessons are taught repeatedly in our schools. Unlike the distributive principle for multiplication, such lessons can pervade life as general premises to be applied in all situations. When they fail, the person whose approach to life has been patterned in this way has only to say that he tried the wrong trick or failed to accept authority with sufficient conviction. Understood so, the failure strengthens the generalization instead of calling it in question. Thus, such premises have the special quality of being self-validating. By contrast, students exposed to "learning by discovery" over considerable periods begin to learn to discover: faced with a new type of problem, they proceed on the assumption that the phenomena are orderly and underlying principles can be discovered, and so they undertake research, constructing and solving analogous problems and comparing the results. Occasionally Gertrude's students have come upon mathematical generalizations with which she was unfamiliar.

Much of my father's work in anthropology has been devoted to the question of how such general, self-validating premises are learned and maintained through life so that they form a set of unquestioned assumptions shared by the members of a culture and permeating all of experience. No bombardment with unpleasant facts about the deterioration of our environment will be sufficient to reverse the trend unless we shift away from an ethos of simple self-interest (including competition with nature) and a faith in expansion and a determining technology. Such premises must be learned at a very deep level, from experience starting very early in infancy and reiterated again and again, until they become the universal truths of our lives, unstated and unquestioned. After Gertrude's material had given us a sense of the many levels of learning and Ted had shown us the importance of integration, we were ready to look at the way in which very abstract premises function in the maintenance of a whole culture. This we did one evening, looking at films of child care which Bernie Raxlen had brought from the Azores.

Bernie was one of the quieter members of the group, sitting in careful attention and listening avidly in the breaks, quiet and neat, with his short black beard perfectly trimmed. He had gone to Hawaii two years before, after finishing medical school, to study psychiatry and, since he had learned Portuguese during a year spent in Brazil, became interested in a Portuguese family at the state hospital. The winter before the conference, he had visited the Azores, where the Hawaiian Portuguese community originates, curious about the relationship between the individual and his family in Portuguese Azorian culture. Bernie spent a busy three weeks wandering and observing, conversing with people and making films.

The Azorians first came to their misty Atlantic archipelago after it was discovered by a Portuguese explorer, in the fifteenth century, and most of the present population of a quarter million is descended from early settlers and remains deeply Catholic and part of an isolated peasant tradition. Everywhere that Bernie looked he noticed repetitive patterns and he emphasized these as he showed us a travelogue of the island: tidy patterns of cobblestones and mosaic; houses the same shape and all equally neat and trim; fields proportioned the same way by intersecting walls and all cultivated with the same tools; and a homogeneous agricultural system, which provides the basis for a social organization in which the rights of individuals are regulated under a tradition of collective property. These repetitive patterns Bernie referred to as redundancies in the ecosystem or recurrent themes in the daily life of the people.

Several months after his return to the United States he began to study frame by frame the films he had taken of mother-child interaction to discover the patterns that prepared children to live in this particular society—and to die there or face death of those they love, I thought, filled suddenly with grief at these pictures of mothers and infants. Many infants must die on these isolated islands and the mothers live with the possibility of their own death or the possible loss of their husbands far away at sea, in the matter-of-fact way that Catholics do, a picture of life which includes its ending as part of what gives it meaning.

It was good for us to have films to look at at that time: films of on-going relationships in families, microcosms of the kind of balance we were concerned with, for each family is itself a system.

The Azores are now beginning to change because of increased communication with the outside, but it is still possible to recognize a balance which has existed for centuries. Ecologically, these islands are intensely cultivated, but the patterns of cultivation are set. Farmers obedient to a traditional calendar follow each year the same sequence of battles with familiar weeds. The coupling between the human society and the plant and animal life of the island is one in which the men can just maintain a constancy, without a vast disparity in power resulting from major technological incursions. Winning a livelihood in the Azores is demanding and time-consuming, depending on farming the stony ground or on long months spent with the whaling fleets.

Social life, too, still shows a stable pattern, recently disrupted somewhat by extensive emigration. Parental and community authority place heavy demands on the individual to subordinate his interests to the whole and accept traditional practice.

Bernie set out to research the question Gregory had mentioned when he introduced himself, of how the individual is patterned by the society and how the relations between individuals are used to maintain the overall cultural pattern. He looked at the way in which a mother handles her child in such basic activities of early infancy as feeding and bathing to see what she might implicitly be teaching the child that would provide an interpretive framework for all later experience and learning, and here he found three principal themes. The first was a theme of teasing, the second was a restriction of the hands, and the third was a sort of briskness or roughness in the mother's handling of the child.

One film we saw of the teasing theme showed the father stretching out his hand toward a child sitting on the floor, coaxing and calling to him while staying just beyond his range. The baby, not yet old enough to crawl, drops his toy and leans forward with outstretched arms toward his father's hand hovering just out of reach. Tantalizingly, the father moves his hand closer and withdraws it, then again returns, while the baby concentrates and strains toward him. Finally the father lets the baby grasp his hand for several seconds and then takes up a similar game with a toy, once again ending the repetitive teasing sequence by granting satisfaction.

Restriction of spontaneous movements of the hands was more apparent on the part of the mothers. In some scenes it was possible to see the child's hands put down five or six times in less than a minute as the child reached out to touch a plant, a toy, or the mother's face. Frequently, as the mother holds the baby to feed or bathe it, she has her arm curved around it in such a way that the hands are immobilized and the body space severely limited, and these actions are also characterized by a general brusqueness, jerking the baby from place to place and toweling it roughly.

The extent to which mothers enforce their control could also be seen in a feeding sequence which became a battle over a final spoonful of mush, where the mother handles the child more and more roughly and constrainingly, and then finally gives way. This last example seemed to me to be complementary to the teasing sequences: an indulgent, playful father encourages exploration but teases the child by delaying reward, yet closure is finally given; a strict, brusque mother constricts the child's activity, forcing her authority, and yet concedes to the child just as the tension is becoming unbearable.

Bernie listed three profound lessons which he speculated that the child would learn from the constant repetition of such interactional sequences: "delayed gratification with closure, a passive, non-manipulative approach to the world, and a hardy, streamlined approach to human relations." The same regularities also appeared in the individual's other interactions as he matured, his interactions with the larger social group and with the land. Thus the coupling of Azorian society with the island ecology followed a pattern set in early childhood learning. Bernie saw the theme of delayed gratification in the delay of waiting for harvest and the patient nurturing of crops and live-stock. Long periods of frustration occur in whaling and in emigrant labor patterns; news, supplies, and even relatives reach the Azores only by long voyaging. The expectation of a life after death, too, is a trust in delayed gratification.

A non-manipulative approach to the world is closely consistent with delayed gratification. "After all, in an island culture, very much subject to the indifference of the elements, cut off for long stretches of time, a stoic, hands-at-the-sides approach to life's difficulties would be natural. Even the Catholicism of the Portuguese stresses above all the adoration of the Virgin, symbolizing the mystic fertilization of a passive female. And, significantly enough, the government of Portugal is a dictatorship, the longest in modern history." The hardy brusqueness of interpersonal relations seemed to fit a rugged way of life, the need to be prepared for long periods of separation and loneliness, and very early transition to roles of well-defined responsibility.

Bernie also saw an acceptance of a given order of things in the neatness and regularity and in the subordination of the individual to the larger community, a "repose in the form which has already been created."

In a stable society, the individual develops in a way which is biologically, culturally, and ecologically consistent. Adaptive change is very gradual, and most of the individual's behavior is preformed to be appropriate. The rightness of his actions is confirmed by his sense of aesthetics and his understanding of the nature of the universe. In a time of change, however, it is extremely difficult to know how to criticize or alter such assumptions. "As compared to what Gertrude and Bernie have been giving us," Gregory said, "the central problems of our conference present themselves backward. We have a civilization operated by people who work with certain, let us say, habits of thought, which are in general non-verbal in those people, habits of maximization of quantity, habits which Barry has called reductionism or atomism. We've been discussing how habits are inculcated in children. What we now need to think about is how such habits may conceivably be changed. If you inculcate into children bad arithmetic habits, Gertrude, do you have to start arithmetic all over again?"

"Gregory, I lost your connecting thought," Bert complained.

"I want to open a school for congressmen, you see, to think straight, and I have very little idea, even in imagination, how this might be done," Gregory said.

I was very much struck, looking at these films of fathers and mothers handling infants, at how completely these small bodies were the center of experience and learning. Bernie spoke of the child's body space and I sat and reflected that the child's body space was its first image of all space. Close-up films showed the mother's hands moving on the child and I thought of the roughness of the towel and the gentler touch of fingers or the movement of water as the forms of the earliest learning about the roughness or gentleness or elusiveness of the whole universe.

As a child, when discussions of child development were common in the household, I was very proud of the fact that I was the first breast-fed and "self-demand" infant a young pediatrician named Benjamin Spock had ever encountered. Indeed, if the present generation of youth is really a product of a method of child-rearing, then I am precisely the first member of that generation. My mother believed that if a child's experience of the rhythms of his or her body were not disrupted by artificially imposed feeding schedules, a natural equilibrium could be established and the child would demand the appropriate quantity and later the appropriate kinds of food. Listening to Bernie's presentation, it was natural to reflect on how it would be possible to learn in infancy to affirm the cybernetic nature of the world, and to try to set that question in the context of the conference. An infant cannot experience the ecological balance or the patterns of the larger society directly—where these come into his experience he can hardly help perceiving only arcs rather than full circuits. However, his own body is a system and it is coupled to the system of the family's life, in which he participates. In demand feeding, time is determined by process in the system, process involving both mother and child. A mother using demand feeding skillfully looks for emergent rhythms in the child's own demands and then emphasizes these, underlining for the child the lesson his own body is teaching. When a mother feeding her child by self-demand is also breast-feeding, the quantity of milk in her breasts and the time it takes to be replenished also serve to establish system times, as the bodily processes of mother and child are coupled. Introduce bottle feeding, where a supermarket on the corner makes the milk supply unlimited, and you have a distortion in perception of the system that complements the belief that the sea is infinite: pump in cow's milk to the microcosm of mother–child relations and perhaps in the macrocosm cities with populations of hundreds of thousands will believe they can heedlessly pump their wastes, partially processed, into the rivers.

Slowly, while some of us lingered and talked, the others slipped away. In the oldest part of the Castle there is a roofless, ruined tower which forms a walled garden close to the sky. Against the rough wall on one side, a stairway ascends to the old chapel, where a massive wooden crucifix hangs, as old as the building itself. Vines creep up the walls of the open tower and thin lines of grass crisscross the floor where the blades have pushed up between the mossy flagstones. One of the traditions of Wartenstein is an evening on the tower, sitting in a circle of deckchairs wrapped in blankets, listening to the stereo and watching the brilliant stars. So when we noticed that the discussion of the film had dwindled to two or three, we went out and joined the group on the tower and listened to the *Goldberg Variations* under the sky.

· C H A P T E R  7 ·

# People and
# More People

ONE OF THE STRANGE THINGS about conferences is that it is often not enough that all members share some knowledge: it has to be reiterated in the group, put on the table, in order to be included in their thinking. What Barry had told us about the nitrogen cycle covered only one aspect of the ecological crisis; we needed, before we could go on, a general statement of the grim future that seems to lie ahead of mankind, and the problems of knowledge in hope and fear that confront us in thinking about it and preventing its fulfillment. We needed, too, a model that included human values and human understanding within the same system as the nitrogen cycle.

Fred Attneave, although he had described himself on the first day as a psychologist interested in perception, showed little interest throughout the week in our more abstract and epistemological flights, and he chose to make his own presentation on the subject of the population explosion, seen in cybernetic terms. "I am astonished," he began, "that up until now no one has mentioned the problem of human population increase. Now I'm just going to sketch this out on the board so I'll have something I can point to. This isn't going to contain anything new; in fact, it's going to be essential to my presentation that there isn't anything really new in this."

121

Fred went up to the board and started writing, talking as he wrote, sketching the larger system in which human society and the ecosystem are coupled. In the center of the board he wrote PEOPLE, with an arrow leading to MORE PEOPLE. Although no one knows the exact rate, world population will double now in about forty years, depending on how you extrapolate. More people leads to INCREASED DEMAND FOR FOOD, yet food production is falling behind the rate of population increase, with two-thirds of the world's population already near the edge of starvation. Thus, it is predictable that in less than a generation there will be widespread, massive FAMINE. Now if, in the year 2000, something like a million people die of starvation in South America, the effect of this in the United States will be tremendous moral pressure and evocation of COMPASSION which feeds back in and reinforces the increased demand for food. This acts as a reinforcing loop, with great pressure to squeeze agricultural capacities by FERTILIZATION and other techniques, irrigation, insecticides, and so on. This will lead to SOIL DESTRUCTION (Barry put in, "You know, in Pakistan, more land is going out of cultivation as a result of irrigation than is going in!") and to deforestation which may affect the balance of oxygen and carbon dioxide, ultimately altering the earth's climate. We discussed how much immediate danger there really was to the balance of the atmosphere, whether from deforestation or industry, and Fred pointed out that this "is a sufficiently redundant net so that you can question almost any point on it without changing the final conclusions." People will not only want food, but also goods, and this will lead to increased oxidation of hydrocarbons in the use of fossil fuels by INDUSTRY, further threatening the $O_2$–$CO_2$ balance. There will also be an increased demand for the industrialization of underdeveloped countries—"for some strange reason universally considered a good thing. In fact, one of the few bright spots here is that these countries are near enough to the starvation level so that they can't accumulate the capital they need. Of course we could create a little more trouble by helping them along more."

In the meantime, all this demand for food will indeed lead to the successful production of more—the effect of more human waste will combine with the effect of fertilization and so on in polluting the environment—and this increase in food will make a loop that leads back to—MORE PEOPLE. Myriad other factors could be added, such as increased transportation contributing to deforestation and pollution, or atomic power as an alternative to the consumption of hydrocarbons, with its own waste problems, but these simply reinforce the basic circuit. In this system, attempts at the solution of problems feed back to an intensification of those problems, with a steady increase of such side effects as pollution. Thus, the attempt to maintain a constant ratio between population and food supplies and other goods leads to an absolute increase in the level of strain on the environment. Postponing the crash simply means that more will suffer when it comes.

The completed diagram, somewhat simplified, looked like this:

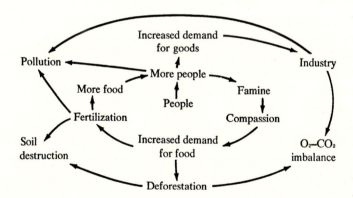

Fred described the common conception of the population problem as one in which the top capacity for food production would rise slowly, although perhaps not so fast as the rate of population growth, and the whole thing would have to level out as the possibilities of food production imposed a ceiling. "It turns out that was wildly optimistic, because in view of the environmental stresses and the way we are destroying the agricultural substrate, it's obvious that this is a very unstable ceiling and one day it's going to fall in, perhaps quite precipitously. And this is doomsday."

Gregory nodded and went on to explore the fallacy of the common-sense assumption further. "There is a general phenomenon here which we haven't mentioned yet. While populations increase along exponential curves, very slowly at first and then more rapidly, environmental capacity to support them increases in something like the traffic curve. That is, if you plot the speed automobiles are going on a particular road against the distance between them, your curve may stay nearly level for a long time and then, as the road gets crowded, it drops off at the next small increment of change." Gregory quoted a story told by Geoffrey Vickers on the BBC, of the man who fell from the top of the Empire State Building and as he passed the second floor was heard to remark, "We're doing all right so far!" "Tolerance curves give you no warning before they crash."

Barry added another fact. "If you take the present world total annual calorie production and divide it by the population of the earth and the days of the year, you get a figure, I think it is 2,700 calories per person, per day, which is about the maintenance level. We've already hit the point where, with a totally equitable distribution, the two curves would touch."

"I think the people in this group essentially know these facts," Fred resumed. "That's my whole point, we do know this. A bright twelve-year-old looking at these facts would be likely to say that people oughtn't to reproduce at this rate. Mankind as an entity just doesn't have the intelligence of a twelve-year-old, but the point is, really, that mankind is not an entity, just a lot of individual people. Individual men may be conscious, but Man is not."

When he had concluded his description of the population crisis, Fred went on to list the impediments to effective action. He maintained that in the case of the population explosion *ignorance* is no longer the problem, although he conceded that there is still a partial ignorance, significantly among political leaders. We had some debate on this, with Barry insisting that educating congressmen was useless unless the voters were educated and pressing them. I found myself again where I had been in listening to Barry's presentation on the nitrogen cycle, trying to assess my own ignorance. Statistics on the population explosion and on world food resources always terrify me and I find it difficult to live with them—to carry them in my head. But certainly I had always considered the situation as one which would get gradually worse, a deterioration to be met, hopefully, by a gradual gain in human responsibility. If the tolerance curve was likely to cave in suddenly and drastically, then we must press on to think about the possibility of sudden quantum gains in awareness, the kinds of pervasive new organizations of knowledge and opinion that accompany insight. Peter said, "People know the phrase 'population explosion' but they don't really know what it means." Barry put in, "There's a fallacy which maintains this ignorance, which says nothing could be this bad."

"Let me put the rest of the impediments up," said Fred, "because some of these things will come out. They know but they don't care: *indifference.* If we want to face this issue we have to turn it around and ask why anybody should care, if it's not going to happen to him."

Fred went on to trace a path through repeated discussions and polemics about the population explosion, cataloging the familiar barriers against this terrifying knowledge. He mentioned *evasion* as lying between ignorance and indifference: "They'll work it out." "God will provide." "Science is wonderful." "By that time we'll send people away in spaceships." A fourth category would be *competing interests.* Peter mentioned the decision of the Ecological Society of America not to do any kind of active lobbying lest it lose its tax-exempt status as the Sierra Club did. He mentioned "supposed national interest ('We need lots of people to have a strong country'; 'They are trying to get us to use birth control so we'll be weak'); economic interests (needing a market for an expanding economy); and, finally, the desire for children." In Fred's view, the whole

family-planning approach must remain ineffectual because people want a lot of children: " 'As many as they choose' is too
damn many!" Peter agreed: "Look at the number of children
in ads."

To complete his list, Fred added one more impediment,
*resignation*: " 'Why should I limit my family when other people
don't?' This is neither irrational nor culpable. You find this
kind of thing formalized in non-zero-sum games where it is
perfectly clear that everyone gets the greatest pay-off if they all
cooperate, but if one person fails to cooperate, then the others
no longer can afford to. One may also encounter resignation on
our level, looking at the impediments and the example of India
and saying 'There is nothing we can do. It's just going to happen.' I hope somebody will talk me out of that."

Listening to Fred's careful separation of the impediments to
a change in the trend toward destruction, it seemed to me that
they were all part of a need for a new sense of who each person
is in relation to others. The evasions he cited all involved a
"they," some other force that would solve the problem, and
most of the competing interests involved a failure to identify
with the interests of the whole. The desire for children is a
curious example of this, since the delight in children need not
imply a separate brood in every household. Listening as a
woman who had just lost a child, I was surprised at how much
my commitment to reversing the nightmare trends we had
spoken of was built on the imagination of a future child. It is
essential to limit birth rates, but it is also essential, I believe, to
the ethical maturity of every human being to be involved in
caring for the growth of another, an infant, a student, a disciple
—one with whom we identify enough to turn our concern for
ourselves into a concern for an unknown future. We must have
as many children as we need to grow into full human beings,
but the day may come when we learn to share them, giving
every adult, whatever his biological choices, a share in the lives
of many children, so that the web of our involvement with each
other is extended into the future.

Barry interrupted. "You passed very fast over the economic

interests. I have the impression that the American economic system is one which cannot operate unless it expands. It cannot operate as a stable state, as Galbraith says. We are seeing ads with station wagons full of children not because there are so many children but because the automobile industry wants a market for those monsters. Another example—the chemical industry is predicated on increasing food production by increased fertilization. If we focus just on social and psychological factors, we'll be deflected from the effective trigger which, I think, is economic."

"We have overdetermination, a redundancy of impediments here. You could get rid of any one of them without bringing about a change," Fred replied.

Gregory said, "In Hawaii we are engaged in a very large road-building program which has been sold by extrapolations of the population curve. Across the country, billions of dollars are involved in the truth of the proposition that the population's going up. I had a schizophrenic patient who said, 'If it's not the way I want it, I'll prove it.' "

Barry went on describing the addiction of the world economic system to a rate of change. "It's no accident that a modern economic system has evolved in exactly this period of world history that has involved the rapid rise of population. It needs the free 'imposed expansion'—the bonus of more babies next year to boost sales. Similarly, I might tell you that our institution in the last year has begun a study of the impact of technical innovations on the ecology of underdeveloped countries.[1] I'm pretty hard to frighten about these things, but I have just been scared witless at the things we've uncovered." Barry explored a number of examples: the destruction of the schools of small fish off the coast of Peru to make fishmeal to feed our chickens, the destruction of the fisheries in the eastern Mediterranean when the Aswan Dam stopped the flow of nutrients from the Nile; stories of soil destroyed and natural controls of pests wiped out. "This whole thing is so embedded in the political momentum of the way in which the world is constructed that almost everyone that we've talked to has simply looked on our investigations as a piece of indelicate obscenity—you know, 'You shouldn't be talking about that now, we're trying to help these people.' "

Ecological intrusion in the underdeveloped countries, however, is only the last step in a threefold destruction of ancient balance, a step which follows almost inevitably on the increase in population, brought about by Western public health measures, and the disruption of the cultures, leading inexorably to an attack on the environment. In a sense, the damage to coupled systems spreads in widening circles, much as polluted streams drain into a river, fouling it as well. This was clear when Barry described the effect of these ideas on a young Iranian engineer who had become involved in his program. "He began to get more and more worried and finally he came to me and said, 'You know, if I went back to Iran and told them what I was learning here, I'd be clapped in jail. The last thing they want to hear is that there are reasons for *not* importing American technology.' One of the very powerful factors here is the feeling on the part of the governments of the underdeveloped countries that the sign of world competence of the other countries is their technology—the way in which they intrude on the environment—and, by God, they want to do it too. One of the critical things that we have to do is to make self-confession, that this has just been a mistake."

"That we are failing," Tolly said.

"We are failing, all right. Now, that leads to my response to your notion of impediments, Fred. The critical emotional problem that we face is to confess. It's very difficult for people to say, 'Look, the whole damn shooting match is wrong and it goes right down the line.' "

Bert had been sitting, deep in thought, since Fred concluded his outline of the population crisis and the impediments to our dealing effectively with it, and now he said, "I felt an extraordinary drama, Fred, in the situation you were painting. Not only are we marching faster and faster toward a certain doom, but we know that we are. I would like to bring into the discussion an analysis of precisely this kind of situation in almost the same terms in relation to a different kind of error, religious error. Error, I think, with a capital E. Augustine takes this up in terms of his own youth and describes himself as a wastrel, thoughtlessly squandering his life, chasing after women and heaven knows what else, and just having a marvelous time of it. Now, Augustine as a religious man some time later thought back on his life and said in retrospect that he was in Error and he didn't even know it. For Augustine, man is part of God's realm and for some reason (I won't go into the Fall) he gets separated from God. Augustine says he was so far from the truth that not only was he doing badly but he didn't know it.

"Then, simply through reading a particular writer, he discovered that he was in Error. Now that corresponds, I think, to what Fred teaches all of us, that we really are going the wrong way and we know it. What, then, is it that really leads us to turn back and, particularly, what is the structure and character of an existence knowingly departing from truth? Can you go along with me in this as being a parallel situation? I mean, can I use the religious imagery?"

"It's very close to a systemic imagery, at least it is for me; I don't know whether it is for others," said Gregory, "but one more point for clarity. Knowing you are in error in St. Augustine's sense does not imply a knowledge of that from which you are in error, yes? He knows there's something wrong. He doesn't know against what background he is wrong."

"Well, he really does know at this point. Of course, he can't know God's realm, but he knows there's a truth he doesn't have and he knows he's not simply separated from it, but is moving away from it, farther and farther from the truth."

"So he knows there's a first derivative in the story . . ."

Bert continued, "This state should be distinguished from the more common-sense state in which we know our goal and are moving toward it but, for some reason, it's difficult. Augustine wasn't even trying."

Fred said, "I'm not bothered by the religious analogy here, but I am bothered by something else. The example of St. Augustine applies to an individual and the population problem applies to several billion individuals. We're in a case where some individuals are not merely aware of error, but they know what the error is, within broad limits. The trouble is that they are individuals, you see, and they can't act for the world."

"Just a brief comment, Fred, on your caveat," I said. "The way you phrase it supposes that man's error is that of having too many children. That would be analogous to saying that St. Augustine's error was that he was having affairs. My father's question is whether Augustine knew what he was away from, that is, while he was in error, did he know what it would be like to love God? He didn't. But perhaps we don't fully know —or perhaps we're beginning to around this table—what it would be like to . . ."—I was struggling for a phrase that would encompass the resolution of all of our conflicts. ". . . to live in cybernetic peace with our environment. It's refusing to do that that is man's error now, not just the next baby."

"Well, he had read an account of what a saintly existence would be, so . . ."

"He both knew and didn't know," Will remarked. "He knew it in the sense that he read the canonica, but he didn't know it in the way of direct experience."

Gregory broke in to underline another aspect of the point he had been reaching for with his question: "A considerable part of the learning experience was a perception of a direction of movement, which does not necessarily involve a knowledge of the starting point of that movement and, of course, only a very dim idea that the other end of the movement is some sort of hell, either on earth or elsewhere. Direction of change is a thing that people can perceive where they cannot perceive the state that they're in."

"I just want to follow Catherine's thought," said Horst. "See, some people here say our whole *Weltanschauung*, our world view, may be wrong, or our understanding of cybernetics may be insufficient. But Fred thinks it's a practical problem, that he knows already a practical key factor, and so already he has a goal, although the impediments are so tremendous. I think that Barry also would protest when Bert says we have no goal."

"My diagnosis really *is* different from yours, Barry," said

Bert. "I don't think the situation is simply one of there being difficulties which as practical men we just have to take steps to surmount. I believe the situation is more like Augustine's second phase, moving away from God, collectively."

"And you're going to try to prove that?" Barry snapped.

"I don't know if I'm going to prove anything," Bert stammered. "Well—Augustine was vastly moved by this situation and he felt really torn to pieces. He knew that his higher self, the self he wanted most, was the one that would go to God, but he found himself doing just the opposite, going on whoring and so on, and he said, 'Whence is this monstrous state?' He just couldn't understand it.

"The idea that occurred to me as Fred was speaking was that as long as we are the kinds of beings that we are, we're going to go on doing the kinds of things that lead us down the road that we are on. The kind of change that seems necessary is the emergence of a changed person. Augustine used the imagery that the man who turns back toward God is a different person. Now, Barry is simply saying that we can use the instruments of practical life today, namely politics, to solve the problem. We wouldn't change, we would just . . ."

"I didn't say that."

". . . go on being political animals, but just be cleverer politicians and politicians who are going the other way. I would like to suggest that the political mode itself would need to be changed, that as long as 'economic' man is there, then we'll go on down this road. If we get out of being economic beings, maximizing our profits and all the rest, and into some other mode, then the economics of the thing just won't be compelling. They wouldn't have any meaning to a moral man, living in terms of different categories. So I suggest that after certain rather fundamental changes, what seems to be impossible will turn out to be matters of common sense."

"It seems to me that the prerequisite of any other value is the valuing of survival," said Fred, "because without that you have nothing else. Now, this is essentially a negative goal. It's a matter of avoiding destruction. You see, there's an important distinction between the paradigm of approach to a reward and avoidance of a punishment. This is a push, not a pull. When you talk about analogies to the bosom of God in this situation, you see, that's a positive state of affairs that's drawing us. Catherine picked up this point and talked about cybernetic peace. I don't think that's the primary nature of the survival problem. We are trying to avoid destruction; the particular way we avoid destruction is for the moment irrelevant. That's a subsequent decision—what we do with ourselves once we have survived—but we have to avoid destruction in order to do any of these things. It's the non-specificity that makes the difference."

As I listened to Fred, I was aware that I disagreed very profoundly with what he was saying, but I was not by any means ready to explain why. If I had tried at that point, it would have come out as an amorphous plea for the vivid specificity of life, opposed to his more pragmatic insistence that we should first pull back from destruction. Afterwards, it occurred to me that the distinction here was related to Gregory's point that the distinction between reward and punishment depends on the definition of the individual. If Augustine had left off sinning for fear of the punishment of hell, his sense of himself as an individual would have remained intact, would even have been enhanced as he acted on the fear of his own flesh seared, his own senses tormented. But when he was converted, surrendering his heart and his will, he had a new definition of himself, defining himself in relation to God. As fire and brimstone preachers learn, the conversions they win are often only temporary and the words of the prophets of doom soon grow tedious. Similarly, if we control birthrates out of a fear of hunger, rather than out of a positive search for a society in which neither man nor nature need be exploited, our control is likely to be arbitrary and sporadic, constantly subject to fluctuating technological promise. New religion, a new definition of who we are and the goals of our society, would allow us to see a small population as a good, a reward, not just as an alternative to mass starvation. Instead of defining ourselves over against nature, whose punishment we fear, we may reach a definition inclusive of the whole natural order and ourselves feel relief when our depredations end.

Fred was suggesting that if a way could be found to overcome impediments we might solve the problem by immediate intervention to control population growth, stimulated by the spectre of hunger in the future. But when you turn to look at population control in wild animal species, it is clear that in most cases the controls are far separate from pressures of hunger and come into play long before any real danger of population explosion. When Fred had finished his presentation, we turned to Peter and asked him to describe such controls.[2]

Peter first took up the popular assumption that natural populations remain stable because death rates have evolved to balance birthrates, an assumption which is nonsensical in the light of natural selection. A certain death rate may be necessary for the whole species, but a system of selection based on the survival of the offspring of individual animals bearing particular traits could never bring this about. Instead, birthrates are themselves regulated. Starlings, for instance, have the biological potential for laying many eggs, but the fledglings with the best chance to survive to another breeding season are those born in a clutch small enough to match the parents' ability to find food; thus there is a selection for an inherited tendency to limit the eggs laid to an appropriate number. In other cases, there is more flexibility, and an increase in the general adult population limits reproduction, as in the "Bruce effect," which causes female mice to abort after intensive exposure to the smell of male mice, which would occur in a dense mouse population.

"Now, perhaps the relevance of these observations to the human situation is this. Our evolutionary history is a reasonably short one and, until very recently, the condition of density under which we've existed has been rather low. There has been very little evolutionary pressure for the development of the kinds of secondary cuing mechanisms found in organisms of greater evolutionary antiquity and shorter generation time, like the birds and the mice. As a consequence of our medical advances and interference in the operation of normal controls on population growth, we suddenly find ourselves in a runaway stage and there is, it seems to me, absolutely no prospect of a natural control comparable to a 'Bruce effect' appearing in Homo sapiens."

Ted asked Peter whether he could give examples comparable to the human population explosion. For correspondence here, Peter turned to cases outside of the temperate zone, in the far north, like the lemmings and snowshoe hares, the lynx, or the snowy owls. Lemming populations often change by as much as three orders of magnitude in a period of three or four years, an incredible increase which is hardly affected by increases in predation.

"Now, what happens then is that as the density increases, physiological and psychological changes occur in the animals, which do two things: they decrease the probability of the animals' withstanding any kind of physiologic or psychic shock and they reduce their fertility. If you collect lemmings or arctic rabbits near the peak of this population cycle, you find that startling them, a slight change in temperature, or any kind of sudden environmental stress will cause a very high proportion of them simply to lie down and die. The fact is that as a result those seemingly uncontrolled populations cave in before shortage of resources starts to affect them."

"So, Peter, you would be contented by a formula so that the homeostasis of food supplies and number of offspring is brought about by feed-forward in the actual organism, but by feedback during phylogeny?" Horst asked. "This of course is what Gregory was saying in the Memorandum when he pointed to the $CO_2$–$O_2$ control in the individual organism. That is an absolutely comparable situation."

"Would somebody say that again for me?" said Tolly.

Control systems that work by feedback adjust themselves through error, so of course they do not work well in situations where error is irreversible. Thus, in the lifetime of a single bird, it would be wasteful to have a control whereby each individual learned by trial and error how many eggs to lay. Instead, clutch size is determined by feed-forward—pre-adjusted for the life of the individual, so that normally the error does not occur. Nevertheless, such a balance must have been reached by a process of adjustment involving feedback through evolution. Individual birds are not responsive to feedback, but natural selection weeds out those that overproduce, correcting error for the species if not for the individual. In the case of oxygen and carbon dioxide, or of the Bruce effect, an even more complex process has occurred. Because oxygen shortage is so serious, the organism cannot wait until it has begun to occur before initiating a correction, so, through evolution, a secondary cue has been developed and correction is begun as soon as there is $CO_2$ excess. Feedback correction of the $CO_2$ level functions to provide feed-forward for $O_2$ level. Similarly, density affects mouse breedings before the more serious result of overcrowding— destruction of the food supply—can occur.

Peter pointed out that you could arrange the mechanisms of population control in a hierarchy from the point of view of their efficiency in maintaining a balance of population and food supply. "The control that operates in the arctic rodents, the lynx, and the snowy owls, which keeps them oscillating but always brings them down before they have impinged too violently upon the environment—that's perhaps the least efficient from the point of view of energy wastage. The second most effective would be the rodents in which fertilization and gestation will proceed but will then be interrupted. The least wasteful model is provided by the song birds, which don't in the first place produce more eggs than they can rear young."

This was an echo of an important idea that Horst had presented years ago at an early Macy cybernetic meeting,[3] the details of which he worked out in his description of how a praying mantis aims at his prey. In his laboratory, Horst still has dozens of slim voracious mantises, some as much as four inches long, grass green or straw colored, from China and Latin America and all over the world. The mantis waits patiently, looking like a twig, and, when some small insect comes within reach, darts out the long front legs that he normally holds in an attitude reminiscent of prayer. When Horst studied the mantids, he discovered that the mantis has no way of altering his aim if he misses repeatedly, no way of using errors for corrective feedback on his habitual shooting.

"The point Horst made, at the Macy meetings," Gregory elaborated, "is that there are two ways of shooting, one being typical of the rifle and the other being typical of the shotgun. If you are dealing with a rifle, you aim it at the bird, look along the rifle and correct your error by the sighting, correct the next error, and, at a certain moment when you feel optimistic, press the trigger. That's one method which is error-corrected in each instance. Each time you aim with a rifle, you are error-corrected through feedback. The alternative is what you are supposed to do with a shotgun."

"You shoot from the hip," Horst supplied.

"Yes. This is the case in which your gun is at the ready and, as you see the duck come up out of the water, you take in a slug of information—its velocity, direction, and probable movement—and you go BANG! having correctly predicted where the bird's going to be. If you are concerned with learning to do this, you have to have a long series of repetitive instances over which you set your calibration so that it will correctly handle the slug of information. This is, by the way, very relevant to species of error based on mental habits."

Horst finished up: "There are two basic possibilities we have: Either it's done during ontogeny by true trial and error learning, or it can be done through evolution by the species, as it is for the mantis, since those which are wrongly calibrated have a lower chance of survival and are in the long run exterminated." Horst went to the board, scratching and mumbling as, in the middle of his explanation, he thought of a new aspect of his account of the relationship between action and perception and began to elaborate it, talking to himself with little cries of delight. "This . . . ah, yes, this will be here . . ." Gregory reminded him of the tape recorder and he returned to his place dazzled.

Barry said, "I'd like to go back to the original purpose of our discussion of the regulation of animal populations—which was, I think, to derive clues for the problem that Fred raised. What I get out of it is that there are no clues."

"That's not what I get," said Tolly.

Barry continued. "I think in a way the message is that we need to look for possible control mechanisms in quite a different area. For example, the question of economic structure, the relative availability of goods, the people's faith that goods will be available for their old age and that they won't necessarily need a large family to support them. This is an enormously complex area. The control is going to have to be related to everything we know about the way our society is organized. And that's a vast job."

"Tolly, you said you had clues," said Gregory.

"Well, it's sort of a platitude, right, that man has made up for the lack of specificity in various built-in control mechanisms by the development of highly elaborate communicating societies—methods of language and coordination of people to people. One of the things we've all been saying to each other is that some of the most profoundly established habits of doing that must change, or we will die. Like, for example, the idea that a man's position and a man's worth are a function of his economically valuable output. That's clearly a very profoundly established idea and I have the feeling that's an idea that's got to go, and there's lots more like that, right? These ideas are clearly communicative control mechanisms which might make up for the absence of other things that are in other species instinctually controlled."

All of these imageries—the way in which a man's position or worth are estimated, the kind of image people have of their own old age, the image of what constitutes a complete or happy family (which in some countries requires a minimum of five or six surviving children)—all of these are part of the cultural calibration that we bring to procreation. The contrast here between man and other species is really not so great as it may at first seem, since the transmission of genetic regulation of the birthrate is also a matter of communication. Learned, culturally coded controls, although fortunately subject to more rapid change, may turn out to have a number of the same abstract properties as inherited ones. As I listened to Peter I could see two models that might be useful. One is based on crowding, using the discomforts of too large a population to inhibit breeding. In order to work with this model, we need to work toward a sense of how large a population must be to support the full human potential for diversity and creativity while yet small enough to escape regimentation and the dreary sameness of our great cities.

The other model is based on the capacity of the parents to care for the offspring. This is the old model, of course, that used to be cited in trying to persuade the poor to have fewer children while the rich could have as many as they liked. But the more we know about the importance of the experience of early childhood, the more we realize that there are many other kinds of resources and that parents with more than one or two children simply give much less to each child. The difference does not show up in food or clothing, but it does show up in the lower incidence of leadership and creativity in "middle" children in large families.

It seemed to me that Peter's examples served as a warning not to think of the regulation of population as unnatural, but to realize that a controlled birthrate is a pervasive characteristic of natural systems, based on mechanisms that have developed over vast periods of time and involved the waste and premature death of many individuals. We do not have that time, but we can study the patterns of regulation of other species, using this example in quite a direct way as we seek for ways of expressing the positive side of a lowered birthrate. Two things are clear: natural populations are not normally directly controlled by hunger and they are not controlled by the taste or convenience of separate pairs of parents.

Peter's material fit well into my musings about reward and punishment, too, since he had given us examples of two ways of maintaining homeostasis, one through feedback, where error occurred and a correction was made and the directly punishing effects of that error might be felt somewhere in the system, and the other through feed-forward, anticipation instead of correction. Species evolve so that a regulated population is intrinsic to their genetic pattern and man must somehow remake his value system so that limitation is similarly built into his social system. Children do this in growing up: they incorporate their parents' commands so that instead of being punished from without for bad behavior, they are internally rewarded for good behavior, and in the process the boundaries of the individual are altered.

"It seems to me," said Bert, "that the greatest elaboration of social-science theory has been the question of social control. There is a fairly good grasp, I think, of different possibilities for . . ."

"Control of whom, by whom?" Tolly asked.

"Well . . . not by anybody. There's just a question how a society is ordered."

"So if we're so smart, why do we have all this damn trouble?" said Barry.

"Can you give me an example of the kind of knowledge you're referring to?" Tolly asked.

Just as Bert was preparing to go into a detailed discussion of theories of social control, Barry interrupted with a procedural proposal that we go no further in trying to specify the exact mechanism of population control. "Otherwise, we're just going to have a gigantic amoeba here, which will make no sense whatsoever. I mean, for example, this whole discussion of social control, my God, that's five conferences' worth of stuff and there's no point even getting into it here."

"I would like not to sidestep the issue of value systems," said Peter, "recognizing the complications it might lead to. Because it seems to me the crucial question is not do we have to stop the growth of the population, and it's not the question of how we stop it, but at what level do we want to stop it—do we want to take it up to where the food supply will be just sufficient, or to some lower level? And that involves social values and attitudes."

"You mean we want to decide on that here?"

"No. I would like to look at that question because I don't have any ideas as to the answer."

Fred said, very reasonably since it was now almost six o'clock, "Why aren't we better off just to go have drinks, forget the whole thing? I'm very serious about this. Can anybody here see any sort of plausible path—any conceivable, halfway reasonable, 0.1 probability path, let's say, leading to something other than destruction?"

"Let me give you now a more favorable experience I have had," Barry answered. "You see, for the last fifteen years, I've been in this kind of Cassandra situation, but in different arenas. The arena in which I was first involved was the whole business of nuclear war, fall-out, radiation, atomic testing, and so on. Now there we can report some success. We *definitely* can."

Barry, more than any of us, had been involved in trying to bring about change in man's dealings with the environment, starting with a public information campaign on the results of atmospheric testing and the dangers of Strontium-90, which was one of the principal factors in the voting of the test ban. He described a number of specific techniques they had used then and later, when the St. Louis group expanded into the national Scientists' Institute for Public Information.

"What I'm saying very simply is that the effort that the scientific community made to bring the facts in a narrow arena, facts that are much more technical than housewives have been accustomed to, before people, in order to allow them to confront the moral issue, succeeded. And I think that it has begun to succeed in the insecticide area and in the area of air pollution generally. One hopeful sign I see is that when ordinary people begin to get the substantive understanding that we've been dealing with here, their morality comes out on the right side."

"Barry, isn't an important factor that the facts are so presented as to allow people to feel that it has something to do with them and their children?" Tolly asked.

"You know the first thing we did in St. Louis when we started this campaign? We organized the first collection of baby teeth. We've taken over the tooth fairy. Every kid that has gone through the public schools in St. Louis in the last ten years knows that there are scientists who are concerned with *their teeth* and the Strontium-90 in their bodies and are doing something about it."

The hour was late and Bernie raised the question of how all this applied to our own proceedings. "Gregory, I'm interested to know how much of this conference you wish to disseminate and to whom, because I have a feeling that we may produce a fine document but it may very well end up like some of the fine documents of the Macy Foundation. In other words, take me as an individual: I don't quite know where in this fantastic labyrinth to start, what to do about it, how to react to it. I mean, I'm emotionally charged up, but I'm puzzled where to put my efforts. I don't know how I would tell my friends, for example, what to do about this. They'd sit down at coffee and they'd say, 'O, Jeez, yeah,' and then I couldn't go on from there."

"We need to devise a series of triggers that will set off the charge that we generate," said Barry.

"Gimmicks like the tooth gimmick," said Gertrude practically.

"There's a question there," said Gregory in a strained voice. "Did we get there by a variety of gimmicks, did we get there by a series of planned triggers?"

"What's the answer, Gregory?" said Barry.

"The answer I expected was no, but . . ."

"What is the 'charge'?" Fred asked.

"The charge is what was described here . . . well . . . this perception of the runaway world that we're living in. I think it's pretty charged," Barry said.

"I think that nobody should be permitted to say anything that he cannot tie directly to the problem," said Ted. "Anything abstract in the sense that we are not directly talking about how to control the environmental crisis. I think we should devote our remaining time to political questions of praxis—what kinds of agencies, what kinds of communications are available, what sorts of messages, possible films or TV series and what can go into them, who doesn't have the facts and who needs them, the kind of rhetoric of persuasion we can put with all that we're worth behind this thing."

Gregory brought both palms down on the table. "I think we might as well stop today, frankly. If we're going to do that we might as well stop today."

"Do what? What Ted suggests?" Barry was aghast.

"Yes. I think it's ridiculous. Because . . . there's one matter which we have not discussed, which is very important, which is the whole problem of public relations."

"Isn't that what Ted's talking about?"

"Yes. But this has not been discussed as a part of the whole pathology we're discussing. As far as I can see, we have a society which is not only going over the brink in population and in terms of $NO_2$ and pesticides and Lord knows what, but is also going over the brink by the rapidly increased corruption of its own communications stream. This is being done in large measure by people with very good intentions, you know, who honestly believe that to increase the G.N.P. is a good thing, and do their public relations to increase the G.N.P. Now we honestly believe that to control the population is a good thing and we're going to try to flood the public relations thing with an attempt to do that. The whole theory of planned public relations and the implications carried on the word 'gimmick' in the discussion of this is a matter which we have not yet thought about and I believe we should."

"Well, I thought that's what I was saying," said Ted.

"I thought you were proposing that we should plan gimmicks."

"No, the question is how one overcomes social inertia, how one gets the information to where it is not. This is the question of public relations."

In effect, one of the things that has tended to happen is that injecting a concern for the environment into the communications stream in America has provided the advertising industry with a new idiom and new fears to prey on, at the same time hideously confusing any rational public debate and eroding the potential concern of the listening public.

"Look," I said, "let's not get caught up in having a purpose that produces pathologies the way other purposes have. But we can, I think, ask the question, what is . . . the loving way of passing this conference on?"

"Something like that, maybe," said Gregory.

"There should be something that we can do that's different from what a group of housewives taking up this question might do with it," Bert put in.

Fred spoke in some exasperation. "I tried to pose the question earlier. It is a question of what are the crucial factors that are involved in getting from an essential understanding of the situation to doing something about it. This is by no means a question of gimmicks. If that's not relevant to the question of conscious purpose and human adaptation, I don't know what is!"

"Gregory, there really was a disagreement of some measure or other between you and Ted, right?" Tolly asked. "Ted, to caricature what he said, said in effect, 'Gee, let's plan our campaign.' "

"That's what I heard him say."

"Okay, like, let's figure out what ad agency to hire and who to hit when with what. Right? Gregory said, sort of with as much emotion as he can evince, almost—I will have no part of that. But we are faced, are we not, with the question of what effects we hope for beyond the confines of these walls? Now where in the spectrum of possible degrees of specific political orientation is our discussion to lie?"

# TOWARD

# AN APPLIED

# EPISTEMOLOGY

*[The Fourth and Fifth Days]*

# The Way We Think
# and Talk

BURG WARTENSTEIN STANDS on a peak looking down into valleys and across them to wooded mountains. The slopes are dotted with small villages like the illustrations in a child's book of fairy tales. The thick green of the slopes seems untroubled by man, but as you look more carefully you can see that this is already an artificial environment. The hillsides are carefully farmed for timber, and the stands of trees are divided by fire lanes. The woods are as pleasant to walk in as a park and, like a park, have been weeded and pruned. After the first three days of sessions we had a free day, and my father and I went walking, counting the different insects we saw as we went: three species of butterfly; a large and showy red beetle; grasshoppers. Thirty years ago there would certainly have been at least a dozen species of butterfly to notice in a day's walk, but even here pesticides had been used and the insect life we found was sparse and little varied.

Will Jones was the only other member of the party who did not go into Vienna. He sat in his room rereading Kierkegaard, with some distaste, for an article he was writing. In the late afternoon the temperature dropped and it began to drizzle, and we gathered around a big fire in the lounge. The others gradually wandered back in time for dinner. Gertrude had been to see the training of the Lipizzan stallions, the white horses of Vienna, to share views with their trainers. Tolly and Horst had driven off together in Horst's little red car and visited the dreary, majestic Hapsburg tombs. Others had shopped and toured in the imperial capital of the Austro-Hungarian Empire, looking for echoes of the gaiety that made the city famous a hundred years ago, as it accelerated to its decay. In the great Kunsthistorisches Museum you can see on one floor ten or twenty of the greatest paintings of Europe—Rembrandt, Dürer, Holbein, Bruegel—and in the anthropological museum, the feather cape of Montezuma, carried to Europe as an imperial gift. Vienna is a city built by men who believed that the order they represented could be maintained forever, and the permanence of the buildings sits heavily on a continent in rapid change.

I was grateful for the day off and happy to spend it wandering out of doors, away from the insistent faces around the conference table, already invading my dreams with their elusive echoes of each other. I felt battered by the effort of understanding and note-taking, and by the cumulative realization of the depths of the crisis facing mankind, the intricately interweaving paths to destruction. I think all of us were weary by then and pessimistic about the possibility of finding real solutions. No one knew if the conference would jell, or what it would look like if it did, and most frustrating of all was Gregory's warning that simply going home and sounding a cry of alarm had its own dangers.

We spent the middle period of the conference on epistemological problems. This means that we went right back to the thesis stated by Gregory in the Memorandum that our failures in relating to natural processes stem from systematic distortions in the way we think and talk about such processes. We have an urgent need to develop new patterns of thought and to find ways to teach these new patterns, which would represent a profound change in understanding, rather than the superficial addition of new slogans.

When we gathered again after the day off, Gregory used

Gertrude's presentation to orient us to the new task. "What we were talking about the other day with Gertrude's material was information available in words or in pre- or non-verbal internal network structure, in that case information on how to perform mathematical operations. Now, in the end, any ideational material has context around it and the question that Gertrude is raising is how you fuse a new piece of patterning into an already existing complex mass. You can stamp it on the surface, so to speak, by having the child learn it by rote in words. It then does not have the sort of interconnection into the whole net which Gertrude wishes it had. It does, of course, necessarily have connection into the whole net, because message material is always assimilated into the whole net, in one way or another. What it has is an inappropriate and insufficient connection with the net so that, when other parts of the net start wiggling and jumping and exchanging impulses, the appropriate resonance can never be touched off. If you diagrammed the net, you would see that there were knots and blocks in it of some kind—but it is in the net, in the sense that along with it goes the creation of a habit of trying to handle ideas in this 'superficial' way.

"Let me put it this way: if you had diagrams of this stuff up in the head, one diagram for the child who has learned, say, the distributive principle for multiplication the 'good way,' and another for the child who has had to learn the 'bad way,' and you looked at those two diagrams, you would find it exceedingly difficult in the 'good' diagram to identify the region in which the learning occurred, because it would be woven into a total composition, it would be a slightly different net; whereas of course if they learned what Gertrude calls the 'bad way,' you'd see the thing stick out like a sore thumb as a discontinuity in the pattern."

"Yes," said Tolly, "and that seems to me to have something to do with the hard-soft business that you and I talked about in Hawaii."

"Ah, right, go ahead."

"Well, I introduced Gregory a year and a half ago, I guess,

to programmer words like the distinction between 'hard' and 'soft,' which is used to describe more or less changeable forms of determination. The distinction was born at the time that it became clear to people in the computer business that programming and soldering were more or less alternative activities; that you could accomplish the same ends with a soldering iron or with a pencil in your hand. That is, by programming you converted a so-called general-purpose computer into a more special-purpose one, in effect constructing a machine, which you could alternatively do with a soldering iron. The critical difference between the two has to do with subsequent modifiability. What you have soldered is laborious to unsolder and rearrange, and what you have programmed and represented on magnetic tape is, relatively speaking, easier to change."

"Therefore," Gregory said, "to go back to Gertrude: If children have learned the distributive principle for multiplication the way Gertrude holds to be the proper way and then later encounter contexts conflicting with that principle, they are going to have very great difficulty and probably a nervous breakdown. I'm sure Gertrude would have a nervous breakdown if she encountered a world where the distributive principle was no longer true; it would be a horrible feeling."

"Ah, but you see, Gregory," Tolly continued, "what becomes clear from this rather pretty look, which started with your very insightful remark about ways of knowing, is that to know different sorts of things there are different degrees of hardening and softening that seem adaptive."

Horst said, "Because either I try to understand the thing or, if I don't have time enough or if I think the subject is too much complicated, I just learn a cookbook rule, and usually there's a proviso that if I get time or so, I lay down and try to understand it."

"May I?" put in Gregory. "There's a very interesting evolutionary point here. By evolutionary process an animal comes to deal with his environment, and his various programs set it up so he will. Here again we have the problem of hard and soft programming depending on whether the environmental variable to which you want to adapt is constant or flexible. If it's always the same, you can fix the thing at a low level and let it be a hard program. For example, you are adapted to breathing on land. The presence of air around your nose is on the whole pretty constant. You can rely on the fact that it's there and, therefore, you can assign the reflexes controlling respiration to your medulla. You also have voluntary control if you need it, but if the voluntary controls are knocked out by concussion or anesthesia, you will still go on breathing because you've got control hard-programmed at a fairly low level. If, on the other hand, you are a porpoise, you've got to deal with the fact that the presence of air around your nose is not a constant condition but a variable condition, and therefore you find that the control over respiration has to be moved, cephalad—I don't know just where it's located but anyway, it's cephalad of where we have it. If you anesthetize a porpoise, he stops breathing. If you knock him over the head and give him a concussion, he stops breathing."

"Yes, and all of this again has something fundamental to do with allocation of resources. That is, it takes more of the porpoise's resources to hold the variable variable," said Tolly.

"And there is an economics of flexibility, so that if you hard-program this, then you can use your soft programming for something else. You can't have it all soft-programmed within the limits of the number of relays in the given computer. In the end, you've got an economics of relays."

Warren McCulloch came in to draw the connection between hard and soft programming as different types of learning and hard and soft programming as contrasting genetically-determined and acquired capacities. "The things we ordinarily think are entirely hereditary are turning out not to be so. The most beautiful example I can give you is from the visual system. It is the work of Valverde. He worked on the famous brown mouse, on which Cajal worked all the time. What he did is the following: he took litter mates, one raised in the dark, the other in the daylight. (I don't mean just one animal; he has oodles of animals of each, but he always picked out litter mates.) Those raised in the dark and those raised in the light differ fundamentally in the connections that are performed in the occipital cortex. The counts are perfectly clear. There is no question but that if you do not have the animals in the light, they don't form the connections."

"May I cap the story?" said Gregory. "What has been demonstrated there is first of all that the neural connections of the normal light-raised mouse are not fully determined by the genotype. Right. But second, what has been demonstrated is that the ability to *alter* the neural connections to fit the experience probably lies in the genotype."

"Surely," said Warren.

"What you've done is to move a level, from the phenotypic description to the capacity to change the phenotype—and the capacity to change slops over into the genome again. You've always got this, whatever aspect of an organism you think of. My skin color alters to some degree under sunshine, so the genotype did not determine the particular shade that I have today—only the genotype plus the amount of sunshine I've been subjected to. But we then can see ability to respond to more or less sunshine as located in the genotype. Some people respond more, some people respond less. It is conceivable that I might be able to learn to tan—not only tan, but learn to tan. But if so, then the ability to *learn* to tan slops over into the genotype. What you are continually getting, which is exactly the same thing that you get with the relationship between, so to speak, top levels of the mind and lower levels of the mind, is that, as you go down the scale, caudad, or as you go from phenotypic control to genotypic control, you continually move into the more abstract, the more relational: what is defined is not a thing, but a relation; or what is defined is not this relation but a relation between relations. This goes for the somatic organization and for the relation between phenotype and genotype."

"I would like to finish the other half of my remark," said Warren. "What we don't yet know about the brown mice is, if you've left them in the dark for a certain length of time, let's say three weeks, and then bring them out in the light, whether they will ever make those connections. That I don't yet know."

"They may be hard-programmed as to the moment at which they are capable of these changes," Gregory agreed.

"Now that wouldn't surprise me at all. Your periods may be entirely biologically locked."

We broke for coffee then, but the discussion continued on the same lines and when we returned to the green table it was to a further clarification of the meaning of "knowing" the mathematical principle Gertrude had used in her presentation. Warren was waiting to give a case history he had mentioned in the break, but Tolly took the floor first, with a mischievous look that indicated he was going to work around to something shocking.

"There are several things involved, you know, in knowing the distributive principle for multiplication. One is how you manipulate those symbol strings themselves just as physical objects. People always talk about these things as abstract, which irritates the hell out of me; they are physical. Well, I mean they're exactly as physical as anything else is. May I digress for just a second, Warren?" Tolly asked. "Can you just wait another minute?"

Warren said, "You're talking my point."

"I gave a talk to a bunch of seventh-graders and tried to tell them about what mathematicians do. I said that in my opinion mathematics is a kind of picture-making art, and I pointed out that there are certain elements that are always involved in picture-making. There are the tools you do it with. There are certain conventionalized movements, component subroutines, like component motions, out of which you construct the model. For instance, if you want to make a picture of mountains and rivers and so on, nobody says that you have to make lines. That's not actually essential, though line-making is one of the kinds of characteristic movements that you can make when you draw that kind of picture.

"So anyway, you have these little picture-making components, which you could describe either in terms of their outcome or in terms of the movement which is involved in making them, and ultimately the thing winds up being a picture because you can identify the relations between its parts with relations in whatever it is supposed to represent. You know, nothing that doesn't have parts can be pictured at all; I mean that's clear."

"Nothing. You can only picture things by attributing parts to them," Gregory agreed.

"Yes, that's right," Tolly said.

Barry asked, "Because you can't represent the thing as a whole?"

"That's right, it just plain doesn't make sense. Okay. Then I said, well how about the mathematician? He has his characteristic sort of components, corresponding to the things that you would call lines or shaded areas or dots for the guy who wants to draw a vase. The mathematician has the things people call 'notations' and there are a number of desiderata for good notations.

"Well, ultimately, I put on the board a sequence of $x$'s and $y$'s, $xyxyxy$ in sequence, and I looked at the class and I said, 'Gee, now, what could that be a picture of?' And some kid immediately raised his hand and said, 'A picket fence.' That made me feel real good. And shortly thereafter somebody else said, 'Ocean waves.' Then we considered, you see, the various kinds of manipulative things you can do to strings of $x$'s and $y$'s and the ways in which those manipulations related to the proposed interpretations—some fit better, some fit worse. In the case of ocean waves, for instance, to take a string of $x$'s and $y$'s and split it in two parts is not so very sensible; in the case of the picket fence it makes more sense. We talked about all different sorts of natural transformations of mathematical pictures, which are made to be diddled. What happens so much in mathematics, of course, is that you make pictures of pictures, and every time you picture something, you naturally leave out a whole lot of its properties and each style of picture-making has its own way of leaving out properties.

"Now really, the reason I'm making all these remarks is because the pictures are no different from whatever it is that they picture. They are just things out there to look at. They're there to be modified and changed and they are all terribly sort of real.

The words 'abstraction' and 'denotation' and so on get in the way, in my opinion, of understanding at this level."

Barry said, "Tolly, what you are saying is that mathematics becomes something real despite the fact that it can be looked on as an abstraction of reality."

"Absolutely. It is just plain a physical thing. The trouble with the usual school thing is not that they teach the distributive laws, but that they don't teach that or anything else. I really like Gertrude's stuff a whole lot, but it seems to me, you know, she tends a little bit to misdirect attention to what the trouble is."

Tolly gave up the floor and Warren began his story. "I don't like to describe a case when I've not seen the patient, and I've not seen this one. It was a child born into a highly educated family. He has neither a vestibular apparatus nor an auditory apparatus and he had a birth injury. He is now seventeen years old. There's been no apparent language development at any time. His father was a devoted chess player and he watched his father playing chess from the time he was a small kid. He began playing chess and he ended up able to beat his father and all of his father's friends. Here is the learning of a game, which you would say is so difficult to learn that unless you could tell somebody the rules, he could never learn it, and that just is not so. Complicated as it is, it can all be learned without any verbal symbolism of any kind whatsoever."

Horst said, "Warren, didn't we agree when you and I were talking last night that it would be nice to have a name for what is common to all representations of, say, chess playing or whatever else? You suggested 'homotropy.' "

"But this boy got it without any representation," Gertrude protested.

"He's got some sort of representation in his head," said Warren. "Got to."

"The trouble with giving a name like homotropy to what is 'common to all the representations' is that it doesn't exist," said Tolly scathingly.

"It doesn't exist, why should it make sense about existing,

for heaven's sakes," said Horst. "What does it mean, 'exist'? Now you become a philosopher!"

"This is the greatest dream that mankind has had, you know, Plato and through history, about the thing that is constant independent of how it's represented. That's what would be really nice to be able to get your hands on and the thing is it ain't. It just plain ain't."

Now we would hear the moral of the discussion of picture-making. Tolly went up to the board and wrote the number two in several ways, 2, II, ii, *2*, a tiny two and a monstrous one, and turned to the group. "It doesn't matter, right? which of these things I do. I mean two is two is two."

Gertrude nodded firmly. "It just has nothing to do with any of these squiggles."

"So the feeling goes, but it just isn't so. There is a profound illusion that it is possible in a systematic sense to separate the representation from what is represented, really deeply buried in our psyches. Well, I stand here and say it is a fundamental error."

This was a very shocking sort of thing to say to a group of intellectuals steeped in abstractions, and Gertrude especially was horrified. As he often did later, Barry decided to speak for Tolly. "Can I help explain this?" Tolly looked wary.

"We mustn't pull the rug from under Barry's feet," said Horst, "because he has gone to great pains to explain that he can talk about specificity as something which exists, you see."

"Ah, but wait, wait. What Tolly is saying is almost the re-verse of what he appears to be saying. What he is saying is that what is general is not something separated from each of the representations, but something which includes all of the representations."

"I wonder," said Horst gloating.

"Let me just delineate it a bit further," Barry continued. "This is now a big gamble—on which side will Tolly fall? I agree with Tolly in this sense: there are generalizations that include within them all of the possible representations of reality, and it is a profound mistake to say that, since the representations appear to be insignificant with respect to the sense, we will throw them away. What Tolly is saying is, you must always keep in mind the fact that the twoness is not there unless you have a representation and in fact it involves all of the possible representations. What he is saying is that it is much richer than the simple concept of twoness; it involves a whole universe of cases of two. All right, Tolly—flip."

"I'm not saying *anything at all* like what you said, see? See, long before I thought the thoughts which I now think, it had already occurred to me in a much more primitive form that the meaning of a symbol should somehow relate to *all* of its connections. I mean, you can think of the intersymbolic connections between things and you can think of the denotative connections, but there isn't any way of separating the connections a symbol has with other symbols from the connections it has with its denotata, okay? I now have thrown all of that out, I think now only of the transactional system of which this happens to be a part. Have I made myself clear? The symbol is nothing apart from its uses."

"Yes," said Barry, glumly, sliding way down in his chair, and quoting Tolly's slogan back to him: "Help stamp out nouns."

Tolly went on to give examples of the relationship between the use of any type of notation and its form, and as he listened, Barry rallied and said, "You know what Tolly is refusing to do? To impoverish the complex interconnections between the abstraction and the various ways of representing it, and between both of those and the (I may use terms wrong, but that's all right), the multiple real situations in which these things come up." Tolly was shaking his head, but Barry persisted in spite of our laughter. "There are three things here. There is the real world. There is the representation of it. And then the abstractions. And what Tolly has been doing here, despite provocation from me, for example, is to insist on retaining the rich interconnections which he sees among all of these things. Now, what strikes me is that we—all the rest of us—have a fantastically insistent tendency to impoverish this complex system in one of various ways, depending on the culture."

"That's what I call 'vulgarity,'" said Gregory, nodding at Barry.

"Right, vulgarization. Now, the difficulty in going Tolly's route, which sort of consists in swimming in a whole sea of stuff, is that people will say, well sure, you may be in love with all of this and that's nice and pleasant for you, but isn't this kind of a helpless way of dealing with this system? The real issue is the question of the cultural or political usefulness of the loving view, which Tolly very beautifully embodies. I don't know that I can prove it, but I feel that the cure to the difficulties that we have been getting into is to learn how to use this swimming technique in a way that is as concrete and capable of leading to manipulation as the impoverished view." Barry was responding to the ideas in Tolly's paper as well as to the immediate discussion.

"Yes, of course, of course," said Tolly.

"'Tolly's Stuff,' meet 'Conscious Purpose,'" Gregory put in. "'Stuff' is perhaps the wrong word—no, the 'stuff that dreams are made of.'"

"Right. Let me say just one more thing about that. We seem to have an inborn tendency, a very insistent tendency, to impoverish anything that we use."

"And so it has to be in fact," said Tolly frankly.

"An economic tendency," Gregory put in.

"Right, that's right. It may turn out that you cannot do this bathing, loving thing and use it at the same time, and that every time you use it, it is going to be impoverished."

"Absolutely," said Tolly.

Fred Attneave came in with his most completely aristocratic tone of voice. "May I just rephrase the point that Barry was making in a slightly different way? We simply have to face the fact that we have vulgar nervous systems."

"We have what?"

"Vulgar nervous systems, in the sense in which vulgarity is being used here. They are vulgar simply because they are finite; they would have to be infinite to represent the universe in its complete complexity. I think it is an exceedingly important fact of life that we have to simplify. It's a matter of trying to find the simplifications that are necessary to our ends. There are good ones and there are bad ones."

"I think one of the things about the nervous system that gives it a potentiality to be less vulgar than one might have expected," said Gregory, "is the enormous hierarchic structure in the thing, in which you get representations in depth. You push that relationship of the distributive law into somebody and it's now in that person, in God knows how many different forms, which interlock with all the other things that a person has swallowed. This sort of complexity in depth seems to me to diminish somehow the vulgarity of the nervous system. Does this make sense, Warren?" Warren nodded. "If I allow something to be embodied somewhere in my head, I have not only allowed that thing to be embodied, I have, for better or for worse, allowed a whole mess of—call it premises of that thing, links between that thing and other things—to come in. I can even dream and use the relationships embodied in that thing in the dream; this will appear as relationships between cups and saucers, mothers and children, God knows what. There's always a funny enrichment related to that fact."

"Another thing that comes racing into my head now," Tolly said, "is a problem that's arisen constantly with my programming colleagues, which is that I have been unable to get them to understand that language-creation and problem-solving are indissoluble activities. Okay? Now that seems to me to have a lot to do with . . . I mean, everyone here is smart enough to see the connection between that and the point of view I've expressed here in general with my numbers, right? Now what I want to get at is the relation between this and the subject of the conference. We have depended through history on a beautifully subtle method, you might say, of semantic and formal drift in our symbolic apparatus. It's clear to me, anyhow, that we can't say in a serious sense that the word 'table' today means what the word 'table' meant a hundred years ago. The semantics gradually slip, old meanings decay, and the formal apparatus—only very gradually and sufficiently slowly—changes.

Well, now of course, the investments in certain symbolic structures have become enormous; our symbolic methods have become embodied in enormous technological complexes."

"Therefore, hard-programmed," Gregory put in.

"Therefore, very difficult to change. And that has, I think,
a lot to do with our continued adaptive capacities."

"Like agriculture," said Barry. "You've got a fantastic problem of unscrambling the problem that I described."

"If programs become maladaptive, if your shark is put into
another environment, or the environment subtly shifts where
the shark is swimming, then he is perfectly doomed to die,
definitely, eventually," said Horst.

"I think one of the problems is that we tend to confuse
consciousness with its uses, which are necessarily impoverished,"
Barry insisted. "But by consciousness I mean the sea in which
Tolly swims so well. It's the works. I think this explains why
Tolly keeps inveighing against the simplifications that derive
from the various ways in which consciousness is employed."

"The way I used it in gathering this company," said Gregory,
"was in contrast to Tolly's sea, as I see it: that which is easily
communicable between persons, especially by language, and
faces certain filtering operations or something of the kind,
which cut out many attributes of Tolly's sea. It was that sub-
traction that I felt needed discussion." For Gregory, the sea
was the sea of mind, with consciousness only a shallow layer
at the surface. Before the conference, he had written:

---

A peculiar sociological phenomenon has arisen in the last one
hundred years, which perhaps threatens to isolate conscious
purpose from many corrective processes that might come out
of less conscious parts of the mind. The social scene is nowa-
days characterized by the existence of a large number of self-
maximizing entities which, in law, have something like the
status of "persons"—trusts, companies, political parties, un-
ions, commercial and financial agencies, nations, and the like.
In biological fact, these entities are precisely *not* persons and
are not even aggregates of whole persons. They are aggregates

of *parts* of persons. When Mr. Smith enters the boardroom of his company, he is expected to limit his thinking narrowly to the specific purposes of the company or to those of that part of the company which he "represents." Mercifully it is not entirely possible for him to do this, and some company decisions are influenced by considerations that spring from older and wiser parts of the mind. But ideally, Mr. Smith is expected to act as a pure, uncorrected consciousness—a dehumanized creature.

---

"Consciousness isn't the soup," Bert insisted. "It's the clarity that comes out of the soup. The thing that you know that you know that you know it. Now, you know that you know that you know it, which is, you have a grasp on it in some way." Bert was our most frequent defender of consciousness.

Poets and clinicians bring to their listening a particular kind of attention, sensitive not only to the single logical path between ideas, but to the multiple bonds between symbols. Unconsciously we all swim in a sea of contexts not dissimilar to the one Tolly argued for. Tolly was arguing against the notion of abstract meanings for symbols separable from their forms and contexts, yet underlying all our conversation of logic and abstraction, each symbol or word used is fitted by each person into multiple contexts deeper than any argument. One of the strange things that was happening out of our growing familiarity, especially out of the attack that Tolly was beginning on our familiar logics, was that this poetic interweaving of ideas was becoming a property of our shared discussion instead of being limited to our separate musings. Bernie came in with a comment on our common thought, and his musing underlined the kind of self-knowledge we might find in Tolly's material: "Just a thought occurred to me about sea. An image came to me first of a sea, Tolly, and then *s e e*—what you see in a concept as you see it and in your mathematics for describing systems. There's the *s e a* of the sea in which you're swimming and the *xyxyxy* of the waves that you're using to explain mathematics, and the See, like a Holy See of the conference. There's, you know, the whole *seeness* of sea or even the *c* in which Gertrude was explaining the *a* + *b* + *c*, and it's not only sea that he's swimming in, but it's this whole sea, which he can't disconnect from that whole thing on the board . . ."

"Is what we've seen going to make the scene?" I quipped.

"I don't know," said Bernie seriously, "and I think *that's* where sometimes you have to say which one are you going to use and vulgarize."

Someone proposed at this point that we should now turn to a cataloging of ills and an attempt to list remedies, but once again Gregory pointed us back toward the abstract discussion. "I think that the conclusion we have reached at this point in our conference is that what I called a science of applied science in the first session is now simply the problem of applied epistemology. The ills with which we are concerned are those of applications of an epistemology which somehow doesn't lie flat against the phenomena which we are trying to represent. This gives us now a much clearer picture of our agenda than we had when we came in. So far so good. We may have to continue the conference for a month, you know, or do it all again, but we are now, I think, beginning to be in a position where we can talk with some care about epistemology. I think we should go on."

Bert said, "Gregory, it does seem to me that if epistemology is at issue in what we're doing, then we really had better listen to the professionals, that is, we'd better give the floor to Will. Amateur epistemology is going to be nonsensical stuff, just as if I were to do biology or if someone else were to do social science. A lot of what I see going on is that when we speak as amateurs the thing collapses and becomes foolishness."

"I'm not an epistemologist at all," said Will, "so you wouldn't particularly listen to me."

"Sure you are."

"I have a kind of minor quirk . . ."

Gregory said, "I don't think Tolly's fifteen or twenty years spent with the problems of representation can be regarded as amateur epistemology!"

This was the context in which we were finally ready to attend to Tolly's approach to the description of systems, turning to it with the explicit sense that a shift to new methods of representation is a real event. Although one might argue that all descriptions of systems are "equivalent," Tolly had prepared us with the sense that a new method of description would involve us in a new world, a world of new problems and new solutions.

# Secreting the Thing from the Process

TOLLY HAD PROMISED US when he introduced himself on the first day that he would be presenting a new approach to the description of systems, one only recently developed and still incomplete, but it was several days before we held in common a sufficient background of knowledge and concern for such a presentation. Earlier, we would surely have lacked the patience to spend the many hours that Tolly asked us to spend in intense concentration on highly formal ideas. As it was, the zest and wonder with which Tolly spread a world of thought on the blackboard, combined with Gregory's insistence that the crisis was located in our manners of knowing and speaking, forbade us to slip away into expressions of concern and political planning instead of focusing on the need for better ways of thinking and talking about the natural world, the idiom of a new kind of consciousness.

Tolly was setting out now to teach us a new language, out of the conviction he had expressed earlier that "language creation and problem-solving are indissoluble activities." He was not, of course, enlisting us in the kind of process involved in learning a natural language, with the tremendous amount of rote involved; instead, he was trying to teach us a new way of arranging familiar units, so that the logic of our natural language was absorbed into another and more fluid logic that made it appropriate to talking about systems. Listening to him, I found that the effort to follow and understand was a direct attack on the premises of my usual speech and thought. It was not so much difficult—he proceeded in very simple terms—as it was alien.

Tolly is one of the few people I have known who runs as if running were not a special variant of walking but a glad, gay thing for people to do. He is good at talking to children and invents games for them to play, and he taught us his lesson from the board like a dancer. He started out, slowly and rather formally, speaking about his view of a theory as a tool, a piece of equipment installed in someone's head. "What I've been doing in my work hasn't been just making philosophy," he said. "I'm concerned with ways of writing things on paper and also with providing the conceptual and semantic background to actually enable a person to use these ways of writing to describe something, ending up knowing something new about it."

When Tolly first started to work on the problem of description or representation, a central problem for work with computers, it seemed obvious to him that he could describe a state of affairs by finding a way to depict a set of objects and defining relationships between them; then change would be represented by a shift in these relations. This is very much our common-sense way of describing things. Yet after a while Tolly rejected that approach completely, to search for a way of representing process. In the old way, which Tolly was rejecting, you might look at a number of leaves floating in a river, diagramming and rediagramming the pattern they formed on the surface, first close, then far, and then together again, but now Tolly was concerned with representing the continuous shifting event of the entire current. He was taking the first steps in meeting the need that Barry had emphasized for holistic methods of description, ways of understanding complex processes that did not depend on breaking them into parts to be studied in isolation from each other.

"Everything I have to say will be clearly understandable to you all," Tolly assured us. "I won't refer to any complicated mathematics, but I am going to have to jog your neurons in various ways in the course of the next hour or two and to disestablish some very deeply embedded habits of thought. I want to show, on the blackboard, a technique for writing, and I want to associate that technique with sentences.

"I'll begin with an extremely simple picture, by way of introduction, and then elaborate it. This will be like those initial minutes in the movies when you see the introductory pictures which give you an idea of the kind of movie it's going to be while telling you who the main characters are, and so on.

"Let's imagine a pendulum swinging back and forth." Tolly hunted around for chalk and then he drew this picture. "This means that for some interval of time the pendulum swings to the right, shown by the arrow labeled R. Here's an occurrence, shown by a point, and then the pendulum swings to the left for some other interval, shown by the arrow labeled L. The occurrence is the end of the swing. You can think of the same picture as representing a billiard ball rolling back and forth on a frictionless table between two reflecting boundaries. Left, right, left, right, and the occurrences are the bounces."

Horst did a double-take. "You mean the *point* indicates the moment it changes from right to left?"

Tolly nodded gleefully. "Yeah. That's right. Unconventional." Once Horst had called my attention to it, I realized that this was indeed unconventional. The minute I stopped thinking that the arrow indicated the direction of the pendulum (which it did not, because the diagram of a light changing from red to green to red would have looked exactly the same), I realized that Tolly was doing the strange thing of using an *arrow* to represent something stable (an "interval of condition-holding" he called it) and a *point* to represent change, the occurrence that initiates new conditions. This was the exact opposite of the convention Barry had used in his diagram, where arrows had represented the transition from, say, organic to non-organic nitrogen compounds, or Fred, who had used arrows to represent causation. It was not yet clear whether these conventions were simply freakish and arbitrary, or whether this choice of symbols was a first step toward new kinds of meanings.

Now Tolly elaborated the diagram on the blackboard by introducing two more billiard balls, still rolling along a plane, bumping into each other on to-and-fro courses between two reflecting sides. Our first billiard ball is rolling right and a new notation indicates this condition of Ball$_1$ moving right: R1. It hits Ball$_2$ moving left (L2) and the occurrence is their collision; after that collision, new conditions, L1 and R2, hold as they rebound. Then Ball$_1$ hits the side and ricochets, while Ball$_2$ hits Ball$_3$ and again reverses. This could go on indefinitely, with Ball$_2$ bounced back and forth between Ball$_1$ and Ball$_3$, each of which bounces off the sides. The points represent collisions, the occurrences after which new conditions hold, and the arrows represent intervals of condition holding.

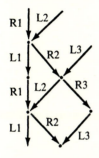

Tolly went on to give the same formal diagram a different interpretation, just as he had done in his children's talk with *xyxyxyxy*, and this in turn gave us a better sense of the use of his notation. Imagine a one-lane, one-way road. We are looking at a particular stretch of that road, which is divided into cells, each of which is large enough to contain one car. The labels 1, 2, and 3, instead of representing billiard balls, now represent cells, alternately free and occupied, while the occurrences (dots) mark a car's passage out of one cell and into a new one. At the boundary of our system, a car has entered Cell$_1$, while Cell$_2$ is still free. The first occurrence represents the car passing from Cell$_1$ to Cell$_2$, so that Cell$_1$ is now free and Cell$_2$ occupied. Using F and O to symbolize these conditions, we can simply relabel the same diagram. Cars enter Cell$_1$ from outside and leave from Cell$_3$, just as Ball$_1$ and Ball$_2$ changed direction by bouncing against the sides.

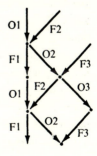

Already I realized that by emphasizing the interactional nature of process, Tolly had taught me a new way of looking at one kind of event, for I suddenly saw that I was looking at an explanation of why a row of cars stopped at a traffic light takes so long to cross when the light turns green; even though a precise division into cells is a simplification, for the cars to get into motion there must be more cells than cars. I thought of my own exasperation on many occasions, sitting fuming in just that situation, feeling that the delay arose from the slowness and inattention of other drivers, rather than from the basic interweaving of space and time in an on-going process.

It soon struck me that the diagrams looked like nets of knotted string. You could follow the alternating conditions on a strand in the net, the lines leading from knot to knot; in some cases following a particular strand seemed to have a consistent meaning. Thus, you could follow strands bearing the same number, which corresponded to balls in the first diagram or to cells in the second, so that you could say that following a strand made it possible to follow the participation of some *thing* in the process. On the other hand, other strands were much more abstract: if you followed letters for the first diagram you would be following a direction of movement, or the momentum passed from ball to ball as they bounced, while for the second diagram the letters represented the states of emptiness or fullness passed from cell to cell. Other possible strands zigzagged through in ways that suggested no useful interpretation to me at all. This was apparently a form of representation which was not biased toward weaving the narrative around the continuity of a set of fixed objects.

The easiest way to follow Tolly's theory into a new way of thinking about "things" is a children's game he was thinking of constructing for building stories like occurrence graphs. "Let's suppose that we want a Momma in our story. Now what's the sensible way of going about constructing a Momma from this point of view? I'm obviously not going to have little stick figures which represent Momma. Instead, you start off by thinking about alternating conditions. For instance, Momma has location, and in the way we usually talk she has one location at a time—she's in the kitchen *or* she's in the living room *or* in the bedroom *or* the whatever, okay? She has activities, maybe more than one at a time. She has mood. Now, there are various synchronies and asynchronies, you might say, in the times of change for these. Then if Momma's in the living room, that's location for her, but it's also a state for the living room; in fact, Momma-in-the-living-room will be a single condition. Of course, the living room, like Momma, is most likely going to be defined by rather a large bundle of lines, not just a single one. It isn't enough to say about the living room that it has a Momma in it. Okay? You can imagine all sorts of building games." When Momma passes from living room to hall, the conditions Momma-in-living-room and empty-hall end, and new conditions, Momma-in-hall and empty-living-room come into being. You can follow a single strand, separating Momma from her context, but the method of narrative does not oblige you to.

"What we're doing here is turning normal practice on its head," Tolly continued. "In most descriptive disciplines the things which describe component parts of states of affairs are sentences. These are molecular structures built up of little components, which designate such things as relations, and also built of nouns, of course, against which I have a very special hatred. I want to pass on this way of thinking by replacing propositions by atomic symbols, which you, of course, are free to write with as long a string of letters as you like. See, that's the clever trick. You cannot, after all, get anybody to talk in some totally different way, but you can let them name conditions, by writing strings as long as they like, just so they recognize that these wind up merely representing atomic symbols from this point of view, $F1$, say, or MLR (Momma-in-the-living-room). Then you can take collections of these and identify them as being some domain that corresponds to a *thing*—in interaction, of course. It is that pattern of interaction which gives us the character of some thing in a context."

"In effect, you're trying to secrete the thing out of the process," said Barry.

"That's right, I'm secreting the thing out of the process."

"And this ties up with what I was talking about the first day," Barry continued. "It can be shown that the rigid structures in cells, what you might call the nouns of the cell, are very likely secretions of the processes. The orthodox view is that there is structure and it transmits its specificity to process, and yet it's just the other way around. Your calculus here is one which I find pleasing because I think it fits in with the ontogeny, so to speak, of living systems, which are in effect really processes. Unfortunately, the structural 'nouns' which these secrete have attracted our attention because we don't know how to deal with the . . ."

Will interrupted plaintively. "Barry, your metaphor about secreting is a splendid metaphor, but it is a metaphor and, when you use it, I see something slowly being squashed. Now, could you translate out of the metaphor into non-metaphorical language, so that I get something that is less vivid but more . . . do you see what I want?"

"The issue," said Tolly, "is to set up, in this context, formal criteria which would allow you to see a certain action pattern as being the interaction of some collection of 'things.' But there may be several different ways of doing that."

"Look, perhaps I can help you," Barry offered. "If you think of the behavior of the systems in a cell which involve the behavior of molecules, you can generally divide them into two large groups. There are those systems in which molecules are interacting with each other, in a vast network of chemical transformations, and then there are structural, time-dependent organizations of these units. Take amino acids, for example: there is a very complicated network of conversions, one amino acid to another, an amino acid to a keto acid, all going around; on the other hand, there are also amino acids strung together in rigid structures. Now this corresponds to a very old idea among biologists, the structure and the function; Gregory knows what I'm talking about. The modern orthodox view is that you can see an origin of that which *happens* only from that which *is*; that is, the structure. That's exactly what Crick is doing. He is taking what I call 'static specificity' and saying that the static specificity of DNA determines the kinetic specificity, the pathways, of this mishmash of stuff that goes on, as well as its own static specificity. What I'm saying is that the static specificity of

DNA is a consequence of the complex, convoluted pattern of processes. Exactly the other way around.

"Now, you see, the DNA orthodoxy fits a mathematical world in which structure is primary and process is brought in by a crutch. There's a nice correspondence between that kind of seventeenth-century or earlier mathematics and the model that we use, and so the model is thought to be beautiful and good and understandable because it fits in with that kind of mathematics, but the mathematics is exactly wrong for the reality, which is just the other way around. The thing that attracts me about Tolly's disquisition here is that, apparently on equally good mathematical grounds, he is going to be giving us a structure with the same kind of aesthetic beauty that fits the realities of a biological system in which process is primary and structure is a kind of impoverished . . . derivation or crystallization from what is fundamentally process." Barry was speaking with great scorn, as if being solid were the lowest, most disreputable possible state. "Now in historical terms, the orthodox view implies the notion that before life appeared there was a chaotic brew of substances floating around and the way we got life was to drop into it one crystal of DNA. This provided the structure around which the patterns of chemistry characteristic of life then organized. I can show, I think, pretty well, that what really happened is exactly the reverse, that the soup organized a gradually evolving kind of process, which in the course of its evolution laid down certain kinds of structures, and that the structures are really, so to speak, vestigia, fossils. They . . . it's very hard to explain . . . it's something like the relationship between the ticket for a train ride and the train ride. The ticket has structure, it says you have been from here to here, but the train ride is the process. I would assert that the train ride gives rise to the ticket, whereas the Watson-Crick approach would say the ticket creates the train ride. That's why I'm interested in what Tolly is saying."

Barry's argument reminded me of a story my father likes to tell about me as a child, when I showed him a "cat's eye" I had been given. When he asked me, I agreed that it could not really have come from a cat, but I had no idea where it came from;

I thought it was some kind of stone. Then he suggested that I turn it over, so I could see the spiral marking on the other side (this kind of "cat's eye" is the operculum or "lid" of a tropical sea snail), and I exclaimed, "It must come from something alive, because it has a spiral." This was true insight, since spirals are produced by motion. Outside of the biological world, spirals can be seen in whirlpools, tornados, and nebulae, and all of these are in motion. A static spiral, like a snail shell, is solidified process, attesting the creature's growth. It would be interesting to explore all of the ways in which we can recognize that a shell or a leaf or a bone, appearing inanimate, is the product, like ourselves, of a self-corrective growth process, not a thing only but the outline of an event. These things we find beautiful.

Tolly goes around with a set of games which he produces without warning, sometimes from his briefcase or his pocket, sometimes from his head, either to illustrate a point or to fill a lull in conversation. One of the games he taught various members of the conference was called "sideways pat-a-cake." The rules of ordinary pat-a-cake involve a series of hand claps between two people. In the version Tolly had learned as a child, each player claps his own hands, claps opposite hands with the other player, his own again, his right hand to the other right hand diagonally, his own again, left diagonally, his own, opposite with both hands, and then his own again. After reviewing these moves with a rather reluctant and self-conscious adult partner, Tolly goes on, "Now I want you to imagine that, as we stand facing each other, two other people stand facing each other at right angles to us, okay? Now your right hand is the left hand of the person standing on your right, and similarly my left hand is his right hand. Okay? Now on the other side, for the second person, your left hand is his right hand—and so on. Now, *those* two people, using our hands, will play pat-a-cake."

Suddenly, confusion is complete. Two people, with deep concentration, grope across the space between themselves, pausing, fumbling, jerking a misplaced hand to a new angle. As the players slowly get into tempo, you can imagine their bodies dissolved and the two ghostly figures whose hands they manipulate taking shape—persons defined not by their physical attributes but by their participation in an interaction. This is vividly what things and persons are for Tolly—participation in process, response, relationship.

Barry was delighted with Tolly's model, but other members of the group were apparently still struggling to understand the system and its implications—the degree to which it differed from more familiar forms of description. Bert Kaplan mentioned Athabascan as a "language in which practically all reality is the reality of movement, since almost everything is expressed with verbs, usually verbs of movement," but Tolly was skeptical:

"Most spoken languages don't have anything that corresponds terribly well to the vertices in these pictures. But the situation is really bad because even in technical language there are no sufficiently convenient ways for representing processes. All there is is state machine language, which is utterly hopeless for anything that is real, and programming languages that are hopeless for other reasons . . . I mean they just don't . . . I mean, do I have to discourse on why I think they're useless and hopeless and so on?"

"Those that will benefit already know why, and there are others who probably wouldn't benefit because they don't know what programming languages are," Gregory said, "so go ahead with your presentation."

Tolly went on, continuing with a systematic presentation at the board, which soon became a tangle of occurrence diagrams. Each one was a schematic narrative, but radically different from the familiar kind of narrative in which a hero passes through a series of encounters, emerging in the end to the happy ever after. Tolly was particularly concerned with narratives that recurred cyclically, like the behavior of an internal combustion engine, the metabolism of a cell, or a store in which the same kinds of transactions are repeated again and again. The partial mutual constraint of the parts of an internal combustion engine, the way they are fitted together, makes them act as a system, and the next step in Tolly's presentation gave us a way to go beyond the narrative of events occurring within a system to a description of the system as a whole.

To exemplify this next step, Tolly described a very simple cobbler shop, just a little cubbyhole of a shop where the Repairman works while the Customer waits, so narrow that a second

Customer cannot enter until the first is served and the Repair-man has no backlog and waits idle if there is no Customer there. No real-life cobbler shop is ever quite this simple, but another system that has almost exactly the same possible states is the drive-in window of a bank.

Tolly listed seven possible conditions that could hold in his cobbler shop, and then pointed out that in the cyclical process in which Customer after Customer is served, these states occur in set sequences; some can co-occur and others cannot. Begin-ning arbitrarily at a point where a Customer is waiting in the Entry and the Repairman has just finished work on a particular pair of Shoes, a stretch of the behavior of this particular system can be shown in an occurrence graph like this:

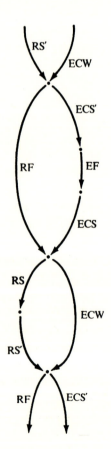

The Repairman is holding
the repaired Shoes (RS′)
and the Entry is occupied
by a Customer Waiting (ECW)

The Repairman is Free (RF)
and the Entry occupied by
a Customer with his repaired
Shoes (ECS′)

The Repairman is Free (RF)
and the Entry is Free (EF)

The Repairman is Free (RF)
and the Entry occupied by
a Customer with Shoes to
be repaired (ECS)

The Repairman has Shoes
to repair (RS)
and the Entry is occupied
by a Customer Waiting (ECW)

The Repairman holds the
repaired Shoes (RS′)
and the Entry is occupied
by a Customer Waiting (ECW)

The Repairman is Free (RF)
and the Entry is occupied
by a Customer with his
repaired Shoes (ECS′)

Et cetera

Such an occurrence graph, like the graph of the billiard balls, could go on indefinitely, and there is obviously a need for a compact description of the parts of this system · and their mutual constraints that could be used to describe its potential for this endless cycle. Tolly's technique for such descriptions, which stand to occurrence graphs as a grammar stands to the possible sentences of a language, he calls Petri nets.[1]

The best way to get a feel for Petri nets is to treat them like a game board. In the Petri net of the cobbler shop, the circles (which are called *places*) represent the conditions whose letter symbols are written inside. The numbered bars are called *transitions* and they refer to the events of the system, corresponding to points in occurrence graphs. To "play" the net, we

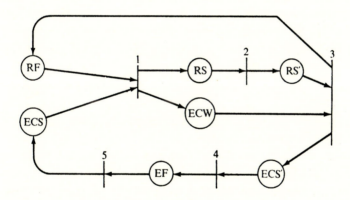

distribute tokens in the places so that they represent a possible set of conditions, say RS and ECW (the Repairman is working on the Shoes and the Entry is occupied by a Customer Waiting); not all conditions, obviously, can co-occur. The state of the system changes when a transition is "fired." Firing can occur only when all the inputs of a transition are filled; at firing, the inputs are instantaneously emptied and the outputs filled. Starting with tokens in RS and ECW, only transition 2 meets these conditions. After its firing, RS' and ECW hold and we are free at any time to fire transition 3. We can continue carrying out this "net simulation" just as long as we like.

So far, this all seems terribly simple and the simulation has a very monotonous form because of the simplicity of the cobbler shop. I had to remind myself of the point of this game, which I was learning through this very simple example, by harking back to a description Tolly once gave me of why games are important. "In most games," he said, "you have a translation from the world into the game that gives the game meaning, streets and buildings, say, or kings and soldiers, and then rules for manipulation within the game, but you don't generally translate back into life. But the purpose here is to construct games that do translate back and that end up informing you about the things you started from in the first place."

I really did not realize how novel Tolly's procedure was until I began to compare the simulations generated by his game of tokens moving on the Petri net with descriptions of stretches of life in a cobbler shop in ordinary language. When you consider the English description of the cobbler shop, you discover that you are immediately tempted to concentrate on the firings, to blur events and conditions, and simply to omit some necessary conditions. For instance, to say "a customer enters," ignores the need for an open entry; in Tolly's method of description, the arrival of a customer at the cobbler shop is represented by the transition from a condition in which the entry is empty to a condition in which it is filled by a waiting customer. Furthermore, the condition of all parts of the system is always taken into account: the entry with the waiting customer does not fade into the background while the repairman is at work, even though any change there depends on the repairman's finishing. A narrative form is precisely the wrong way to describe the behavior of a system or of a Petri net, as it is also the wrong form for describing the network of interactions in an ecosystem. A description of state sequences, which might be represented by little cartoons, would do the job for this particular Petri net, but as we considered more complex examples, it turned out that the occurrence graph was more versatile.

"I want to point out that one of the kinds of uses that I feel that this descriptive discipline can be put to, even in its baby form," Tolly continued, "is to draw your attention to certain things that your attention normally is not drawn to at all, and I'll give you an example of that right away. It is not ordinary to think that a typewriter key must talk back to you or else you can't push it. I haven't thought this out particularly; it's sort of an on-the-spur-of-the-moment construction and even if it's not perfect, it will make my point."

Tolly went to the board and started working out a Petri net of a man typing. According to his axioms, no condition can survive a transition, so striking a key involves entering a new state for both the typewriter and the typist, by definition different from the "ready" state before the strike. Then the event of striking the key again must depend on additional shifts to new input conditions for both man and machine, which bring them into readiness. "The point is that after I've hit the key once, in order for me to push the typewriter again, the key has to tell me that it's in ready position to be pushed again."

"That's really not true," said Fred. "It probably is in principle, but haven't you had a key stick and try to hit it? You don't necessarily wait for this information back from the key to hit it again."

"Yes, but I'm not defining a strike of the typewriter key simply as a movement of a finger. A typewriter which has gotten stuck is like the table surface on which you can pound, but you're not operating the typewriter any more. The typewriter being used as intended, which is what I'm trying to build a model of, must signal back to you that it is ready to be pushed again."

"It must, surely," said Gordon.

"Okay, now let me point out, there are two different ways in which I can get the signal back. One way would be if I actually have to see some signal before I can strike again with the intention of producing an effect at the other end. Then there's another situation in which the typewriter key responds so fast, relative to the speed at which I can iterate my movements, that the signal is guaranteed. Within the system, the guarantee is equivalent to the visual check."

"You don't need to wait then?"

"See, there's perhaps a philosophic point or something that the communication system nevertheless has to be looked at as including a return signal. From the formal point of view it looks alike, whether it comes about because you wait to see that the typewriter's in up position or because your nervous system happens to be so constructed, relative to the spring tensions in the typewriter, that you're guaranteed not to respond before the spring has, in fact, pushed the key back up again."

"You can have an internal representation of the mechanism that eventually replaces external feedback," Horst added.

Gregory said, "This is a dreadfully important point. May I say what I think and see if this makes sense? What happens, as I understand it, in this typewriter example, is that the diagram forces the designer of the total double system—man *plus* typewriter—to make specifications about the nature of the man and the nature of the typewriter such that over repeated instances they shall fit. The alternative to dealing with repeated instances in the specifications of the man and the typewriter is to have a specific signal in each instance. Now the step from the situation in which you have the signal in each instance to the situation in which you handle this at the next level up, by the specifications, is the step that is relevant to the question about handling higher logical types in this business."

Bernie then compared the sticking of the typewriter key to the jolt that occurs when calibration is in error, as when you mistake the number of stairs in the dark. "When something goes wrong with a cuing mechanism it's not that the motion continues, it's that the mental organization changes, the chap invokes a different set of programs altogether," Gordon ended. Literally a breakdown in the system.

Some of our ecological failures can be illumined by the typewriter example. For many eons, we could act in relation to our environment as if the "ready" signal were designed in: our inputs were small enough so that the readiness of a watercourse to receive new wastes could be taken for granted and we slowly developed traditional rotation systems that ensured the readiness of land to yield new crops. Our demands and our inputs have now altered and increased exponentially, yet still we forget that every event involving ourselves and a field or a stream or an estuary leaves both of us changed, and the same action is possible a second time only if both have undergone a process of restoration and new readiness. Otherwise the action is not the same but different, perhaps a second step in a cumulative process of degradation.

Tolly had returned to his seat and had been sitting quietly, as various members of the group explored the typewriter example. "Notice," he remarked, "if I sit here and talk, it is easy to ignore the fact that there is a signal coming back to me all the time. I mean, is the continuation of looking a signal? It is, you see. I *must have* the return response which tells me it's okay to say my next sentence."

"It is exceedingly difficult to say more than about thirty to fifty words over a telephone without a response from the other person," Gregory agreed.

As if the response to his most recent example assured him of our readiness to untangle new nets, Tolly returned to the board. Now that we had the rudiments of the two forms of notation, occurrence graphs and Petri nets, clearly in mind, he was able to sketch new examples lavishly, often intertwined and unlabeled. At this stage, although we lacked the proofs and theorems, which would have been necessary in a presentation to a group of mathematicians, and had skimmed very lightly over the formal axioms governing this writing system, we had the basic techniques. It took quite a while, however, before its implications became clear, as Tolly went on to define further concepts useful in the interpretation of graphs and nets. In the meantime, we took a break, while I amused myself by reflecting that one could describe the break not in terms of me and the coffee I drank, but in terms, say, of the progressive transfer of fullness from my cup to my stomach or of emptiness from my stomach to the cup.

# Human Freedom
# and Finite Resources

AFTER THE BREAK, Tolly directed our attention again to an occurrence graph of billiard balls that still remained on the blackboard, drawing a dotted line across it, which he described as a "time-slice" and labeled *a*. At that point we asked a lot of questions about time. Gertrude wanted to know whether the length of the arrows indicated duration and whether having two points at the same level in the diagram meant that the two occurrences were simultaneous; the answer was "no" to both. Then Gregory wanted to know whether the time slice represented simultaneity and Tolly drew in a second time-slice, *b*. "The only meaning the arrows have is what connects to what—nothing to do with their lengths. This graph is like a net and you can make a time-slice any place where you could run a scissors through, dividing it into two parts, except that you can't cut through the knots. There are ways of launching the billiard balls that would make the set of arrows gathered ·up by *a* simultaneous and other ways that would make those gathered up by *b* simultaneous—a very rough approximation to the meaning of a time-slice is that it represents *possible* simultaneity.

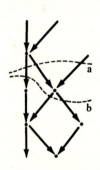

180

The system guarantees the priority of some events vis-à-vis others, but not all."

Barry said, "It's strange to call that a time-slice, but I guess you want us to live with that strangeness."

Warren asked, "Would you have any objections to making your arrows out of rubber?"

"No."

"Would you have any objection to 'time' being circular?"

"No. Oh, by no means. As a matter of fact, it will turn out that way." Warren looked content. "Time will be both circular and many-stranded."

Tolly went on to say that if it is possible to locate two points on a single strand of the net, following a series of arrows down from one point to another, those points are in sequence: they are ordered, with a set before–after relationship; similarly for two intervals of condition-holding. Looking at the graph of the billiard balls, it is clearly possible to follow the arrows down from R1 to R3 (see pp. 166–7) or to the next occurrence of R1, and so on. But it is not possible to follow the arrows on any path from the first interval of the condition L1 to the first interval L3 or from the same L1 to R3, and there are many other such pairs in this graph. These pairs of arrows are not ordered.

When two occurrences are independent of each other, with no necessary time ordering, they are called *concurrent*, as in the statement "After supper, Isabel stretched, Jason fell asleep at the table, and Roger loosened his belt"; these events are *ordered* in relation to supper, but concurrent in relation to each other, although they do occur in the same system.

At this point Tolly turned and faced the room squarely, on fire with enthusiasm. "I maintain that it is impossible, just simply impossible, to make sense out of the notion of information without the notion of concurrence." Everybody blinked. So far, we had been trying to follow Tolly along a path where few of the landmarks were familiar. We were playing his game to see where it would lead us and now he claimed that it would lead to a radical redefinition of some of the basic terms of cybernetics and information theory. There was a burst of argument as Tolly tried first to explain his assertion and finally to persuade the group to wait until later for further clarification.

As our understanding of it developed, concurrence turned out to be one of the most important concepts we discussed. It was curious to me that this should be so, because so far the emphasis had been on man's failure to realize how tightly and intricately interconnected, through how many different pathways, systemic events are, and yet concurrence emphasizes the independence of events. It is a particular kind of independence however—independence that develops out of complexity within a general context of detailed interconnection. Moving to a systemic rather than a lineal concept of causation is sometimes resisted because, with so many links, it seems to be an overwhelming new form of determinism. It is not or, if it is a determinism, at least it differs from the lineal determinism of a tumbling row of dominoes. All human actions are possible outcomes of previous events, and all the circumstances of our lives are subject to complex mutual constraints. However, the pathologies that result from our pursuit of purposes that seem good and reasonable are evidence that there is a weakness in our theories of what follows from what, either temporally or causally. Part of this failure arises from ignoring some necessary conditions and some outcomes, as narrative leads us to focus on only a portion of the process described in an occurrence net. But part of this failure is related to the old philosophical problem of human freedom. Because we have not yet understood the nature of freedom and flexibility within systems, our focus constantly shifts from an assertion of absolute determinism to the intuitive affirmation of the experience of choice.

Tolly presented concurrence as the basis for a new rhetoric of human freedom, a formulation that was only just taking shape, so that he could not go a great deal further than asserting that the concept was essential. The concept of concurrence is a way of looking at an occurrence graph or a Petri net and locating those aspects of a system that are not determined, the area that lies open for accident and coincidence and human choice without changing the nature of the system, to be contrasted with actions that necessitate systemic disruption or change.

To understand concurrence, we had to look at a second, more elaborate cobbler shop. In this one, Shoes are not passed

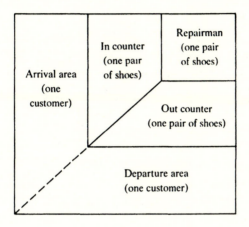

directly between Customer and Repairman, but placed on an In counter for the Repairman to pick up if he is free. The Customer Waiting may move on, any time after depositing his Shoes on the In counter, to a Departure area, through which he will exit when his Shoes are ready. The Arrival and Departure areas each can hold only one Customer, and the In and Out counters, as well as the Repairman, can each accommodate only one pair of Shoes at a time.

The Petri net Tolly drew on the board for his new and enlarged cobbler shop was harder to read than the first one, since the neat little diagram we were staring at with such perplexity seemed to be folded back on itself. Actually, Tolly had designed the diagram to show how areas of local cycling were interconnected. Thus, the In counter at one point in the system (lower right) always either had Shoes or not: transition 12 represented the placing of Shoes on the In counter, and transition 2 their removal by the Repairman. That portion of the

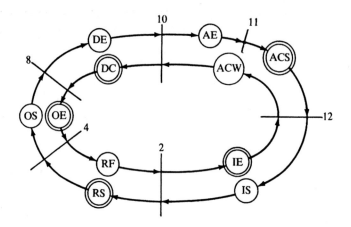

KEY TO SYSTEM CONDITIONS

| | | | |
|---|---|---|---|
| OE | Out counter Empty | IE | In counter Empty |
| OS | Out counter has Shoes | IS | In counter has Shoes |
| DE | Departure area Empty | AE | Arrival area Empty |
| DC | Departure area has Customer | ACS | Arrival area has Customer with Shoes |
| RF | Repairman Free | ACW | Arrival area has Customer Waiting |
| RS | Repairman has Shoes | | |

system just goes round and round, while at the same time its state affects other parts of the system. Similarly, the states of the Repairman, the Out counter, and the Arrival and Departure areas provide local areas of cycling, all linked together by the movement of the Shoes alternating with an idle and empty shop —this is the cycle that characterizes the whole system.

Using the same fiction of a game played with tokens, Tolly began a simulation with tokens in the places shown circled on this Petri net: One Customer is in the Departure area, while the Repairman works on his Shoes; a second Customer has entered but has not yet laid his Shoes on the In counter. Now, the most important thing to notice about this situation is that two and only two different things can happen next: ·the new Customer can put his Shoes down on the In counter (transition 12), or the Repairman can finish the Shoes he is working on and put them on the Out counter (transition 4). *Which* of these two things happens next is entirely unspecified by the system. Relative to each other, within the system as described, they are not determined.

Tolly recorded his simulation with an occurrence graph, firing transitions in the order: 4, 8, 12, 10, 2, 11, 4, 8, 12. Then he reminded us that only points directly connected by arrows on the occurrence graph were sequenced. Starting from the same conditions, the same occurrence graph, with the same interconnecting sequence of points and arrows, could record several other sequences of firings, for instance: 12, 4, 2, 8, 10, 11, 12, 4, 8, 10. The occurrence graph is "ambiguous" about the relative ordering of some events when this has no significance for the system being modeled. This is its great advantage over a state-sequence diagram.

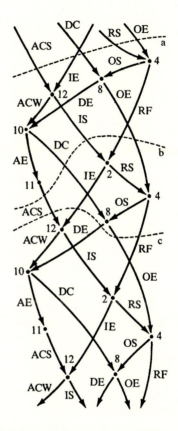

By definition, all pairs of occurrences on an occurrence graph which are not ordered are *concurrent*: the repairman finishing with one pair of shoes and the decision of the new customer to put his on the counter are concurrent in this system. Tolly drew three dotted lines across the graph with the side of the chalk, each one crossing a set of concurrent arcs, and labeled them *a*, *b*, and *c*. These were time-slices, and now we could understand what he had meant when he said that a time-slice represented "possible simultaneity." In a net simulation, each possible arrangement of tokens corresponds to a time-slice. The first slice corresponds to the original distribution of tokens in Tolly's simulation, and you can try and visualize the others by checking the conditions back against the key. As was true in the beginning of the simulation, time-slices do not, in general, have unique immediate successors. Either of the following two slices could be the immediate successor of $a$:

$$ACS - IS - DC - RS - OE$$

or

$$ACS - IS - DC - OS - RF$$

As Tolly talked, I found I was relying heavily on an imagery I had got from Warren: if, as Warren had suggested, the arrows were made out of rubber, then there would be a way of spreading each occurrence graph like a net, letting some arrows stretch and others contract, without violating any of the before-after relations that were actually fixed in the knots, so that any one of the many alternative time-slices could be a straight line. Will protested that *in fact* the movements of a customer from one area of the shop to another and the stages of the cobbler's work—or alternatively Isabel's stretch and Roger's loosening of his belt—must always be in some relative sequence, but Tolly insisted that saying this is meaningful only if some observer is watching both or their actions are checked against a clock. Otherwise the net is pulled and stretched and time is a result of process.

I had a feeling of vertigo listening to Tolly. As we met in that castle, moving from topic to topic and from room to room, I knew my husband was driving across Europe: Stuttgart, Florence, Barcelona, London—the places he would linger I knew, but Tolly was telling me that until we met again in London we were moving in different times—that it would be nonsense to say that I went down to dinner *at the same time* that he drove out of Stuttgart. Then I thought of the concurrence in each of our efforts to understand Tolly. Spoken words, which all of us would hear, glances exchanged, interactions, all created

transitions involving our separate strands of growing understanding, but each of us interiorly moved into new and different
states after each utterance, setting off concurrent trains of
thought. I looked around the room where people sat in different
postures, papers and pencils now scattered at all angles. Barry
had slid down into his chair, so that just his head was visible,
and scowled in concentration at the blackboard. Gertrude was
frowning, listening as a mathematician but not completely ap-
proving. At the blackboard, Tolly was tense and gleeful, his
hair standing up in points and a tangle of half-erased diagrams
behind him.

"See, I think that none of these process models really make
any sense unless one ultimately sees them as related to us,"
Tolly continued. "So far, you know, these look like pictures of
billiard balls bouncing or cobblers' shops in operation, and it
looks as if I haven't said anything about observers, but I *really*
have, I really have."

"You've never said anything except about observers," said
Gregory.

"Yes, that's right. Us. Us is really what it all comes from."

The observer in Tolly's system is closely related to concurrence. The notion that two unconnected events can be ordered or simultaneous in any meaningful sense supposes that
there is some universal observer, who can see them both and
connects them by his knowledge, or some universal clock to
which both are causally hitched. It was precisely this that Tolly
was rejecting with his notion of concurrence. This seemed to
me to be closely related to a story he told about Carl Adam
Petri, for whom Petri nets are named. At their first meeting, in
1962, an historic event for both of them, Petri remarked that
you cannot synchronize two clocks without a channel of communication between them. "And I looked," said Tolly, "and I
didn't understand why he was telling me this or why I should
care, but I had the very strong feeling that I had better find out
what that meant. And I've spent four or five years trying."

In an occurrence graph of the operation of two synchronized
clocks, their synchrony would be a connection between them

and their movement would never be concurrent. This would be true whether the condition that connected them were an observer who sat and noted that they were synchronized, someone who was actually adjusting the settings continually, or simply the guarantee that having been started up together they would never get out of step, since the guarantee would be a continuing condition. Without one of these conditions, what sense would it make to say they were synchronized? Similarly, Tolly said, a car pulling away from the curb at 49th Street and another driven by a stranger pulling away from the curb at 110th would be concurrent—unless there were someone in a plane whose observation set these events in a meaningful before-after sequence. The presence of an observer determines system constraints by defining sequence and simultaneity.

During his presentation, long before we had the idea clearly in mind, Tolly had made the radical assertion that, without the notion of concurrence, nothing sensible can be said on the subject of information, and now he was ready to explain it further. "In the absence of concurrence, there is no way of saying what it means for two things to act independently, which is a prerequisite for the passage of information." And also, clearly, a prerequisite for any understanding of individual freedom.

We floundered around on this for quite a long time, trying to get concurrence clear and to work out its relationship to information theory. Two or three people, Gordon and Warren at least, were agreeing enthusiastically with Tolly. Barry was pugnaciously challenging those who seemed to understand to explain what they had that he had missed. Others preserved a discreet and bewildered silence. Bert Kaplan wandered out of the room.

"See, when I first encountered information theory," Tolly said, "I saw that it had no interpretation of what it might be to receive a message—what must one posit in the world in order to have a receiver! A message sent from one place to another has a synchronizing effect, so in order to make information possible you have to have some kind of asynchrony, which is concurrence."

"Let's see if I've got you on this," Ted said. "You're saying that you can't have the exchange of a message without a system that has some unconnected points?"

"Yes. And it's sensible to talk about me talking to you only insofar as we think of you and me as independent."

One of the ways of specifying the meaning of concurrence in occurrence theory was the axiom that two intervals of condition-holding might never bear the same label if they were concurrent, that is, if there were no path between them. "Now, what does that teach us?" asked Tolly. "Supposing we have two pendula, which are swinging, and we have them oriented in such a way that you can talk about each of them as swinging to the right . . ."

"These are two different conditions," said Warren.

"Right, that's the point. We are not allowed to say the condition 'pendulum swinging to the right' applies to both pendula. Okay?" And similarly, it seemed to me, when we are talking about a society, in which a tremendous number of individuals are part of the same system but are in concurrence with much of the system at any one time, even though they may be doing the same things or holding the same opinions, we tend to distort our whole understanding of the network of causal relations by speaking in statistical terms.

"What is beginning to impress me," Barry put in, "is that your entire system has specificity built into it at all points. You are systematically excluding non-meaningful events. You see what I mean?"

"I think I just barely take the trip."

"In other words, wherever you see a possibility for a lack of significance, you're simply casting it out."

"Yes. Let's take an example where there would be a temptation to have two concurrent intervals bear the same label. Let's suppose that we have a screen, okay? and two holes through which that screen can be observed, so that independent observers can arrive at those holes without interfering with each other. Now, supposing you flash a message on that screen. That's another situation in which one might want to give two arrows the same label. However, I will insist that you label them differently for each observer."

"That's exactly what I mean," said Barry. "You refuse to accept the notion that there is an independence between what is seen and who is seeing it."

"Absolutely, absolutely. One hundred per cent."

"You are simply, inherently . . . you've got a congenital tendency toward specificity in anything you're doing."

From here Tolly went on to talk about conflict, which throws a different kind of light on the problem of determinism. Conflict occurs when there is a place in a Petri net which feeds two alternative transitions. The simplest possible case of conflict would be a net like this. Starting with a token at R, two different transitions could be fired, since R is the input for both,

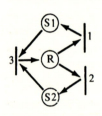

resulting in either of the states S1 or S2. In a long net simulation, an occurrence graph would be produced on which S1 and S2 would appear in a random order, as heads and tails do in a series of coin tosses, since nothing in the system as diagrammed determines which of the two transitions will be fired. Such a determination requires some information from outside the system, some interface with the environment. An expanded net, taking in more of the environment, by including more relevant conditions in the definition of the system, could remove that conflict.

"The appearance of conflict has something to do with how I happen to define the boundary," Tolly pointed out. "And it's as a function of boundary definition that the thing called 'information exchange' makes its appearance."

Later, as I worked through what we had heard from Tolly, I found that I spent a lot of time musing about the problem of how to define the boundaries of systems. In all of the models we considered, the system was receiving some input from the outside—vehicles, a customer with shoes to be repaired—and releasing some output. The same was true of my aquarium, for which sunlight and water to replace evaporation loss were needed, and the same is true of the Azores or any ecosystem. We speak of these things as systems because of a particular pattern in their internal relations, but in every case they are coupled to other systems so that you can, if you like, imagine them as subsystems of a larger system: each individual is a system, but so is a family a system; each country of Europe is a system, but so is Europe a system. In a sense, the impossibility of a perpetual motion machine means that no on-going system can be entirely autonomous.

In my first understanding of Tolly's ideas, I had felt that he had thrown away the notion of the individual along with his "nouns": Momma ceased to be completely separable in his narrative and became instead variably involved in different interactions. Yet at the same time, Tolly was leading us to a new sense of the individual through his emphasis on system boundaries and on concurrence. It seemed that these notions would be helpful in understanding the separateness of consciousness from the rest of the mind too—as the growth of a child within the womb is independent of the mother's knowledge or the body is aroused to passion or anger independent of the conscious mind's justification and explanation. Within our bodies vast numbers of processes go on all the time, often concurrently in Tolly's sense, but there are messengers in that system, such as the hormones, which function to limit concurrence. Then the edge of the individual is not his skin, but a pattern in the ripples of an occurrence graph, a change in the quality of interconnections. When you define an individual, you are choosing to bound your system so that you can predict as much as possible of what occurs within it, without referring outside—that is, you minimize what Tolly called conflict in a Petri net; and you bound your system at points of high concurrence. In my aquarium, hundreds of necessary before-after relations in events were independent of what went on outside, but at certain crucial points there were connections from that bounded and individual world to the wider one: the fish would gather in the front of the tank when I fed them, and you could not know when they would change course and swim forward unless you knew about the patterns of my day. But the fish could learn when to expect me, and by their adaptive learning would be more closely coupled into the larger system, with less concurrence between their movements and my own.

"Now this suggests that the growth of the net might give rise to changes in information exchange," Barry wondered.

"Well certainly, when you redefine those boundary lines."

"Now that again relates to one of the puzzling dichotomies between the new orthodoxy of inheritance, the molecular view, and what biologists have believed for a long time, which is that information is generated during the growth of the organism." Tolly looked somewhat dubious as Barry went on. "The question is, do you have all the information in the fertilized egg, which is just translated to a new form as the organism develops, or is the egg much less informed, so to speak, than the adult, in which case you've got to visualize a source of information. Really, of course, it has to be something like the 'boot-strap theory' of the nucleus which says that the particles that you can get out of the nucleus have no self-sufficient existence inside, where their properties are determined by their neighbors and vice versa. You know, if I understand what you've said just now, you could get this boot-strapping because of the proliferation of the network as it grows, giving rise to new possible . . . new sources of energy input."

"Yes, you know it's all still very far away, from the point of view of our actual modeling capabilities." Tolly was looking rather weary.

"If you're supposing that there is some sort of growth process represented here," said Gordon, "then at some stage I'm impelled to say I will use a different sort of description of the behaviors. As I understand it, I will define a new Petri net."

"Well, look, Gordon, you have to recognize what you're looking at is a baby, I mean this whole thing is really still sort of weak, pink, newborn."

Gordon smiled engagingly. "I'm fascinated by the biological or psychological relevance of this sort of modeling. I think, like Barry, I'm trying to jump in at the deep end and say, well, look, I would like it to be terribly relevant, please."

Peter Klopfer was worried about a related problem. "All the examples you cite, Tolly, and those that have grown out of Barry's lecture are based on cyclic or iterative processes. At least in the time scale with which many of us work, we're dealing with processes that are not iterative. When a duckling hatches or a kid is born, an event takes place and something is changed. It's never the same again. One can even go beyond individuals, if one takes ecological communities in succession through to climax. Again, there is within that very long stretch of time, from the earliest to the latest successional phase, no iteration, no cycling. It's only within the components of the larger system that one gets the cycles or, I suppose, if one takes the universe as a whole and an infinite period of time."

"*Ja*, I think, definitely, I agree with Peter," said Horst. "The interest of someone studying the growth of an animal, which has its own history, is not in the system in little time slots, which you can do with your . . . you know, you take the beast's breathing, that's what Peter meant by saying parts of it are probably cyclical. But if you want to look at the whole development of a beast and predict its future development, then I very much doubt that it's possible to do this with your method."

"Wait a minute—impossible because of a lack of data in the end?" Gregory asked.

"No, my claim is that that's part of the true nature of such systems as organisms."

Tolly hesitated.

"That is what I meant when I said that in the development of an individual there is an increase in the information content," Barry persisted. "In other words, Peter is saying that this is not the kind of repetitious thing that one sees with billiard balls and, therefore, what we are dealing with is a way in which the system has got to either generate or acquire new information . . ."

"Acquire, acquire," muttered Tolly.

"Now as I remember," Barry said, "something you said, Tolly, led me to believe that the system had properties that allowed it to grow in complexity at the expense of the surrounding network?"

"Yes."

"And I asked a question about that, Tolly, that at least tentatively satisfied me that this language will provide exactly the answer that Peter and Horst want."

"Now, you say you want to talk about a development that you regard as potentially predictable from the scientist's point of view," Tolly answered. "You think of this as having a beginning and an end—I mean, the animal gets born sometime, goes through some developmental history, and dies. And the resources are finite resources, okay? Its body is only so large and the environment will supply only so much of whatever it is that's required for its growth. Then, without making any claims at the moment about how much of some total developmental cycle can practically be encompassed in nets or the equivalent of nets, in principle it all works just fine. It's something that in principle is repeatable. It doesn't matter whether you ever see this chicken or this particular ecosystem again.

"There's another element of confusion in this. Don't think that all systems are as determined as a set of billiard balls rolling on a frictionless surface or even these very schematic cobbler shops. The fact that most of the examples I've shown were determinate has nothing to do with the nature of my descriptive device. In more complex Petri nets, you can have a lot of conflict and a lot of possibilities for the influx, you might say, of information from the outside, which is not built into the character of the system."

Will reformulated the question of cycling to refer to historical events. "Back twenty years or so ago, I began drawing pictures, Tolly, that looked strangely like your occurrence graphs, because I started listening to historians. Historians talk a foreign sort of language. They say: 'What are the causes of the French Revolution?'" Gregory winced. "They do, Gregory, they do!"

"I know they do," he said.

"They talk just as if they were dealing with a great big god damn billiard ball called the French Revolution, which was about the same sort of thing as another one called the Industrial Revolution. Well, I began to make analyses in terms of things that I called 'influence strands' and 'nodes' on influence strands.

For instance, if we talk about the French Revolution, one node would be the 'Oath on the Tennis Court,' but then you'd open that node and inside that node you would find other influence strands with intersections on those strands and these begin to look very much like your occurrence graphs. Well, now, okay, two questions. First, when you are trying to deal with something even as small as the 'Oath on the Tennis Court,' let alone the French Revolution, aren't you going to be dealing with so many conditions that you have to cut out an immense number of relevant ones and make it highly artificial? That's the first question and it cannot be answered simply by saying, 'The baby hasn't grown up yet,' because what I'm asking is whether this baby is ever going to grow up—*this baby,* you see? Then, quite apart from complexity, what do the words *'in principle* predictable or repeatable' mean? Do such things ever repeat? This is different even from Peter's ducks, you see, because the duck repeats itself in the next generation of ducks, but do you ever have a second generation of the French Revolution, Tolly?"

"Yes is the answer to that."

"But you don't in actuality. Now, what does it mean to say you do in principle?"

"Yes. I guess what I will rest on, in my answer 'yes,' is kind of, you know, my religion, which is the finiteness of everything."

"Okay, if we get to religion, that's all right."

"That is, I think that history forever is as much an absurd fiction as God. The French Revolution is a meaningful term only in a finite context." A transcendent God, of course, has to be ruled out of Tolly's system; otherwise he would be the universal observer removing all concurrence and setting all events in sequence. As I explored this later on, it appeared to me that Tolly was not so much asserting that a second French Revolution, identical to the first, would someday occur, but that as the context broadens, the notion of the French Revolution loses its specificity so that it becomes meaningless to say it does *not* repeat. This is again a problem of the observer.

Fred Attneave wanted to know whether Tolly could specifically design a set of axioms that were necessarily historical and would not allow the system to repeat itself. So Tolly pointed out again that it would always be easy to represent nets with information supplied from outside, like an endless sequence of coin tosses that never repeated itself. Bert Kaplan wanted something different of history: "In history, aren't there events that are truly productive of new possibilities?"

Gertrude spoke up in a clear voice: "What I want, what I thought I was hearing yesterday, was a device that would make it possible to make predictions and to check them empirically. It seems to me that's what we have to have."

"That's right. And anything you can predict is in principle repeatable," said Tolly.

"There's no difficulty in depicting in your system what the engineers call a runaway?" Gregory asked. "A system that progressively deteriorates to its own destruction?"

Tolly was perplexed. "To its own destruction—that's a much more difficult question. I mean I don't think I could call a thing that destroys itself . . ." Gregory then distinguished between the problem of representing something like a steam engine, so connected up that it follows an exponential curve of increased velocity, and the problem of representing its eventual breakdown. "The thing that's giving me pause," said Tolly, "is the question of any increase without bounds. The technique as so far developed deals strictly with finite resources and, although it can take resources in from outside the system, it can't take anything in without bounds."

Gregory: "Nothing can."

Tolly shook his head. "Thinking something like that through . . . I just haven't performed that experiment." After quite a lot of discussion it became clear that the present axioms of Petri nets exclude the possibility of, say, a cobbler shop that broke down due to a bottleneck. If it is unstable and breaks down, it cannot in the end be described as a system at that level, although it must be a part of some system. On the other hand, you could build nets within the present axioms that would fail and you might have an important debugging technique to discover formally that a machine or a traffic plan or the abuse of Lake Erie will not work.

At that point Ted said he wanted to ask a few questions. Gregory looked at him warily. "You have two or three questions, right, on a piece of paper there? I'm getting traumatized about people who want to put three points on the table at once."

"Then let me just ask two that are strictly . . ."

"ONE!" Everyone laughed. Saving up questions is like the repairman saving up pairs of shoes while the customers—or the comments that have caused the framing of a particular question —go on their way. Then when the questions are voiced they are concurrent with all the other lines of thought in the room and the system of groping talk loses its intricate interconnection.

"One or two of my questions are absolutely relevant here," Ted said stiffly, "or I wouldn't be bothering you with them. This is my third question, leaving out the one on stability."

"Here's the question that I will not ask, here's the question I will ask," Tolly laughed.

Ted continued, "In all of the examples that you've given, the plot seems to revolve around a bottleneck. We have a cobbler shop where only one customer at a time can be handled or a road section that one car at a time can cross—things of this sort. This is a question, it seems to me, of channel capacity. Now, suppose we have a cobbler shop where they can easily handle twenty customers at a time, but they never get more than ten, so that, in a sense, we've ruled out the readiness question because it's a constant—they're always ready. Is your system extendable to larger channel capacities where this kind of traffic or queuing problem is not really the crucial one?"

"I'm trying to think of what the reason is for bottlenecks having been prominent and I haven't at the moment got a good answer," Tolly mused. "There's no difficulty with representing cobbler shops where the traffic that is presumed to flow is greatly less than the capacity of the cobbler shop. But it seems to me that forms, structures, insofar as they have something to do with functional things, always represent some way of handling the facts of finite resources . . ."

"A twenty-customer capacity is exactly the same thing as the example I gave of a screen which is visible through two holes," Tolly continued. "I pointed out that that visibility is doubly represented by two conditions which are capable of being swallowed up, one by the viewer at the one hole and the other concurrently by the viewer at the other hole. So also, the cobbler shop which has a capacity of twenty has twenty ready states, ready to be consumed concurrently."

"Maybe what happens is that such a system breaks down into twenty parallel Petri diagrams."

"Then probably it's just plain twenty cobbler shops. I mean, is the cobbler shop really a unit, in the sense that various working parts influence each other somehow? If a thing has been constructed as a single cobbler shop, then somewhere there will be queuing, somewhere there's going to be some machine which is a scarce resource. I think the business of systems and all comes into being only as a result of scarcity of resources."

"I wondered if this was a limitation in the method that you're presenting," Ted said.

"No, I think it's a limitation of the subject matter. I mean, that's what has now occurred to me. It seems to me that that's really the subject of systems in the first place." As soon as we begin to think of the natural environment in cybernetic terms, I thought, we have to think of it as finite, processing real quantities with limited capacity, offering limited resources.

Barry came in with an illustration from biology. "In photosynthesis there are processes that occur in the light and processes that occur in the dark. Now, the light process is not influenced very much by temperature, but the dark process is, and they're sequential. If you now look at photosynthesis and examine its overall sensitivity to temperature changes, this would depend on which of the sequential steps is limiting in the overall rate. If there is plenty of light, for example, then the dark process is limiting, and the whole system is sensitive to temperature. If you ask the question of how the system as a whole responds to an outside influence, the open segment, of the type that Ted's talking about, won't be so relevant. What is relevant is that there is a sequential segment which is of Tolly's kind.

"The same thing occurs in the kinds of enzyme systems that

we were talking about when we discussed toxicity," Barry continued. "For example, foodstuffs float around freely in the juice of the cell and the place that's really critical in determining what happens is where they sit down on the surface of an enzyme to be processed. That is limited in its capacity and there are elaborate analyses of the role of foodstuffs, poisons, and so on, in affecting enzyme processes, which relate to exactly this kind of saturation. In fact, they're ludicrously like this. If we think of the active sites, where the small molecule of foodstuff can sit on the enzyme, then that site is either ready, occupied, or releasing the transformed substance. One of the very interesting things that could be done would be to look at some of these enzymatic processes using Tolly's notation. Now, the feeling I have is that what happens elsewhere in the cell, where there is not a saturable point, is irrelevant. You can think of the cell as a network of bottlenecks which determine the distribution of available materials." Not surprisingly, I thought, problem-solving that aims at relieving bottlenecks is almost inevitably frustrated by the development of new bottlenecks. Scarcity is a fact of life—we can only try to choose our scarcities. Thus, we can examine our proposed interventions to determine the ways in which they will shift or create bottlenecks. Indeed, we can go further and recognize bottlenecks as determining the characteristics of the system, and pick and choose the bottlenecks to give the system a particular form.

"In any case," said Tolly, "an extremely interesting subject is the development of measures of capacity which have to do with these nets, which I so far know very little about."

Barry had been drawing the moral of Tolly's remarks at every available opportunity, but now he said, "I'd just like to take two minutes to tell you what I've gotten out of all this, because I think it's easy to lose sight of its importance by asking too much and I think this is the point of Tolly's remark about the baby. I have tried to list the ways in which the properties of Tolly's approach correct misleading tendencies generated by the kind of conceptual processes that I have been taught to use—that may be personal and idiosyncratic, but I rather doubt it.

"First there is, I think, a serious tendency in natural science to isolate the observer from the object observed. This has become so serious as to require very profound corrections, all of which are imposed or introduced as a crutch to the methods which actually generated the difficulty. Newtonian physics had to deal as though the object were not influenced by the person who was observing it. Now, having built on that concept, you find modern physicists going to great pains to prove that it is not true. Wigner[1] has very carefully generated a mathematical proof that there has to be an interaction between the observer and that which is observed, and this leads him to really detailed considerations of conceptual processes. Now this kind of misdirection is avoided, at least psychologically, by Tolly's presentation."

Gregory interrupted: "The Holt method will not coerce the old-fashioned scientist away from his old-fashioned thoughts; he can still think old-fashioned and use Tolly's graphs. All it does is permit him to think better."

"A second point is this," Barry continued. "I think, just personally, that another difficulty quite common in modern science which is helped, to put it very crudely, by Tolly's approach, is the relationship between process and time. Biologists particularly have had to go through great tortuous arguments to begin to sense that time is a consequence of process, rather than something handed down by the Lord, which biological objects obey like a clock. Your sense of time is a consequence of process, and all of you who have just traveled know what I mean. Now the whole notion of a time-slice takes time off the pedestal of absoluteness that has troubled biologists for a long time.

"The third thing that I found very useful is the destruction of the noun. And this turns out, in my way of thinking, to be beautifully subtle. The peculiar thing is that, while he seems to obliterate them, Tolly has actually discovered a new way to create nouns, because he has an indefinite way of tacking together descriptions of processes. We have tended to think of nouns as being primary and the process as secondary, whereas actually I think it's the other way around. That other-way-aroundness, again, drops immediately out of Tolly's presentation."

Horst interrupted to ask Barry why he was making an armored attack and bringing two hundred tanks to go through an open door, whether he felt Tolly had to be defended.

"No, I'm not doing this to defend Tolly at all. He doesn't need me. I'm simply recording my whole response to what he's said. Let me mention one last point. In general, interactions—reciprocal effects—are emphasized by what Tolly says and, again, this is something that we have to learn. When you try to get graduate students to understand how to teach, they start by thinking that teaching consists of filling themselves with knowledge and then putting it out. After that, they may notice that there's somebody out here listening and, long after that, they'll notice that there's some response. Now, you see, Tolly's approach says that when you walk into a room full of students, there are going to be interactions and what happens will depend on your watching their eyes and facial expressions and altering what you do accordingly. Well, I wouldn't understand most of the mathematics, but I do understand the consequences of the approach, I think, and it is a highly biological device, which we don't have so far."

"Well, I'll make a quick comment," Tolly grinned. "I do need Barry. Now let's break."

# Purpose and Control

By THE END OF Tolly's preliminary description, we had several different topics hanging suspended, a dozen different things that people wondered if they could say in Tolly's language: would occurrence systems represent history, or hierarchies, or standard cybernetic notions like information and control? And just what did these terms mean anyhow? Two or three conversations were going on simultaneously, with the cyberneticists running an argument among themselves about the meaning of their terms and beating away at Tolly, and the less mathematically inclined rather bewildered by the whole debate.

Gordon Pask had identified himself on the first day as a cyberneticist interested in microsystems of interaction between men and men and men and machines, especially from the point of view of control, and he was the member of the group most anxious to engage with Tolly on a technical level. He was small and quick and difficult to follow, with a small head, the lower part of which was often engaged in supporting a very large pipe, while his eyes seemed always to be peering toward the most bizarre implications of what was being said. At first glance, no two people could possibly have been more different in their styles of discussion. It was perhaps inevitable that they would fight before they could agree, especially since Tolly had offered a portion of himself to the group and Gordon's style of debate, always edged with disparagement, seemed to engage him on a level of triviality.

Gordon began, "I use models to represent processes like learning, social evolution, or even biological evolution. In order to do this, it seems, in the models we have at the moment, that it is necessary to construct hierarchies of control. It seems to me that the question that requires answering is not a very complicated one, or one which is outside the baby stage of the theory to comprehend, and the question is simply this: How, in this theory of yours, Tolly, do I represent control?"

Tolly hesitated between rejecting the question entirely, as phrased in terms of an inadequate terminology, and trying to answer. "See, first of all, control is another one of those words which has seemed to me in need of being made technically nice. But—let's say I have a large net, which I divide in two parts, and I want to think of one part as controlling the other, determining its behavior. Is that it, vaguely?"

Gordon continued drily to a more precise specification of what he had in mind, but instead of answering him in his terms Tolly decided to clarify several of the technical terms of classical cybernetics—information, control, and the decoding of a bit, the traditional unit of information—at the same time. He drew a new net containing conflict at one point, like the net he had used to illustrate conflict, but with a number of other, conflict-free transitions added. The conflict represents a choice between two concurrent sequences each of which, once started, is strictly ordered and entirely determinate. Information enters from outside the net, determining which of two conflicting transitions is fired, but after that branch point is passed, the information is converted to control: only one thing can happen.

"That's the first time I've ever seen someone able to make the difference clear between information and control," said Horst gleefully.

"I mean, it's so infuriating!" Tolly said. "Can you imagine, with fifteen years of cyberneticizing, computerizing, etc., etc., I have never seen a picture that made clear to me what it might mean to decode a bit, or the difference between control and bits? After all this fuss and talk about information—it just seems incredible to me!"

Horst was terribly excited. "*Ja*, and I recently had to give a talk to a German cybernetic society, and I tried to explain to them Norbert Wiener's double definition of cybernetics. See, he never made that clear, why do information and control fit under the same heading?"

"The change from synchrony to concurrence is what is critical here," Tolly continued. "After that point where the information is converted to control, you have two streams that are determinate and move along independently of each other, whereas the bits of information coming in, which determined that it would first go this way and then that way, were strictly sequenced. That's the essence of the issue of the decoding of a bit."

Barry said, "What I like about this is that, looking at it the other way around, when the control appears, the information disappears, because the essence of the information is that there shall be two alternative opportunities."

"That's right. Precisely. After that, there are two officers who are standing at the beginning of the two streams, who have nothing to do but shout 'go' to their slaves down below, and all they're doing is standing there waiting for the 'go' sign."

Warren was disapproving. "I say that the diagram of the decoding of a bit shows the effect of information on a physical process, but it doesn't answer Gordon's question, and I'm unhappy about it. This seems to me a chain of command, and control is *not* command. In all problems of control, the main issue is to listen to the thing which you control. You can have a chain of command all the way to the Almighty if you want to and it flows one way, but control is forever to be ready, so when you say 'go' to the guy, you know that he's understood what he is to do. You've got to listen to him, otherwise you can't do it. The control problem is a closed-loop problem; a command system can be one-ended. Look, suppose you're drilling troops; the first thing you do is you order what is to be done and you listen to that come back. You yell 'Right by squads,' and it comes back 'right by squads.' Only then do you say 'March!' "

"Why?" Tolly asked.

"Otherwise you've lost control; you've only got command. It just doesn't work. It never has worked. If you want to control something you have to have information as to the state and activity and whatnot of the thing being controlled. It's quite different from command. They're very distinct and people are always getting mixed up on them."

"Yes," Tolly answered, "but the reason you have to wait for the return shout is. . . I mean the problem that's being solved is your receiving the ready signal." There wasn't a chance for Tolly to elaborate on this, but it seemed to me that the difference between control and command was closely related to the problem of the typewriter that talked back. In Tolly's system, the necessity of an explicit "ready" condition before any process could be initiated seemed to obviate the need for a distinction between command and control. From his point of view, what Warren was referring to as command was always, if it worked, of the nature of control.

This is a point about the coupling of systems that we had been converging on from several different directions. We had started from Barry's description of the cultural climate in which we see ourselves as technological masters of nature, manipulating it as we will. Then, when Barry spoke of DNA theory, he referred in passing to the characterization of DNA as the "master" molecule of the cell, with all other molecules its "slaves." This is another manifestation of the belief we have in this culture that it is possible to be separate and yet to rule, to dominate without being affected by what is dominated. This is a fallacy. There is a sense in which all rule is possible only by the consent of the governed, since it depends at the very least upon some common understanding—some contract about the interpretation of the royal dictates. God cannot be a "tyrant crown'd." Another way of looking at the same matter is to notice that a king needs subjects, or he is not a king, and, as the humble–proud Israelites knew, a god needs worshippers. We act, in our treatment of the environment, as if we have no need to wait on feedback from the environment; in our proud domination, we deny the fact that we are affected by the response to our acts.

In Tolly's system, the ready signal from the typewriter (which is equivalent to the "Yes, sir" of the private) becomes necessary when there is the possibility of concurrence between typist and machine. They are engaged in separate, unordered sequences of events, so that information flow is possible between them. The separate process of our consciousness sets us off in just this way against the natural world, and indeed against all the other processes going on in our own bodies that proceed concurrently with our conscious thought. Actually waiting for the signal from the typewriter is unnecessary when the typewriter is so constructed that the key is guaranteed to return to place before the finger can strike again; this kind of timing calibration is an analogue to the situation when the power ratio between man and environment was such that man could do relatively little damage.

The ecosystem we try to rule does talk back: smog and depletion, the eutrophication of streams and the development of insecticide immunities in pests are its messages. As long as we are unresponsive to them, our dictates to nature—our attempts to manipulate it—are of the nature of what Warren was calling command. Gregory was dealing with a similar problem in the Memorandum when he described Alice's attempt to use a flamingo as a croquet mallet. An ordinary croquet mallet is an extension of the player's own limb; player plus mallet function as one component. But the flamingo has purposes of its own, which develop concurrently. Alice does not understand—and therefore cannot control—the flamingo, and in her efforts to follow the play she is driven to try and treat the flamingo simply as a tool, an *it*, and inevitably fails.

There was no hope of working out the relationship between what Warren was saying and Tolly's system, however, because suddenly six different strands of terminological confusion about control, command, and information seemed to be going at once. There was a very irritating and confusing wrangle for a while, with a sharp exchange between Ted and Gregory as Gregory tried to sort out the argument. Tolly had lapsed into complete, exasperated silence, glowering, his black hair standing out from his head in all directions.

Will made a tentative effort to find his way into the confusion. "May I see how lost I am? In the language that's now being used, Tolly has . . ."

Tolly blew up. "We've sailed off into the stratosphere, it's that simple. A balloon cut loose. And I mean, I'm feeling a certain level of irritation. What I put up there was simple in the extreme."

"In the language we are now using," Will said, "what is on the board is information and command, not information and control?"

"That's right."

"I don't agree." Bedlam.

"It's control over command if you like," said Barry magnanimously.

"No, no," said Horst. "Now Barry has tried to understand this in his marvelous way—you know, he uses metaphors."

"I'm sorry," Barry said.

"You always do this. You don't try to talk Tolly's language and get information from him."

"That's because he's a good teacher; he elicits my language."

"Yes, of course it's helpful to the rest of biologists. But I want an answer in his language. This Petri net of the decoding of a bit . . ." Horst fumbled for words and finally asked Tolly to draw an occurrence diagram to match the Petri net which still remained on the board. "We are so well trained, you see . . . we have spent so much time on occurrence diagrams, equivalent to several years . . ."

Tolly started a simulation and then carried it through, and Horst was content.

As soon as there was a pause, Gordon returned to the attack, doodling on the blackboard where he stood, his head tilted, his body slanting sharply backward or forward from the ankle, rather prim and very clever. "I'd simply like to investigate to what extent the notion of *goal* can be described as a property of some representation like Tolly's and to what extent the notion of goal is imposed by somebody who defines the system in the first place. As Minsky and others have pointed out, before we can ever represent these sequences of states, we have got to state the purpose of the machine. We must say, that thing is a typewriter; that thing is a society and I want to look at it as a machine; that thing is an insect and I would like to look at it as a machine. We're in fact asking what it's used for, what its purpose is. Unless we did that, we would not be in a position to designate the states of that machine. We could draw arbitrary diagrams on the blackboard and we could have some rules for manipulating the diagrams but, in a perfectly good sense, we would not have designated a machine or a system."

"Is this really true?" Gregory asked.

"I think so," said Gordon drily, raising his eyebrows and smiling faintly.

"Say I have a machine," Gregory said, holding up a matchbox, frowning at it and turning it from side to side. "I don't know what it's used for. I study the interrelations and interactions of its parts. And I make what seems to me to be a diagram of a sequence of states for it. I form a hypothesis: it's for milking cows. Now somebody comes in later and says, *no*, that wasn't for milking cows, that's for timing speeches in conferences. Now, with this new piece of information, I go back to my sequence diagram, which was constructed with the wrong hypothesis. That diagram will be useful to me in constructing a new diagram, won't it?"

"Well, it would be surprising, but it's conceivable. What I would like to submit is what you actually stated a little bit earlier—namely, that you must have a hypothesis first; I would submit that in order to draw a diagram of these funny connected parts . . ."

"This I think is probably true, yes. That makes sense."

"Now, if you've got a rather elaborate hypothesis," Gordon

said, "that this is a machine for milking cows, and it turns out it's for timing conferences, it's unlikely that the fruits of your previous labors will be of any use to you at all. They might even be positively misleading. But in the case where you set up sub-hypotheses, of course, they might be. I think the essential point is that your hypothesis comes first. I don't really mind whether you're talking about an insect or a typewriter or a milking machine."

Warren set this problem in the context of the history of cybernetics. "The first meeting of the group that eventually became the basic conference on cybernetics was occasioned by the capture of two German devices. The navy men who started to open the first one were killed—it had a destruct mechanism in it. So they took the second one to Princeton and brought us over to have a look at it. We don't know what it's for; we don't know how it does it; we don't know what's inside. How do you find out? One thing they took for granted was that it would have some purpose."

Both Barry and Tolly seemed to disagree, and Horst interrupted to interpret for Barry. Barry shook his head. "The only reason I was unhappy is that I was thinking—I'm very parochial —I was just thinking about the insect."

"But even the insect—Barry, I claim that you can do this with my praying mantis," Horst protested. "I did exactly like it, I had to worry in the end about what its goal might be."

Gordon said, "I think the most beautiful example of this that I know of is the work done by Jerry Lettvin and Warren's group on the frog's eyes,[1] where absolutely no progress was made until somebody said, well, the frog is a machine for eating insects, at which point it became possible to determine what intentional definition it had, as it were; what its perceptual filters were."

"But you see," said Barry, "that's just my point. The frog was a machine for eating insects even while no one recognized that."

"That's correct. I agree. Now I'm going to come to that, because what I'm talking about at the moment is what in my paper I called 'goals *for* machines' as against 'goals *of* machines.' There's really quite a lot of difference here, between the descriptive and the prescriptive mode." From here, Gordon went on to relate the notion of goal to the notion of control. He pointed out that when someone claims to control a simple device like a light switch, this is possible because the switch has been built to be useful in a particular way: the knowledge that the device will work, necessary to convert command to control, is provided by feed-forward in the specifications, a goal *for* the machine. With more complicated devices such as thermostats, two levels are involved, and control is built into the machine. The goal *of* the machine is still set by feed-forward, adjusting the setting of the thermostat, but it is maintained by a continuous feedback control process within.

"I want to inquire to what extent the existence of such relationships is part of such a construct as yours, Tolly, and to what extent it is restricted upon the sorts of diagrams you can draw. I think this is important, because in the two cases of feedback and feed-forward control, the crux of the matter in distinguishing between the notion of command and the notion of control appears to reside in the existence of just those relationships between levels, such that if they are satisfied, then a state of affairs called the goal state is maintained. Could you perhaps, if you don't think I'm talking nonsense, make a few comments?"

Tolly listened rather indifferently. "I don't think by any means it's nonsense," he answered slowly. "It's sort of an area of discourse I'm just plain not at home in. As I commented to you privately before lunch, I don't like the distinction between feed-forward and feedback control because I don't believe that anything whatsoever can be fed forward without a feedback. I mean I really don't think I've got anything very useful to contribute. One sits down and builds some models and inspects a collection of them and sees whether or not they are interesting." He paused. "It's true that I personally have a kind of emotional prejudice for representations which are level-free, okay? I used to be very enamored of the idea of levels, piled on levels, piled on levels, and so on. I don't like them any more. I'd be much happier to see the phenomenon that I recognize as level on level on level as some structural fact that you can identify in a picture that is fundamentally uniform. What I said when we talked before was, 'Sure, I can construct a net whose action I can think of through some intermediate coded step as representing the construction of some other net, which then does something or other.' That really isn't at all what I would try to do. I mean someone else is welcome to it. I'd never do that."

"What would you try to do?" Gordon asked.

"I would ultimately try to build an absolutely uniform soup that looks like lots and lots of what I put on the board, which I would then be capable of interpreting as acting in that fashion."

"This would be a very different project, wouldn't it?"

"Hmm."

"At this point," commented Gregory, "I think I'm right in saying that you diverge from the way organisms are made."

"I would have thought so," Gordon agreed.

"Gregory, in reply to you, I don't think that there is an issue as to how organisms are made, at all. I think there's only an issue of methodological preference."

"I can immediately see why this difficulty arises," said Horst, "because, as I think we said at cocktails and as you have seen now, Tolly is looking at everything from the stance of the artist. He is not really concerned with analyzing some patient or some beast or some cricket or something, and the artist has every right to reject what doesn't really fit. I feel that if I'm listening to Gordon he has a totally different stance; he would study the desert if it's there, you see. He has everything so well thought out, you know. If you listen to him you feel that, well . . . many people around the table must feel like me that I can't . . . the flow of information is too fast, and my channel gets clogged up. There is apparently a well-ordered universe there, but it's very difficult to grasp it at that speed. It would be nice to slow him down a little bit, to see if he can order cybernetic systems, because they must be ordered."

I knew we would have to explore the question of levels

further, since it has been central in Gregory's thought for many years. I remember once picnicking with him in Central Park when I was about thirteen years old, on a visit of his to New York. Then he talked about the theory of Logical Types of Whitehead and Russell.[2] He took a pen and pointed out that it was a member of the class of all pens—but that the class of all pens was not itself a pen; you couldn't write with it, or put it in your pocket, or compute with it along with a number of individual pens. Similarly, he said, the class of pens was a member of the class of classes—which could not be a member of itself. The logical error of confusing the class of pens with individual pens, or making the class of classes a member of itself, generates paradoxes like the famous one of Epimenides the Cretan who said that all Cretans are liars—one Cretan encompasses all Cretans in a statement that yet includes himself.

This notion of a meta-level that acts as an operator had already turned up several times at the conference. We had spoken of knowing whether you know something or not—the meta-knowledge of ignorance—and the learning of general premises that then structured all subsequent learning. Gregory had asserted that it is precisely this structuring, in many levels, that makes the human nervous system less vulgar than it would otherwise be, providing a certain depth and richness. Organisms are constructed hierarchically because this is the central form of economy of communication pathways in the Creatura, making summary and generalization possible. If, in fact, the operative causes in the biological world are differences and relationships, then logical hierarchy is unavoidable.

This was something that struck me later in the conference, when Tolly taxed me for talking about relationships. "See, I went through this business of parts and relations and it just didn't work. If you're going to think about representation, you're just going to have to throw all of that away; you're going to have to think about process." Tolly and I were walking through the rainy mist along a road leading further up the mountain from the castle. "Tolly," I said, "it seems to me that the only thing that makes it possible to talk about parts and relations is that one deals with levels, because you end up having to talk about relations between relations, and so on. I think it is not accidental that you reject both of these approaches at once, because they go together. I think you missed the boat, when you were talking to Pask: it isn't true that you just have an emotional or artistic dislike of levels that you can't justify. Or at least, if the dislike is emotional or aesthetic, it's still right at the center of occurrence systems and everything." I found myself incoherent when it came to spelling out exactly why this must be so, but I walked on feeling that here was a key to many of the questions we were struggling with.

We went on as the dusk gathered and finally we struck out across an orchard. We came to an old unharvested cherry tree, half wild, with clusters of tiny sour cherries hanging everywhere, just above reach, and Tolly shinnied up to the center of the tree. "You know, I think maybe you're a clever girl to see that about rejecting levels and rejecting parts and relations." Somehow the mathematical talk was lost as Tolly climbed higher and higher, sliding out on the branches and tossing down mounds of cherries that we took back to the castle to share out at dinner.

When Gordon and Tolly discussed it, however, I was aware of the question of levels only as one aspect of a conflict brewing between the two of them. When Tolly had described his dislike of hierarchies, Gordon resumed his presentation and began to spell out his sharp divergence from Tolly. "Let me say why I'm a protagonist of hierarchies. I'm for them because I do a lot of work in psychology, you see. Now, let's take the following simple situation: I set up an adaptive training system. What's this look like?"

Gordon walked to the board. "It's good to know why these preferences exist; they exist because of what the person making up the description sees in the world. What I see in the world, because I have quite a lot to do with psychology, is something like this." Gordon drew a cartoon on the board, a stick-figure man with a hat on. "There's a student here, and he's being taught some quite difficult skill and presented with quite difficult problems that would in fact be insoluble for him without some

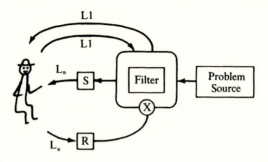

learning—say problems in code learning or teleprinting or pattern recognition." The box labeled S represents the stimulus—problems being presented to the student, which come from a problem source. The student's response, R, his attempted solutions, are fed back into the apparatus. Between the problem source and the stimuli going to the student is a sort of a filter or external computer, which simplifies the problems for the student by partially solving them in a variety of ways. This external computer might be said to cooperate with the learner by adjusting the form of the stimuli on the basis of the learner's responses. "It would be nice to think that such a system would be stable. This is true up to a point and then funny things begin to happen—what I would like to call 'participant interaction.' The student begins to use his responses to adjust the machine, not to solve problems. This chap is beginning to play with the machine."

At this point it becomes impossible to interpret the subject's responses, since they may either be efforts to solve problems or attempts to influence the machine in its way of posing them. The solution is to introduce a second language. The language for posing problems and expressing answers, $L_0$, is retained, and the subject is given a second language, $L_1$, whereby he can express his preferences to the machine and the machine can decide whether or not to accept them, depending on whether the man's own understanding of his individual style of learning is correct. The machine can also tell him how well he is doing in this language and even tell him something about himself, his whole performance. $L_1$ is language for talking at a higher level about the events in $L_0$. Both of these languages ("he signals by pressing buttons in front of him actually—well, the hardware is very simple and degenerate") must be separated from L*, the portions of the English language used in getting the subject's initial agreement and instructing him in the device. Gregory had interpreted the communication disorders of schizophrenia as being similar to confusions between $L_1$ and $L_0$, so that there is a confusion of messages and meta-messages that indicate at what level a message is to be interpreted.

"So you mean this to demonstrate the necessity of using levels in teaching live subjects?" Gregory asked.

"Controlling. In any controlling of human subjects, in interactions, and so on."

"Supposing I go to your lab and collect what you do and say, what the machine says, the subject, and so on, and ask Tolly to make a Petri net or a Tolly graph or whatever . . . Tolly, you'd write it so that Pask's levels just wouldn't appear?"

"They'd be reconstructable."

"Uniquely so? Or could one come out with all sorts of alternative levels arrangements?"

Tolly shook his head. "I don't know yet. I haven't tried the experiment."

Gordon went back to the board, carrying his presentation of his model of a learner much farther, still with the cartoon student in the little hat hooked up to a variety of boxes. When he returned to his seat Tolly spoke in rage—or perhaps contempt.

"Since it was agreed on the first day that our conference had among other things political purposes, I feel just irrepressibly moved to make a short political speech. I would like to go on record as distressed at the cultural climate which leads us to talk about either people or societies like machines. That is to say, as Gordon said, you can't really talk about machines without talking about their purpose, and I think talking about the purpose of either people or societies is absurd. I think people and societies are the source of purpose, but have none, and to treat them as if they did leads to dreadful consequences."

"May I go on record as not disagreeing with this, but wishing, of course, as usual, to argue about it?" said Pask politely.

"I would like to go on record as being equally as distressed as Tolly," Barry affirmed. "I think that one of the beauties of Tolly's approach is that he can perfectly well take all levels and, well, the natural situation, and show it. Then if you want, on your own risk, to say this is a machine, this is control, this is purpose—then you know you are doing it. Now the old way of doing it is to start out with pre-existing designations as to what is machine, what is purpose, what is goal. Those have a cultural origin, which is what Tolly is objecting to." Aside to Gregory, Barry said, "I'm trying to explain the connection between Tolly's political speech and his scientific one."

Gregory agreed. "Yes, we have to."

"And I really feel that culturally this is bad news," Barry said.

"And I think germane, really germane, to the subject of the conference as a whole," Tolly added.

"Right."

"Now wait," Gregory said. "We have not dealt with Pask's 'descriptive purpose.' We've dealt only with *pre*scriptive purpose, and when we deal with *de*scriptive purpose, this will answer these points, won't it, Gordon?"

"It will cast some light, I think. I don't think you can answer them, you see; in a sense I have a certain sympathy with many of the points that are being raised, but . . ."

"One of the other ways of saying the sort of thing I was talking about in my initial Memorandum is in terms of the relationship between descriptive and prescriptive purpose," Gregory continued. "If you regard the one as the other, then you get to these pathologies. This is what you do when you call men machines."

When Gordon finally made his presentation, we got a clarification of terms that had been appearing on and off in the discussion from the beginning. He had been insisting that, in the case of machines made by man, the goals were prescribed by the designer and these prescriptive goals were a property of artifacts. Depending on whether the machine had an internal control system or not, these might be goals *for* machines or goals *of* machines. On the other hand, he still insisted that it was necessary to speak of insects or societies as having goals from a descriptive point of view, because it would otherwise be impossible to understand their functioning.

In the discussion of command and control, Gordon had added a further and related strand of complexity by insisting on a distinction between state-achievement commands[3] and simple commands. State-achievement commands, of the type "Go to Venice," may be very little specified. A machine to fly an aircraft has embedded in it the underspecified goal of achieving a certain state, which may involve all sorts of complicated adaptations and adjustment. Not only has the goal been built in, it has been built in in a way that allows considerable flexibility in its achievement.

In general, Gordon was trying to make the machine analogy more reliable by insisting on a differentiation of different kinds of machines. A list of examples might show the way in which the different notions cut across one another: a typewriter and a can opener are machines with no goal *in* them, and a prescriptive purpose *for* them; a thermostat is prescriptively purposed, with a specified goal built *into* it; an automatic pilot of an airplane is also prescriptively purposed, but the goal embedded in it is underspecified. Goals of natural systems are always descriptive, but they vary from the rather highly specified goals of some subsystems of a praying mantis, for example, to very highly underspecified goals like those of the adaptation of a whole species. This gives rise to some interesting speculations about evolutionary goals, which were explored in Gordon Pask's paper.

---

The existence of goals of machines is probably the main insight of cybernetics. It leads to some interesting possibilities, such as: (1) the goals of a given goal-directed mechanism (though compatible with the goals of its designer) need not be compatible with *our* goals and, of course, the machine might be more powerful than we are. (2) In a community of goal-directed mechanisms, it may be the case that individual goals are more or less at odds with one another. If so, competitive and cooperative interaction can readily engender group and subgroup goals that act in the manner of social norms, leading, for example, to the establishment of roles and the division of labor.

For the moment I am anxious to distinguish between the sorts of goal that can be built into an artifact or inferred to exist in an organism. I shall designate these goal types "normal" and "evolutionary." Normal goals are built into a machine by specifying a set of differential equations or (in the case of a computer) an algorithmic program, which, on execution, leads to the goal or goals concerned. Normal goals appear in models of the descriptive mode insofar as it is possible to infer causal relationships, or mechanically interpreted rules, determining the activity of the organism.

An evolutionary goal is built into a system by prescribing a principle of minimization (or maximization) that is treated in a calculus of variations, for example, the "survival of the fittest" principle. If the system is a computing machine, we invoke, instead, a class of heuristic programs.

The broad distinction between normal and evolutionary goals is cogent enough. To show this we need only examine the different ways in which we observe evolutionary and non-evolutionary systems and the very different methods for identifying a model with an evolutionary system and any other system. With non-evolutionary systems (like machines with normal goals), the model (whether prescriptive or descriptive) is related to the real thing by an analogy in which all of the properties have defined relevance, either "relevant" or "irrelevant." No analogical properties are "possibly relevant." None have "undetermined relevance." In contrast, the analogy whereby the evolutionary system is identified with its model *does* have at least *some* properties with undetermined relevance. These are analogical properties that may become relevant or become irrelevant as observation or experimentation proceeds. Since the logic of these two situations is en-

tirely different, it is justifiable to maintain and to stress the
distinction between the two types of goal.

Further, this distinction is highly pertinent to the issue of
consciousness and purpose (or goal-directedness). In particular, I would like to take up Bateson's reference to the narrow
and rather arid goal-directedness of the patriarch Job.

The point is this. If an organism is conscious of normal
goals only (that is, if it can at least list them and describe the
algorithms or procedures it uses to achieve them), then it is
right to equate goal-directedness with narrowness and the
conceptual rigidity of the idealized (or burlesqued, whichever
you prefer) committeeman. But this point is no longer universally true if the organism is conscious of some of the evolutionary goals in its repertoire. "To love" is just as much an
evolutionary goal as "to survive" (and, to my mind, a more
laudable one). The consciousness of evolutionary goals, whatever else it may entail, does not have the norm-determined
fixity of Job's utterance or the automatic character of a man-
tid's strike. It would be unwise to equate the most important
features of conscious purpose with the description, possession,
or attainment of normal goals, because I believe it can be
argued that man works primarily with evolutionary goals. He
aims to find meaning in his environment or his memory; he
is imbued with curiosity; he seeks to learn and to control; he
seeks competence; he seeks identification with certain other
men and other groups; and, last but not least, he wants to love.

# The Metaphor
# of the Machine

WE HAD ALL BEEN STARTLED by Tolly's criticism of Gordon's approach, and as I watched his face across the table I could see an unresolved discontent still smoldering. We came to the coffee break, and I missed the interim development of the discussion, but as we filed back to sit down again around the table, I heard Warren saying, "He's not gruntled, and I don't know why, and I'm not sure he does."

"And I made a sort of nasty comment out there," Tolly picked him up, "in which I said that the climate which makes it possible for Gordon to put boxes on a blackboard, one of which has as its content a man with a hat and the other one of which is a machine, is a cultural madness, which I feel I want to make political speeches about. Gordon very properly asked what in the world could be wrong with it; after all, the man agreed that he would like to participate in the experiment and gave his assent to the temporary goals that were set up. And I said, 'I realize that what you say is right and I'm not quite sure why I'm objecting, but I sure am objecting.' Now in the meantime I've thought of a few things that shed light on what I feel. I'm not sure how clearly they'll communicate.

"For instance, in my view, my body has parts only very

rarely. That is to say, it has parts when I go to the doctor and at other times I would say it doesn't. That, I realize, is not the common way of talking. Most people would say I have an arm that is dropping from here to here and a hand from here to here, yet I would sit here and say that isn't true. Also, at some times I am a learner, let's say, in Gordon's experiment, and at other times I'm not a learner in Gordon's experiment. Perhaps a part of the reason why I feel these strong objections is just the uncommonness of the view I expressed in the first place about my body and its parts. It is not customary for people to think of themselves freely in this sense as either having parts or not having parts at will. If we were versatile in the sense of being able to declare freely in different contexts, now I am a learner in Gordon's experiment and now in a certain radical sense I am not a learner in Gordon's experiment, then perhaps I would not feel so strongly about those pictures up there.

"I made a speech in Texas some time ago, in which the subject was men and machines, and in it I gave the specifications I would write if I wanted to get the large electronic firms in the United States to construct a device that I would agree to call a chess partner. The first thing I'd write down is that I want the damn thing to understand the rules of chess. Now how do I know that the damn thing understands the rules of chess? Presumably that at appropriate times it can make appropriate moves, according to the rules as I understand them, on a chessboard. What do I accept as evidence that it does so? Would I insist that it should be able to make appropriate moves with anything that I'm accustomed to call a chessboard, whether it be big wooden pieces, or a small magnetic set with little buttons, or one of those pocket things which you shove into slots, or whatnot? Or would I say all that doesn't matter and be quite content to sit at a display with one of those conventional pictures of a chessboard and, say, lettered identification of the pieces? I don't want to resolve at the moment the question as to what I would specify, but only to draw your attention to the issue that there is a question here of specification. I could make an even more radical demand, after all; with someone with whom I might go out to the forest, we could agree that the pine cones are pawns and so on, but let's leave that out.

"The next demand I would make is that it should appreciate my brilliant moves if and when I make them. Now the same question arises all over again. What evidence do I accept for its performing that function? For example, would I insist upon an image of a human face that breaks into a broad smile or says 'Ah!' or 'Good show!' or would I be content with a printed message on a typewriter that says, 'You have just made a brilliant move'? Would I be content with a print-out E-42 which I look up in a code book on the side of the console, where I find a line numbered E-42 which means that I have made a brilliant move? Here the question of specification is harder.

"Now my next spec would be that it should feel bad if I beat it and once again the same set of questions arise of what I will accept as evidence. I can very well imagine a situation where I play with a man who at the end of the game shows nothing whatsoever which you could see on a movie camera, no change in the tension of his body, no raising of the shoulder, no change of facial expression, and yet I *know* that he feels bad, having been beaten. If anyone would like to argue later about the epistemological questions as to what it means to me to say 'I know,' I will be happy to discuss it with them. In any case, I stick to saying 'I know.' "

Gregory asked, "You're sure that if you mated him by accident and didn't know you had and he gave this signal which isn't a signal, that is, is invisible and cannot be detected on a movie film, you would still know? Or is it only the fact that you know you've mated him that enables you to 'know'?"

"That could well be. That might be part of the necessary context."

"That's what you'd feel if you were he," Gertrude said.

"Right. By the way, if somebody should ever ask me why I would demand all this, then I guess the answer would be, well, I wouldn't want to play chess with it unless it did all that."

As we were laughing, Will commented that if Tolly played chess long enough with the machine, he would come to know that the little print-out, E-42 or whatever, meant it was sad or glad. Barry was shaking his head.

Tolly said, "That . . . I mean, sure, that could happen. As to whether or not I would regard it as good is another question. This could happen. This could happen in society all over. There is no question about that. We could no doubt transform ourselves in such a way that the device which prints out E-42 is accepted by me as feeling sad, but that involves an essential transformation of me. That makes me different from what I now am."

"And that's why you're angry," said Barry.

"Why on earth do you object to that?" Fred asked. "Why do you object to machines that are really like people—isn't that what you're saying?"

"The issue is not whether they *really* are, there is no such thing as a machine that *really* is or a machine that *really* isn't. The question is whether or not I agree that it really is or really isn't. It has nothing at all to do with objectively verifiable fact. There are learned discussions that take place on the question of whether or not machines can think, which I regard as absolute and total nonsense."

Barry said, "I feel the way Tolly does. If you accept the dictates of, shall we say, an impoverished aspect of nature, you can then play a kind of chess, but it will be a new game and there is no way of playing that game short of changing yourself. The rage that I feel about what's happening in the environment is that it has led to a change in the attitude of human beings toward life, including themselves. Take the city—the city is, in a certain sense, Tolly's mechanical chess player. It is a way of making ourselves live and it has changed what we consider living. Now, you say, well, what's wrong with changing? I don't want to argue that, because that's simply a matter of taste, I suppose, but I think what Tolly is saying and what I want to say now is that when you say that the box is a chess player, then you are covering up the fact that this is transforming you, and I am unwilling to allow people to be transformed in ignorance."

Gertrude said that she didn't feel any such rejection of machines. "I'm willing to hold the goal of getting machines to serve us that come closer and closer to what an intellect can do, as long as we don't say that they're the same thing. I like to think of this as a closer and closer approximation instead of the intention of ever reaching the goal."

"But the trouble is, Gertrude," said Gregory, "it's a two-sided approach. It's not that the machines get closer and closer to us, but . . ."

". . . but we get closer and . . . well, but as long as we keep that in mind, isn't there a possibility that we might be introspective enough to resist this change?"

"You see, if we take that attitude, then what we should do is retain the goal, which is people. We have it. We don't need to make people," Barry declared.

"We want this kind of thing to serve us instead of becoming the pattern for us."

Gregory said, "We want prescriptive purpose in the machine. Now, if you start dealing with that which is prescriptively purposed, you get an asymmetry of relationship in your interaction and you end up as prescriptively purposed yourself."

"Barry, I don't see the relevance of your comments at all," Fred said. "If we were able to build a machine that was not only intelligent, capable of feeling pleasure, pain, appreciation, with a sense of humor, would you consider this degrading to man? Or would you extend to this machine the same respect that you extend to man?"

"If my grandmother had wheels, she'd be a trolley car," Barry muttered. "You have described something which *is* and *can only be* a man. If you want something with all the characteristics of a human being, you will have to accept the way in which nature produces human beings."

"We're all entirely free to invest machines with personhood," Tolly continued. "There is nothing whatsoever to stop anyone from doing so. You say, *if* we could build a machine that can feel pain; I can do it today provided only that you will agree with me to accept certain print-outs as betokening certain meanings, and there is absolutely nothing that is distinguishable between that situation and what you now accept as somebody's feeling pain or pleasure. Nothing. In other words, there is no question of science, there is no question of fact involved here. Nothing that has to do with technological advance, nothing that sages should argue about as you did a minute ago, when you said 'if it were possible,' right? if we got clever enough engineers to design a device that can *really* feel pleasure. Now what does that mean?"

"Nothing," Barry agreed. "If you treat a machine as you would a person, you have changed yourself, and that's what the argument is."

"Only by the same token that you would change yourself, Barry, if you did a lot of other things," said Gordon. "You change yourself in interaction with me, we're changing ourselves continually. Any specification of this goal of being a person is surely something to do with the sort of interpersonal interaction that does go on. Whatever else does it mean, Barry?"

"There's nothing scientific here. What's happening is that I think Tolly and I are expressing a normative idea, which is that we believe in and want to see happen those changes which result from relationships among people. I think I can make the case that the kinds of changes that are enforced on people by endowing machines with 'peoplehood' are bad."

We kept slipping over the edge of the old and worn-out argument about whether a machine could be constructed that would be like a person, as if the issue were technological capability rather than the interactional system that includes machines and people. Will judged it time to bring in a little historical perspective:

"I can conceive of this discussion going on in Rome and I can see a patrician saying, 'If you call those slaves people, you're diminishing personhood. It's really a very shocking thing to include them among people. Everyone knows they aren't people. They are tools . . .' I beg your pardon, but that is what very eminent and distinguished people did say—Aristotle, for instance."

"But they were *wrong*!" Barry shouted furiously. "They *are* people!"

"I can just see people a hundred years from now saying, 'Those poor Americans living in the twentieth century, they didn't realize that these computers were people too and they treated the computers simply outrageously!' Or there might come a time when people would say, 'White machines are okay, but black machines . . .' "

"I don't particularly like people," Warren snapped. "Never have. Man to my mind is about the nastiest, most destructive of all the animals. I don't see any reason, if he can evolve machines that can have more fun than he himself can, why they shouldn't take over, enslave us, quite happily. They might have a lot more fun. Invent better games than we ever did."

Several people nodded or murmured their agreement to Warren, while Tolly and Barry stayed ominously silent. "Barry," said Gordon, "you seem for some reason to be adopting the point of view that the machine exists outside of you, independently of you. In fact, you prescribed it at the beginning. Maybe it had some kind of evolutionary program and it developed; then you interacted with it and you modified it and it modified you. It knocked you and you knocked it. Now, surely this is exactly the same sort of process that you're talking about when you talk about the development of something like a subspecies of the human species who were called slaves. They were under certain constraints so that their behaviors were constrained, their initial learning was different, they were in effect acting as a very different sort of creature to most human beings in the Roman society. They were later put into a situation where they were educated in a different way and had different social conventions, new interactions, and they didn't become slaves any longer. I cannot really see a distinction between man's social potentialities externalizing themselves in respect to other men and externalizing themselves in respect to artifacts which were after all initially created by men. I certainly wouldn't like to be governed by any machines I happen to know at the moment, they're all pretty crude, but . . ."

Tolly sat in stolid silence, while Will looked for historical analogies and Fred Attneave tried to turn the discussion to a dispassionate comparison of properties of men and machines. Finally Tolly broke in: "I'd like to ask Warren if he has been busy making a calculation to decide whether the nitrogen cycle will hold out long enough for us to build those clever machines that will play, as he said, better games than we do. If it will hold out long enough, then it seems to me he could leave here forthwith, for then there should be no further concern."

"We may even create a world that isn't fit for machines to live in," Gregory remarked.

"I have a very strong feeling that this question is an utterly familiar one," Warren said. "We'll make one kind of artifact at one time and another kind of artifact at another time, but once you've started making computing machines, you're not going to stop them from evolving. I have no objection to it, if they make one that plays a better game of chess than I do."

"Yes, well, I don't think that any machine *plays* any chess at all," Tolly replied. "There's no disagreement about facts, you know, no disagreement about the possibility of constructing extremely well-fitted and clever devices, only a question of what attitudes you and I shall take toward them. Like, for instance, you talk about them playing better games and I go blind. I can't imagine what you could ever mean by that. I can't imagine what that 'better' might be, I mean, better with respect to what criteria?"

"More fun."

"Yes, more fun! I don't understand what that means either. What's more important is that I think it is not something which is subject to understanding, period."

"I've gotten a little tired recently," said Ted. "I've heard a lot of this kind of thing in exhortations from the podium, a new kind of Frankenstein's monster: 'the computer is about to overwhelm us,' or, 'let us return to the truth of human nature' (which probably was defined for these people ten thousand years ago), or the 'inhumanness' of this or that or 'returning to a human scale.' I think that man is still in the process of finding out what is human, and we can't predict for our successors ten thousand or a hundred thousand years from now. I see human nature as emergent, not a prescription for what shall be from now until all time, and I don't like being frightened or having my aversions aroused by the spectre of the machine. I think all of us are people who work with machines. Certainly you are, Tolly. You contribute to this evolution of artifacts, which is what they are, from the most trivial to the most beautiful. The thing you've put on the board is a machine and it's something to which you frequently apply the term beautiful. I see no reason why not. We are perhaps at a turning point, like the Luddites and others at the beginning of the Industrial Revolution, where we have to decide whether we can live with these things we're creating. One thing that I think would be useful is not creating these spectres and Frankensteins or raging about competition with the human species or replacing the human species or a degradation of it. I'm fairly convinced of the resilience and the continuing evolution of human culture and human beings, and I think that we're going to continue to be able to handle our creations. But we're expressing values; I think we've suddenly switched to an entirely other plane that smacks of irrelevance."

"If you speak of the Luddite approach," Barry answered, "as not simply destroying the machines, but assuming that they wanted them somehow used more humanely, the fact that this kind of Luddite assault on the early machines in the Industrial Revolution has failed is exactly what is driving us to destruction. The Industrial Revolution transformed the concept of machines into something that we could use to transform the world, and that concept was faulted in its inhumanity and, as a result, it may kill off humanity."

"You could make all the same remarks about the development of a spoken language," Fred shrugged, "and say it's got us into all this trouble. So let's stop talking."

Horst shook his head. "The first axe prehistoric men made . . . you see, you have to show that this is something different from what happened throughout the development."

"The point that I was trying to make," Barry persisted, "is that a mechanistic generalization about the world is the cultural cause of the kinds of difficulties that I talked about, a generalization from inventions."

"Right," Gregory agreed. "This is not the same as the first invention!"

"De la Mettrie, *L'homme machine*," supplied Horst. "About 1750."

"I'm now worried that the generalization about the nature of machines is about to take another giant step forward," Barry continued. "We are not learning the lesson of this past failure in developing an appropriate attitude toward what you spoke of as our continuing evolution, Ted. I see nothing but an exacerbation, intensive exacerbation, of exactly the difficulties we're in now if we just sit back and say well, we're doing this, let's see where we get to. I think we will get ourselves destroyed!"

"If we have, as it seems from the way we've all lit up, now arrived at the nitty-gritty of it, then I propose that we discuss this question rather thoroughly." Ted spoke sharply. "Other kinds of frivolities could be dispensed with, including some of the things I had intended to say."

"This is certainly the nitty-gritty of it," said Gregory.

Bert had returned when technicalities ended. Now he said, "I can't imagine that. This is such a cliché. I think we all understand everything that could be said about this." We were in the curious position that the technically oriented members of the group were more insistent on discussing the man-machine problem than the more humanistically oriented members. Those who felt that it had been discussed fully a century before were not the ones who were in the center of developing technologies.

Gertrude joined in, in a shrill, exasperated voice that echoed the tension that had been growing in the room. "I don't see why we can't consider machines a part of nature too and think of the whole planet, at least, as a unit. I feel a genuine grief when I see a good field washing away, whether it is from plowing by machinery or from overgrazing. Why can't we accept that the machines and the cattle are a part of nature, but keep in mind that anguish is anguish and agony is agony, no matter what organism is feeling it. In the same way, we don't want to see a great painting destroyed. Just because some of its parts move under some conditions is no reason that a finely built machine, like the more and more beautiful racing machines of Ferrari, should be excluded from that company. You can feel an aesthetic reaction to a machine, but the mistake is deifying it."

"This isn't the level at which we are," said Gregory, "this isn't where the nitty-gritty lies. I think, really, that we are reasonably agreed that man is going to use and elaborate his tools and they will even involve electronics and all this mess; nobody has any objection to that." He raised an eyebrow at Tolly and Barry and they nodded. "The objection comes at the point at which human thought takes a certain shape because of that. The problem is how to go on thinking like a biologist in spite of having tools."

Fred said that was just fine if someone would spell out what these attitudes are, so Barry referred back to Will Jones' list of types of ignorance and his own presentation. "We simply lack a biological understanding of the consequences of our capability of building machines, including machines like a herd of cattle, because that's a machine too, when you lock them in a pasture."

Will protested that we were mixing two questions. One question concerned the empirical matter of the effect of machines on human beings and on society, and the other was the moral or epistemological question of what is a person: "The answer to that question concerns, I believe, not the empirical characteristics of the things that we call persons, but our attitudes, and one of the most important attitudes is respect. This is formulated first by Immanuel Kant, not in quite this way—that anything toward which we feel respect is a person."

"That's not Kant," Bert protested.

"It's an extension of Kant."

"We are awfully close to discussing the pathologies that arise when you don't obey the Categorical Imperative not to use persons as tools," Gregory put in thoughtfully.

Will went on to suggest that just because they were not treated as persons, slaves did not behave like persons and Barry blew up. "What about slave revolts? What about the way they treated each other? Or all . . . I mean the whole thing now in Black history is exactly that. There was one culture behind the scenes and one culture out where the whites could see it."

Bert said, "Christianity developed precisely out of the slave situation."

"And might have been a mistake generated by treating people as non-persons," Gregory added.

Ted spoke tensely, with a totally different anger from Tolly's: "We are trying to prescribe what behaving like persons is. It's extremely difficult for a person under any circumstances not to behave like a person, and the repertoire is great."

"There is a very pure criterion in this thing," Bert replied. "Machines and racing cars don't exist to themselves, and the existence that the thing has for itself is what we mean, I think, by consciousness. It goes a very long way toward establishing what we mean by a person; it exists for itself; if it doesn't it's not it."

"You have all talked as though there was a fixed heritage of machines that dated from the Industrial Revolution or somewhat earlier," Gordon said. "It seems to me that the notion of machine that was current in the course of the Industrial Revolution—and which we might have inherited—is a notion, essentially, of a machine without a goal, it had no goal *of*, it had a goal *for*. And this gradually developed into the notion of machines with goals *of*, like thermostats, which I might begin to object to because they might compete with me. Now we've got the notion of a machine with an underspecified goal, the system that evolves. This is a new notion, nothing like the notion of machines that was current in the Industrial Revolution, absolutely nothing like it. It is, if you like, a much more biological notion. Maybe I'm wrong to call such a thing a machine; I gave that label to it because I like to realize things as artifacts, but you might not call the system a machine, you might call it something else."

Gregory referred to his own definition of purpose in the original Memorandum, as that operation within a system that makes a previously true proposition go on being true, a descriptive proposition about the system. "We describe a machine with a governor as operating at a certain speed. Now, the purpose of the system, in a certain sense, is the maintenance of the truth of the proposition, 'this is the speed of the machine.' And in order to maintain the truth of that proposition, we start altering other things to make it true. Now, most self-respecting animals change themselves in such a way as to maintain constant truths about their relationship to environment, whereas what man does more and more is to change the environment in order to maintain a constancy inside himself. When this happens in evolution, the logical process is toward ecosystems that sustain *only* the dominant, environment-controlling species and its symbionts and parasites, like fungal colonies and concentrated forests of conifers. This habit of man's of changing his environment rather than changing himself is one of our central concerns here. First I act on the environment, in order to maintain a constancy about myself, my blood sugar, or something, and then I start doing it to my friends and I parasitize them in the way that I've discovered how to parasitize my environment. Is this a different definition of purpose?"

"It corresponds, doesn't it," Gordon replied, "to the idea of purpose inherent in underspecified goals—the maintenance of a constant?" Then the mechanistic generalization to which Barry referred was perhaps the spreading notion that all parts of the environment, including other persons, are means in achieving our purposes, with a flat confusion between prescriptive and descriptive purposes, and the easy assumption that all such purposes could be specified.

Horst asked Barry if he was, in effect, challenging the engineers to construct a machine with the gene mechanism in it; Barry pointed out that the hub of his critique of the Watson-Crick theory was that in order to make an amoeba, the genetic code isn't enough. "You've got to have the whole shooting match." In the end, Barry maintained that "it's very likely that in order to achieve the kind of self-duplicating machine that an amoeba now is, what you'll have to do is get yourself an Earth and start the whole works going."

"I would dearly like," said Tolly, "to see us stop discussing what is life or should the machines take over. Let's bury the hatchet and ask where we go from here in relating the cultural climate to the ecological problems that we've talked about and how we can influence it."

Tolly's plea was a signal to adjourn for the day. All of us were tired and irritated. We had come from Fred's presentation with a kind of purity of intention to try and find remedies, and struggled with Tolly's theory in the hope that it would give us an immediate new way to phrase our concern, but the day had ended with wrangling, exposing sharp disagreements in the group as we tried to relate the scientific material to questions of value. Some reacted with rage and others with clichés. We were all weary.

I tried one day to summarize some of the ways in which Barry's and Tolly's ideas interconnected that had not come out in the discussion, in the hope that this would contribute to the notion of applied epistemology, because it seemed to me that there was a very close analogy between Barry's outrage at reductionism and Tolly's objection to the mechanical chess player: the mechanical chess player results from a reductionist approach to the question of what a chess player is. In a letter Ted wrote to me months after the conference, he described the conference as being almost Manichean in the way it fell into talking about dichotomies as if one side were evil and the other good, where it was really a matter of the "evil" side being simpler and often leading to dangerous oversimplification. During the conference, just as an experiment, I had gone through my notes listing these pairs of terms, most of which came from Barry or Tolly or the responses to them, in two columns, even though they involved rather different kinds of entities.

*Means*, including machines and the treatment of men and biological systems as means, were contrasted with *ends*, and *overspecified goals* were contrasted with *underspecified goals*. Perception in terms of *things* (nouns), and *parts*, and *lineal causal sequences* was contrasted with perception of *processes* and *wholes* and causation occurring in *circuits*, in our commitment to *holism* as against *reductionist atomism*.

I put *matter*, as representing a set of assumptions about how to approach the objects of science, on one side and *mind* on the other. "With some of these pairs," I said, "we can look at the way in which someone, at an historical point in time, made a division, as Descartes did between 'mind' and 'matter', so that there was a time when the mind-matter dichotomy supposed that one might talk about mind and one might talk about matter but the twain would never meet. What we have had historically is a gradual pushing of the boundary point in such divisions from the center over toward the complex side. There continued to be a feeling that there was *something* they couldn't talk about in mind, but they kept moving over by a direction of metaphors from matter, using simple properties of matter to try and account for more and more of mind. Similarly, we would like to be able to break underspecified goals down into finer and finer pieces so that we could deal with them all as specified, break wholes into parts, and so on. It's as if there had been a recurrent intellectual imperialism where first two spheres of discussion, say mind and matter, were separated, with a kind of explanation appropriate to each, and then this was followed by the effort to get one to 'eat up' the other." I had put my concepts in two columns on the board, the simple ones on the left and the complex on the right:

| *seeking simplification* | *acknowledging complexity* |
|---|---|
| reductionist approaches: | holistic approaches: |
| things (nouns), parts, | processes, wholes, |
| lineal sequences | systems |
| overspecified goals, | underspecified goals, |
| means | ends |
| "matter" | "mind" |
| secular | sacred |

"We have had a set of examples," I said, "and a set of dialogues, where somebody, usually Barry, has said, 'This is dreadful! We must think in terms of the notions on the right!' and then somebody else, Will or Ted, has said, 'Don't dichotomize! the other is still valuable!' In a very small number of those cases, we have gone on to say that if you move your intellectual imperialism in the opposite direction, from the right to the left, you get some kind of sensible result. That is, you can get the eddy in the river by looking at the flow of the current; you cannot get the overall pattern of the current by starting with the eddies. You can use holistic analyses to predict atomistic properties, processes to account for things, but not vice versa. So then we have had a set of comments about the possibility of projecting the properties of mind down, in terms of levels of complexity, in order to get a mind-like understanding of more and more material order, rather than vice versa: a materialistic understanding of more and more of mind.

"In a funny way, the problem of who you're going to play chess with is similar. If you define a chess player in terms of a function that can be performed by a machine—if, that is, you *simplify* the function and then move in and judge your human chess player on whether he can beat your machine chess player —you get a very serious alteration in your human being, and this has been part of our passion and our vehemence. If you regard human beings as, in addition to being able to play human chess, able to build machines that fill a few of the functions of playing chess, you don't get quite that point of panic. If you look at a machine as similar in some ways to a person, you have a basis for finding it beautiful; if you look at a person as like a machine, you coarsen your perception of both. And as Pask keeps telling us, our idea of machines is itself a dreadful oversimplification. The general strategic point is that the motion that makes it possible to love the things you're looking at is the one that tries to extend your constructs or your metaphors from the right to the left, from the complex to the simple, just the opposite of the prevailing trend. And moving from the left to the right gives you vulgarization."

Gregory sat for a minute frowning at my lists. "Yes. It becomes very subtle or difficult because—you see, if I'd been drawing that diagram as representing what I've on the whole been trying to say . . . it keeps slipping and sliding . . . have other people been suffering from this? If you wrote 'mind-matter' as one word on the complex side, and 'mind-matter' as two words on the left . . ."

"Yes, that's what I meant by letting the right eat the left, rather than vice versa."

"No I don't want them to eat each other, Catherine. I don't want one to eat the other, I want them to . . ."

"You want them to merge," said Barry.

"To merge. Yes. Quite. Now, when they merge, you are still left with the fact of human natural history, with the fact man does, and is going to, use two universes of explanation, one applying to Pleroma and the other to Creatura. What is important is to know that he is using two universes of explanation, to be disciplined at every point. We're always using one language about the other world: we talk as though ideas could push each other around and exchange energy, which they can't, and as though they existed in the Pleromatic world, which they don't, and so forth. Do I . . . am I intelligible at all? Let's for a moment dissect Tolly's motto, what is it, 'Trample on nouns'? not 'Trample . . .' "

"Oh, 'Help stamp out nouns.' "

" 'Help stamp out nouns,' that's the word. Now, 'Help stamp out nouns' is a command closely comparable to the famous joke that anybody who goes to a psychiatrist ought to have his head examined. You see? Any noun that has that degree of concreteness, in the way you think about it, should be trampled on. But of course no noun should have that degree of concreteness. All stampable nouns should be stamped on and anybody who goes to a psychiatrist should have his head examined."

The lists as I put them on the board included two items that had never been discussed in that form, "sacred" and "secular." I sensed, in the way the sphere of the sacred has been narrowed over the centuries, a comparable phenomenon. When mind and matter were separated, there was for a little while a region where science, which was thought to deal only with matter, was not allowed to enter; similarly there has been a continual narrowing and withering of the area of the sacred. Yet, just as we were moving toward finding the characteristics of mind immanent in the complexities of matter, so I believe we must move toward a pervasive sense of the sacred, applied

to the whole of the Creatura and to the whole physical universe
as it is made meaningful in human experience. When Gregory
first posed the question of possible correctives to the maladaptive effects of conscious purpose, he wrote:

---

Attempts have been made in the last hundred years to
create social systems with a minimum of symbolic, supernatural, and ritual components. Education has been secular-
ized, and so on. But could a social system be viable with only
laws and ethical principles and no fantasy, no play, no art, no
totemism, no religion, and no humor?

---

# A DARKNESS
# UNOBSCURED

*[The Last Two Days]*

· C H A P T E R   1 3 ·

# A Human Family
# on a Ledge

NOW WE WERE APPROACHING the end, still unsure even of what
we wanted that end to be. We had grown to a sense of passionate commitment and then stayed our wish for action, to
spend two days untangling the dense figures Tolly spread before
us on the blackboard. Out of a weaving of the wonderful and
the banal was coming a new understanding of the importance
of context for the significance of any comment made and, indeed, our gradual approach to resolution came by the construction of contexts and the weaving of an imagery that would
begin to combine our most highly technical discussions and our
wonder.

The last period of the conference began with a presentation
by Bert Kaplan that acted, for me at least, as a new statement
of the problem, brought into relief by his use of aesthetic and
religious imagery. Bert had missed a number of our discussions,
but he had been very present and audible between sessions. He
had come to Burg Wartenstein fresh from a visit to Esalen, the
personal-regeneration-by-group-process center on the edge of
hippiedom in Big Sur, and he had spent many hours arguing
with Barry about the meaning of that experience and the kind
of spiritual depth at which people needed to change.

Bert had been unhappy and bored during the technical discussions and, like many of us, had wondered at first about his relevance to the conference. He apparently found himself at odds with the cyberneticists through his sense that cybernetics was oriented toward circular systems or systems that varied only slightly in maintaining a steady-state. The emphasis in our discussions seemed to have been on stability, with a rejection of change. Compared to this rather pedestrian notion, he found the notion of historical change, qualitative discontinuities in the history of an individual like St. Augustine or a society, such as come about through shifts of consciousness and leaps of imagination, infinitely more stirring. Answering him, Gregory argued that an understanding of stable systems, even very simple and repetitive ones, was a necessary basis for understanding parametric change. Throughout his presentation, Barry leaped bristling into the debate at every opportunity, challenging Bert's focus and his understanding of cybernetics. "He's not talking about the real world; he's talking about the world of ideas. You can get very misled by regarding the cybernetic approach that has been described here as being reducible to a closed circuit. In fact, Bert, you'll then be in a non-informable, non-controllable idealistic realm, which is maybe where you want to be!"

Doggedly, Bert set out to contrast nature, as essentially ahistorical, with the history of mind. "I think of Hegel spinning out his marvelous history of mind on the lecture platform before large audiences, everyone entranced by the brilliance of the development of mind, but outside the lecture hall nothing developed at all. Large numbers of people listening to Hegel had exactly this idea of a contrast between a historical movement of thought and the static, heavy quality of life outside. Well, now, that's the kind of division I'd like to suggest, a division between, you know, the heaviness of actuality and the lightness of reason. This really brings me to the idea that I'd like to elaborate this morning, history seen as the possibility, for human existence, of progressive development out of what is."

Barry reacted to Bert's preamble like a bull to a red flag. "*Now* what is it that you're talking about—the development of thought, of ideas? Are you talking about what Hegel talked about, or are you talking about what Marx talked about?"

"Well, both, because Hegel really did talk about both. The only thing is, all Hegel could do on a lecture platform was talk his thing. The notion of transforming thought, taking actuality and changing it through work, was the crucial concept in Marx. It is really best given in the idea of a sculptor hacking away at a block of stone; he has the idea of the thing in mind, but what he has before him is a block of stone and through his own work he imposes his concept upon the material with his hands, chopping, hewing, and finally what you have is a transformed block of stone. Nature becomes the embodiment of the idea."

"That's Hegel, not Marx."

"Er, yes, okay. It's both really."

Barry noticed what he was doing and subsided. "I should let you talk."

"Well now, I think history is the point, as we confront the situations that Barry and Fred have described, because unless there are basic or real historical changes, unless history is made, nothing will happen. History is movement that gets someplace. Kant asked why there is such a thing as history and he came up with the notion that history was possible only in a human existence; that reasoned consciousness was the ground of this kind of movement. Hegel took up this notion and said—it's his main point—that consciousness, or mind, is a historical phenomenon . . ."

Barry interrupted again. "It's a cause of history, right? and without it you don't have this kind of development, this movement, isn't that what Hegel said? Of course, he's wrong, because this kind of evolving movement is exactly what is characteristic, for example, of living things and also of the universe as a whole, regardless of man or reason or Hegel. Now, I'm sorry I made that little speech." He subsided abruptly and slid down into his chair, folding his arms and glowering. It seemed to me that Barry was himself speaking within two different frames of reference. One was perhaps a hangover from the old hubris of science that regarded ideas as "idealistic," as "not part of the real world." At the same time, Barry was affirming an evolving movement throughout the universe. In fact, ideas are causal and systems of ideas do develop: but the philosophical ideas that concerned Bert were only a special case of the causal effect and emergent intricacy of differences and systems of relationships. The ideas and aspirations that fire men to build empires or to shift to radically new styles of life are comparable to the slight variations between light and shade that cause the plant stalk to twist—not light, but a difference in light, an abstraction. The biological world ponders and acts, and there too, as in human society, qualitative change results.

"Well, the image I always have, thinking of this, is the Leonardo painting of 'The Virgin and St. Anne' in the Louvre," Bert went on. "Like many of Leonardo's paintings, this is divided into two parts. The background shows mountains and streams, painted in rather a cold, distant—it's a weird land-scape, and the mountains have a funny shapelessness to them. Leonardo has written about this and it represents his notion of nature: mountains rise and fall, streams shift to a different course, earthquakes bring the mountains up, rains wash them down, and the winds crumble them to pieces, until new earth-quakes raise them up again. Nature is just in senseless motion, one blind cataclysm after another. This is the background of Leonardo's painting."

Barry was looking extremely disgusted with the proceedings, and Horst came in to mediate. "See, Barry's unhappy, but I want to make him look at something he may have forgotten." Horst then set out to find examples where contemporary physics might recognize movement of the sort Bert was describing, but Barry shook his head impatiently. "My difficulty is that I think Bert is setting up a straw universe to knock down."

"No, no, I don't think so."

There was a storm of cross-talk while Bert, who had gone to the blackboard, waited patiently, his shoulders slightly hunched, as Barry's denunciations rained down on him. Gregory cut in sharply. "Bert is setting up a universe step by step, and of course the early steps change as he sets up the later ones."

"Now, could I try my hand momentarily at interpreting

Bert?" said Will. "I think it would be easy to make Bert's notion of history sound nonsensical. It may be mistaken, but it isn't nonsensical. And I'll start from something you said, Barry, which I jotted down. You said that Bert 'is not talking about the real world; he's talking about the world of ideas.' Now, how's that for atomism? If you assume that there is a real world which has a real history in real time, independent of human conceptual systems, then Bert is talking nonsense. But Bert's position is that it's impossible to get at this supposedly real world independent of some sort of conceptual system, so that if the real world in real time is filtered through successive conceptual systems, then the history of these conceptual systems, which is what Bert would call the 'history of consciousness,' I think, is highly relevant to anything you'd like to say about the 'real world.' "

"Let me give you a ten-second statement on this," said Barry. "I believe that there is a material universe, which at one time produced man, and that when man appeared he in very distinctive and unique ways intruded on the nature of that universe, resulting thereby in a change in man, which, again, changed the way he operated on the universe—and the two things interpenetrate. What Bert is doing is making a separation of the two, or else swallowing up the part of the universe that existed before man and has continued into consciousness, which is again an idealism. But I think he should be allowed to finish."

Bert had been sketching in the composition of the Leonardo painting on the board and now he nervously continued from the point where he had been interrupted, tripping slightly over his words. "As I was saying, this Leonardo painting has a background of mountains and streams, trees and forests, but it . . . it's just a chaos. Leonardo takes up the painting of the little family in the foreground, Mary, Jesus and St. Anne, in a completely different way. They're on a bit of a ledge that's rather indistinct and some people think that they're in a precarious position, but I don't see that clearly myself. What's striking is that this human group is painted as a family, whereas the background, nature, is painted in rather cold, abstract terms. Mary is lovingly holding the baby, the baby obviously content in mother's arms, and St. Anne, Mary's mother, is looking at them and loving both. It's just a—a marvelous little human reality, because there's a symbolic character to this family. Jesus, the one who's being taken care of and loved, is not just any baby, he brings the word of God, that is, he's a historic event. Now, Christianity may be regarded as a theory of human history as a gigantic, cosmic drama in three or four parts. A certain number of events are specified by Christian theology as the significant events in human history: the Fall is the first, leaving the Garden of Eden or being pushed out; then, I'd say, wandering in an alienated, separated condition; and then, at some point in history, the truly historical event occurs, the life of Jesus. Christianity regards it as historic in the sense that it's a life that makes a difference. For Christianity this is the life that made history, the Word of God."

"That's nineteenth-century Christian theology," said Barry. "I know very profound Christians today who will absolutely disagree with your description of Christianity."

"He's speaking about Leonardo's Christianity, aren't you?" Warren asked.

"Yes. Well, the Christian view of history is that, at some point in this historical movement, an event occurs, the life of Jesus, that is crucial. It indicates the end of history. Christian theologians believe we are living after the Word and before the apocalyptic event, that is to say, we're living in the last days.

"Now my own understanding of the situation is this: that the good news, which to me corresponds to the philosopher's *concept* or to the intellectual's *understanding* of this situation, doesn't automatically change anything material. However, now we live with the idea, and you get to heaven by transforming the idea into actuality through work, like the sculptor. Most of us may say we don't have anything like a complete understanding, as the Christian thinks that he does, but we do certainly understand a great deal more than is actually reflected in social life, and we do have the problem of transforming that idea into actuality.

"Well, now, to get back to the Leonardo painting. The human family is separated from nature. I must say that the question of whether nature has a historical development just doesn't seem crucial for me. I can have it either way, because I do feel the truth of the fact that the human family has its own history and what happens in nature just doesn't—in any way I can understand—impose itself on this purely human drama. It's for this reason that I'm a Cartesian and I believe in and I feel the separation of the course of the natural order, with what's going on in it, from human history. Now, in the long term I'm sure there won't be the separation and we'll sink back into nature, but at the moment it just feels to me as though the issue is human history and not . . . Now I know that most of you in the conference feel there is a, what was the term you used, a linkage, or coupling, between these two . . ."

"That's what the conference is about," said Barry.

"Well, I feel that that's really a different view." Bert went and sat down. "I feel that what's happening in purely human terms is the thing that is happening, that the human family is upon a stage. We have our own drama that has nature going on as its background." Bert was consistently faithful to his own mode of thinking, maintaining it with great integrity against Barry's pressure. Feeling my own shock at that phrase "sink back into nature," I could well understand Barry's attacks. The tendency to separate man from nature can even, tragically, be found in the basic rhetoric of the ecology movement. Thus, one of the most discouraging aspects of the current awakening of concern is its expression in terms of "environment," and yet it is difficult to find a better form of expression. The very use of the term implies a separation of man from nature and a conception of the entire planet as a stage for man's action, with which we are concerned only to make it more pleasant or more readily exploitable. When a man says that his environment is deteriorating, it does not immediately occur to us that his relationships need changing. The only word in English that may perhaps express our relationship to this planet and the system of life upon it is "home." When a man says that his home is going to pieces and becoming unlivable, we do not fail to remember that he is a part of it and is himself involved in any change.

Gregory said, "I would say that Leonardo's statement, as interpreted by you, Bert, is precisely the statement of what brings us here, that the moment you separate the human organization from the larger natural organization in this sort of way, the moment you say they're a totally different sort of thing . . ."

"You're on a ledge," Warren put it.

"You're on a ledge. By God, you're on a ledge! Not only that, but you're going to have all sorts of what we've been calling pathologies developing within your human family and, of course, all sorts of pathologies developing in the natural system, which is not an essentially random system such as Leonardo represented. And so on."

"May I resume my *Mittelmanning*?" Horst asked. "You see, this is the point where Bert indeed may be totally wrong. But I feel that he may be right in pointing out that we might have to change man radically, give him a new morality or something, otherwise we might fail. You see?"

Tolly began to speak. "I'd like to say in advance that what I have to say is not an expression of disrespect for Bert. I have very violent reactions to what I've heard and I will not be able to express what I feel in an entirely coherent way. So it will just have to come out as a number of disconnected statements whose connections will perhaps dawn on you to a greater or lesser degree." Tolly was speaking very slowly. "I've wondered from time to time about myself—and I'm speaking as an amateur— as to which of my tissues is the hungriest, whether it's my brain or my stomach or my penis. I have the feeling that most men must have another tissue which is hungrier than all three of these, which is one which demands cosmic certainty, and I feel that that appetite is our undoing . . . There is more than a superficial connection between the anger I feel listening to Bert talking about Leonardo and St. Augustine, and the anger I felt in 1958 when I talked to Marvin Minsky, who said that it would be so nice if we would produce an order of being in the form of robots that are improvements on ourselves, ones that are not subject to such ridiculous infirmities as disease and death and such very limited capacity for ratiocination . . . that is, I see St. Augustine and Marvin Minsky as in league against *me* . . . I also want to say something about that sculptor Bert described. In my eyes the rock sculpts the sculptor, as much as the sculptor sculpts the rock. On the first day when Barry talked about man and nature, I made a marginal note, which I never voiced, which was: 'man does not deal with nature; man is of nature.' . . . I think there's a difference." Tolly pounded the table and tears appeared in his eyes and rolled down his cheeks. "*I want to dance and I want to sing.*" Then very quietly, "And you are to understand that remark as if you had looked out the window . . . and seen a cloud pass by. It takes space to dance in and air to move with my voice and people to hear. Those are conditions that are not maintained in and of themselves . . . anyhow that seems not to be enough. I think another difficulty is that . . . there is this feeling everyone has that reality is heavy. Things are never good enough. The cycle of pain and pleasure is not good enough . . . increase the pleasure, more, MORE . . . as if the one could exist without the other. Also the endless wish for simple solutions. Most ugly messes are created in small degrees and can be cleaned up only in small degrees, lots of little things that have to be done, to correct for lots of little things that weren't done. Anyone who has ever run a house knows about it. In the end you call it a big ugly mess and it is, but it came about in little steps, many of them, taken or not taken. There are no single answers, no simple solutions. We are here looking at a scene which was put on the board by Fred and by Barry . . . and it's an ugly mess . . . to me. I'm not in the very least interested, not in the least interested to consider on what ground I regard it as an ugly mess; that I think is a *hideous* question, no one should ask on what grounds do you say that's an ugly mess . . . I say it is. Say it with me or don't . . . and let's look to remedies. I mean there are lots of them, not single ones, revisions of attitudes, the arousing of religious feelings which I take as real, exercises such as Barry's been carrying on for ten years and . . . a *humbling* of people.

"I had an exchange with Gertrude yesterday on the subject of humbleness. She quoted G. H. Hardy and said that Hardy said that we create what we observe . . ."

"No!" she said indignantly.

"Then said what?" He turned to hear her protest.

"No! 'Mathematics lies in the world around us and what we vainly consider our creations are merely the record of our observations.' "[1]

"Right. That says it better." Again he faced the group. "I said in reply, what we observe is the record of our creations. She said, that's less humble . . . and I said, it could be argued that it is more humble. I said, Hardy has expressed with that remark his wish to erect a platform for man in general and himself in particular, from which to produce eternal verities, and I deny to everyone, myself included, of course, the capacity to produce eternal verities."

"I think it would help to read a biography of his . . ."

"It wouldn't help me a bit! The words are unambiguous . . . Well. I guess it's the end of the speech."

An epistemological problem had now been posed for us in at least three ways: in the question of whether, as Hardy and Barry implied, the world was there to be known and knowledge could have a kind of certainty; in Tolly's position that all knowledge was a relative human artifact, an on-going process; and in the curious divergence where Tolly made this view a basis for humility, a similarity between man and nature, while Bert, building on Hegel, used it to glorify humanity as opposed to nature. Now Barry asked to respond to Bert and Tolly, moving from epistemological theory to the implications of that theory for action. "Gregory, let me discuss what Bert has said and what Tolly has said. I have assumed that Bert's motivation for his carefully worked out ideas in what he said is a concern for the human family, for love between people."

"I got it at Esalen last week."

"No, I think you probably brought a good deal of it to Esalen. Now, I think that this kind of motivation and the purity of his expression of it is a very valuable feature of modern society—by modern I mean this week's. It's something that is appearing in a new way, certainly in the United States, and it is an important and meaningful feeling. I think that what Bert has brought to this table is an expression of that.

"Now what he has done with it, in my view, dehumanizes man. I think that Bert's understanding of his problem is *so wrong* as to destroy the very thing that he is concerned with and, in that sense, he is in league with the robot-makers. And I think that what weighs so heavily on Tolly—again I'm guessing here—is that he happens to have a peculiarly sensitive feeling toward both sides. That is, what we see all the time now is a destruction of humanity, which comes from two opposite sources: one is to deny the soul of man, which is wrong. Obviously man has a soul; you're a beautiful example of that, Bert. So is Tolly. So are the rest of us. That's so! What the robot-makers do is to deny it and that is a direct, one-to-one destruction of humanity. But the peculiar thing is that you can also destroy humanity and the soul of man by insisting on its isolation from the rest of nature. The thing that enrages me is that in some sense this is regarded as more humane. There is no difference, to me, in how you destroy a man; if he's destroyed, that is inhumane.

"Now let me give you some examples. The whole notion that nature is here for us to work on, the sculptor working on the rock, has I think been largely to blame for the kind of mess that we have been talking about. You just look at the chemical companies and what they tell you over and over again—we are the sculptors, we understand the nature of the rock and we will make it into something new. Every one of the practical, hard, modern intrusions that we've got is ludicrously related to this very simple idea."

Bert interrupted here, to draw a line between the image of human beings as a part of nature, like the birds in the trees or the animals in the fields, and such a picture when it includes the possibility of reflective consciousness, of man as philosopher. "That's a development, in addition to the natural order and harmony, that's as real as being in nature, or rather more real to us, because it's the reality of our development. It's the development of a reflective creature of nature." Barry was still fuming as Bert talked, and when Bert had finished, he wound up his own vehement denunciation.

"You have expressed very clearly, very, very clearly, the cause of the dehumanized end of your consideration. You have said over and over again that there is a way in which man is different from nature and I agree. And the way in which we can express that difference is in terms of consciousness, ideas. You then go on, which is the tragic Hegelian error, to say that those phenomena—consciousness, ideas—have a history of their own, that they represent a world unrelated to that 'cyclic, cold nature,' and that the way to live is to develop that independent human conceptual history to the point where it is good; then we will know the good thing to do to nature. Now, it seems to me that what you've done is perfectly clear and I think it is simply tragically wrong. The fact of the matter is that we are a product of nature and we have this peculiar, tragic tendency that Tolly expressed so beautifully, an appetite for isolating what we regard as unique to us, our consciousness, raising it to heaven, and saying *that is the way it is going to be.* Now the reason why it's tragic is that I think you can trace most social tragedies to just that kind of absolutism. I will trace Hitler to it, I will trace Vietnam to it, and I will trace the destruction of nature to it. The reason why it is so dangerous is that it is simply not true in nature that there can be a history of pure idea, because the whole notion of what an idea is depends on the context in which we exist. That's what all these anthropologists have been telling us! Now I've preached to you, but that's what I wanted to do."

As Barry subsided in his chair, his fury spent for the moment, Warren asked for the chance to comment on the history of the idea that mind could be spoken of in isolation from material events. "I think I know Descartes fairly well. What Descartes did was to say, I intend to look at things as a physicist. You can have a mind or a soul or anything else you want to call it, only it is not to be used as part of the explanation of physical events. He looked at the nervous system above all else. He postulated the nerve impulse as a carrier of information and he formulated the first coding theorem. He saw that what we see must be switched from coding in space to coding in time. But he never got as far as understanding the specificity of nervous activity. It is not that one impulse differs from another, except in where and when it occurs." In which case the specificity of nervous activity depends on context.

There was a curious irony in the contrast between Bert's phrasing of Cartesian dualism and that which Warren was attributing to Descartes, for after all Bert was speaking after the triumph of physics. As Will and Warren kept emphasizing, the split between mind and matter was necessary in Descartes's day in order to allow physicists to get on with the analysis of matter, which they had to see in terms as simple and determinate as possible. Bert's was the cry of the humanist a few centuries later, trying to preserve the things he cared about in human life, human creativity and freedom and love, from the triumphant expansion of a kind of materialistic analysis not complex enough yet to do more than reduce them to the caricature that can be seen in so much of experimental psychology. Mind is not a fiction, nor can it be accounted for in the terms of traditional physics, and so it seemed useful to believe in transcendent mind.

What we were learning from the cyberneticists, however, was to think about matter with a new kind of complexity. We were learning about ways in which matter could be and is organized throughout the biological world, what Gregory called Creatura, so that mind-like properties were immanent in it. One might almost go back over the discussions and try substituting the word "mind" for the word "system" wherever either occurred. Then "mind" becomes a property not just of single organisms, but of relations between them, including systems consisting of man and man, or a man and a horse, a man and a garden or a beetle and a plant. Some mind-like properties seem very simple when they occur by themselves, but together they suggest a way of thinking which neither reduces mind to a model of billiard balls, nor sets it off in contrast to matter, but allows for a search through all orders of material complexity for forms of organization comparable to our own. This is perhaps a basis for a new kind of respect for the structures of the world in which we live.

Mind is immanent where there are a number of parts, moving and mutually constrained, forming a system which is self-corrective, maintaining constants about relations between the parts and relations to the environment: a steam engine with a governor. Mind is immanent where energy is stored so that the system can be responsive to abstract cues. Mind is related to purpose, especially to the kind of goals which Gordon called evolutionary goals, and any material system with an evolutionary goal deserves to be called historical in a sense going beyond the simple fact of change.

Warren continued: "That we are able to perform a good physical analysis of how our brains are actually working is fine. But . . . I am sorry, but you cannot attack that problem without looking at the much more general problem that whether you are an engineer or a biologist, you live in a world in which you have to consider values, in which there are purposes and intentions. There are things in that world on which you can bark your shins. Now, the object of most of us who work in cybernetics is to look at the whole of nature, not a fragment. This is a nature in which there are words that carry meanings, there are creatures for which things are good or bad, and so on. This is unthinkable if you won't let me have values out yonder. It is these aspects of it which tend to unify our world again. It doesn't matter whether it happens to be in a machine or in a man, the problem we look at is the same problem. If we're talkers as well as tool-makers, then, by golly, you've got to think it all the way through about your talking."

Warren glared around the room as he came to an abrupt stop. In the sudden silence, Peter began tentatively to speak. He pointed out that although human perception and consciousness must be seen as an outgrowth of natural selection, if, in fact, our consciousness were always under this control, the kinds of maladaptation Barry and Gregory were talking about would have been unlikely to occur. "I am suggesting that Bert's notion may have a certain validity, that the development of consciousness may have proceeded to the point where, to some extent or other, the operation of consciousness escaped the control of natural selection. Then one could develop a system of ideas or ideals, which does have a history of its own, quite independent of the nexus we call nature."

"And is unfortunately unnatural," said Barry.

"Sure it is! And if the escape hadn't occurred, why of course our present dissonances wouldn't exist. I'm not saying this is a good thing, on the contrary; but I am suggesting that it is possible and indeed perhaps quite crucial, to accept the possibility of looking at the history of man's ideas as something that has an independent existence."

"Sure, I favor reading Hegel," Barry shrugged. "Absolutely. As an example of the pathology of this terrible appetite that Tolly talks about. I favor it. I, in a sense, delight in listening to Bert, as an example of that same pathology in modern guise. But if we don't understand the dissonance between that kind of idealism and us in the world, it'll kill us. The dreadful thing that is happening in many quarters today is that this particular pathology, which has a tragic history, is being elevated to a way of life." And yet, I thought, what Bert is saying about man's distinctness vis-à-vis the rest of the natural world is still true and there must be a way of expressing it that will not trap us into violating and exploiting nature. We need to love and still acknowledge difference, without accentuating that difference in the poetry of our courtship. In a strange way, here we stand at the end of centuries of history, in Bert's sense, and eons of evolution. If we now behave, with our tools and our knowledge, in the natural way, we are doomed. We need to become, uniquely in the history of life on our planet, a species that does not compete with every skill and weapon to monopolize resources and guarantee the survival of as many of our immediate offspring as possible. Instead, we must begin not only to include ourselves within our understanding of nature, but include our understanding of nature within our understanding of ourselves, consciously fostering natural balances because we have a vision of the whole, rather than simply moving within it. We need to see ourselves as parts of the system, and we need to develop an internalization of that system, like an actor turned director who must discipline his wish to steal the show.

"I'd be the last man to stand between anyone and his pleasures or to stand between anyone and his traps," said Tolly. "We all build our own traps. So long as that activity doesn't destroy the world. But we now have the problem of scale. There are people playing their games at points in the system which are sensitive, like the oxidized forms of nitrogen in the nitrogen cycle, so that it's not just a question of live and let live any more. I mean, you know, I really have nothing against the military buffs going around planning battles and building weapons or Marvin Minsky building incredibly clever devices or Warren playing with neuronal circuits. Oh, it's like at Harvard, for instance, as contrasted with what I saw at Princeton; you know, at Harvard there are social clubs and the guys who want to be very exclusive and socially tremendous can do so without disturbing anybody else, which I think is just fine. I look at that with the same amusement as I look at me. At Princeton it was very different: The social clubs literally governed life. There you just couldn't exist unless you were willing to play that game. It seems to me our problem is that there are people with their toys and their traps that are making it impossible for us to exist and, for that matter, themselves."

My father on the first day had suggested that the social disorders of the present, in the cities and on the campuses, were a sign of a change in the folk theory of mind-body relations. These we had come to see as isomorphic with theories of man-nature relations: If transcendent mind dwells in man's body as a foreign overlord, so man dwells in nature; on the other hand, if the notion of transcendent mind is rejected and we have a simple materialistic notion of mind as explainable and manipulable in the same terms as the simplest components of man's body, it is in these terms that we will see ourselves and deal with others. "In my view," Barry answered, "there are two classes of traps, two classes of pathology—the Minsky trap and the Kaplan trap. Now, in many ways we have seen much more of the Minsky difficulty lately than of the other one, but anyone who lives on an American campus has sensed Bert Kaplan's trap waiting for us the minute we get out of the Minsky trap. Frankly, I have been in anguish over this day after day, and it's accelerating. This is the notion that the way to regain the humanness of a world dehumanized by technology is to align oneself exclusively with the internalized, conceptualized goals so well expressed by Bert. It has the great virtue of being a form of protest against dehumanization; the tragedy is that it will equally well destroy us."

"That's quite true, but this isn't what Bert was recommending, surely," objected Peter.

"This we don't know yet," said Gregory, "so Bert should have a new chance to state a position. Bert?"

"One way some of these kids are thinking is this. They see the 'system' as monolithic. It seems to them to have a very strange solidity and stability and they say, that machine just has to be stopped, so I throw my body into it to mess it up. The stability they see is the villain. Now what I say is that that system, including the human beings in it, has to become different, go somewhere else, get off that road. The kind of road it's on is really the same as the kind of system that it is. It must change. That's why I was interested in the notion introduced earlier, the possibility of systems whose point is not homeostasis but change."

"Bert, you have again beautifully illustrated what's wrong here," Barry said. "I assert that it is factually incorrect that the Establishment, the 'system' against which the kids and you are revolting, is stable! That is everything that's been discussed here. Fred beautifully illustrated its intrinsic instability."

"Wait," Gregory interrupted, "the sense in which Bert used the word 'stable' was not a technical sense. What he means, Barry, is that unless something happens, it will continue to move in that direction. This is actually a definition of instability."

"No, in fact, one of the motivations that I see for the kind of attitude that Bert has expressed is exactly the notion that the 'system' is so monolithic, so all-powerful, that there is nothing that can be done in it; it has to be totally denied by changing man. My view is quite different. Just the other way around; that the system has within it, by virtue of the way in which it is developing, what Marx spoke of as the seeds of its own destruction. It cannot work. It will be changed or destroyed. The question is, will it be changed in a way which will totally destroy man and nature or will we be able to act, again to use the Marxist terminology, as midwives to a humanistic change? If you don't understand that the system itself is changeable and changing, if you regard it as a monolith, then you immediately fall into your trap."

Gertrude complained, "It just seems as if people are too willing to destroy things that are good for somebody somewhere. Somehow, there ought to be a distaste for changing something that could be put to a good purpose for anybody into rubble, just as there ought not to be a destruction of crops and meat in order to raise prices. Any time that anything that's good for somebody is changed to *junk*, why to me there's been a pathological treatment of this system of nature. It just seems to me that if everybody felt that way, there'd be so many more nice things for all of us."

Horst set out to rephrase Barry's two traps. "The Renaissance man has two different kinds of possibilities. On the one side, he builds machines, monsters, Manhattan towers—man against nature, you see. On the other hand, he has his soul, his mind, his inner part; the other trap I think is the Romantic trap. I wonder whether Bert is a Romantic, is he really? The hippies may be a modern-day Romantic movement. But I wonder whether Bert's suggestion is really exactly the same?"

"I'm a middle-aged hippie," he acknowledged.

"That's right," said Barry scornfully. "Exactly. You're a professorial hippie, so you talk about Hegel!"

Bert led the discussion to the cargo cult again, by pointing out that, whether you are building Romantic castles with no substance or Manhattan towers, a great deal depends on what kind of gain is anticipated. The post–World War II Manus represent a basic religious impulse, the anticipation of a total transformation of life. "Now you see, I love your cargo cultists, Ted, but I feel they're just deluded, because they don't imagine the right cargo. They expect refrigerators and lawn mowers and that sort of thing to come in and save them. Well, we know, because we've got it all, that it doesn't save. In my terms, in religious terms, this is worship of the wrong thing, it's idolatry. The question is, what is it that's worthy of worship? What kind of religion is the true religion?"

"A non-worshipful one," Barry muttered.

"Oh, no," said Gregory.

"See, Kierkegaard goes through all this," Bert continued. "If you worship another person, well, that's reasonable, you can give your life to another person; that's marriage. But it turns out that that doesn't work, simply on the grounds that, good as a person is, even a person isn't enough, isn't worthy of worship either. The question is, what is?"

It was unfortunate that Gordon Pask was out of the room, or he might have drawn the parallels between the questions of worship and idolatry and the different types of purpose he had described. Instead, there was an outbreak of cross-talk. Both Fred and Barry wanted to speak, but Gregory insisted, "I want to hear what Bert does think is worthy of worship."

"Well, I've never really thought of that question . . . I suppose the only answer I can give you is this whole human family, this image of people being nourished by and nourishing each other."

Gregory concluded, "Yes, that does separate man from nature." Barry agreed.

"It seems to me that the kinship-with-all-things business becomes a religion, kind of," said Gertrude. Gregory nodded. "Those of us who were brought up, say, in the Christian tradition, go back and find lots of things in the Synoptic Gospels that support our point of view, and so we say this is the view of Christianity that we want."

We were nearly ready to adjourn, but Tolly, who had hardly

spoken since his impassioned response to Bert's presentation, now asked if he could read a second passage from Alan Watts into the record. This passage[2] concerned the fear of death: death as a void, filled with fantasies of judgment and punishment, fantasies of an experienced nothingness or even of a dreary heaven. He read it, two or three pages, with no explanation, yet setting the memory of death, with all the associations it must have for everyone around that table, floating in the current of our talk. After he stopped, the pause lengthened in the slowly darkening room.

"The one point I wanted to inject before we break," said Gregory, at last, without commenting on Tolly's reading, "was the rather curious fact, which I'm sure is relevant, that an ancient ecosystem—the primeval forest, the desert, the Everglades, the arctic tundra—for those of you who have ever seen such things, of which there are not many, is an incredibly beautiful thing. Now, there must be a reason why, to an organism who is also interested in automobiles and in the maximization of wealth, with all sorts of other peculiar characteristics we've noted in man, these funny, interacting masses of, you might suppose, quite irrelevant organisms, most of which you can't even eat, should have beauty. I leave that as a question."

"And perhaps much more crucial, why, to some people, are they not beautiful?" said Peter.

"There are also people, I'm sorry to say, who, if they walk down the road in the evening and see a snail on it, will by preference step on the snail—it's just as simple as that. And if they go ashore on a Galapagos island and see a bird that doesn't run away from them, will immediately hit it over the head." He shook himself abruptly and stood to leave, and around the table small eddies of conversation began as notes were gathered and we prepared to scatter.

We were on our way to rest and dress for the festive evening of the conference. It is a tradition of Burg Wartenstein on one evening of every conference to invite the two musicians who play at all the Gloggnitz weddings up to the castle, so this was the evening when we danced and we sang. One man plays an accordion and the other a strange instrument called a *Teufel-geiger*, the devil's fiddle. The devil's fiddler dances with his instrument which, in addition to its strings, has bells and chimes; the player holds it by the neck, resting the base on the floor by his feet and bowing it—then suddenly he lifts it, beats the base in rhythm on the floor, pivots and spins, while all around him are dancing polkas and waltzes. This was a relationship between a person and a tool that lifted the tool into almost human life, like a ship.

And how fine to see this rather stiff, shy group of people dancing, after so many days of watching heads and shoulders across the conference table. By the time the dancing began, we were already very gay, after a festive meal with the women from the Wenner-Gren staff in dirndls and an unending flow of white wine from very *kitsch* Viennese wine servers, glass spheres with spigots at the bottom, supported in wrought iron stands shaped into the tendrils of vines. How differently these people danced, my father breathless and gay in a silk Hawaiian shirt, lifting his knees high; Will debonair with careful old-fashioned courtesy; Tolly spinning his partner in faster and faster circles. We found our limbs, we could move again, and surely with care we could make each other as human as that player made his spinning, tinkling fiddle.

Later on we gathered around the fire and Tolly began to lead us in singing. Expanding his chest and gesturing with bravura from group to group, he wove our voices together in a series of rounds new to all of us. "Ah, Robyn," began one ancient round,

> Gentyl Robyn,
> Tell me how thy leman doth
> And thou shalt know of mine.

The singer goes on to complain to the bird that his sweetheart loves another and refuses his suit. "My lady is not so," the bird replies, "I cannot think such doubleness . . ." "Ah, Robyn," the voices of the first group boom out, complaining to the birds of the duplicity of conscious purpose.

Warren was pacing in the background and when I called to

him to join us he complained that he could not hear, was deaf to high notes, so I went and stood, resting my chin on his angular shoulder with my temple pressed against the side of his head so that he could feel the vibration of the notes. "Viva la musica!" we learned to sing next.

## · CHAPTER 14 ·

# Diversity and Love

WE HAD ALL BECOME accustomed to life in the castle by this time, enjoying the surroundings and the rhythm of the day. The main rooms were lined up on one side of a courtyard with a gate at one end, and through that gate most of the men went out across the drawbridge every night to their rooms in the remodeled stables. My room was in a tower above the gate and I could look out my window and see them toiling up the hill before a session, or wandering to and fro as their errands took them. First to awaken in the morning was Peter, who slipped out before dawn and walked all the way down to Gloggnitz and back, or found new paths through the woods, searching for birds with Gregory's field glasses and breakfasting on berries. The last to sleep in the evenings was usually Warren. He was staying right in the castle, so he had no need to retire before the gates were locked at midnight. When we gathered in the lounge after dinner to drink brandy around the fire, Warren would sit debating the perplexities of America, bright-eyed and intent, seeking out Bernie or Tolly or my father, and as one person after another slipped away he would remain pacing around the darkened halls far into the night.

Evening after evening, an intricate web of conversation was spun in the different rooms of the castle and beyond the castle gates. Even within that short period each of us had established patterns and relationships, surprisingly disparate ones, sometimes very different from what we saw around the green table. Outside the conference room, too, we had the company and advice of Lita Osmundsen and the Foundation staff. They led us through the ritual of graceful meals, a hostess at each table. Looking along the dining room, I could sometimes see a table where someone from the New York office of the Foundation sat gazing into space, stranded between four mathematicians, while at other tables I could watch a flirtation or a carefully tended conversation between people who had been quarreling during the day.

Lita Osmundsen, the chatelaine of Burg Wartenstein, usually listened in on the discussions and would remonstrate with my father for the long hours we kept, urging him to be a firmer chairman. Meanwhile, often perplexed and depressed about the direction of the conference, he kept doggedly bringing us together for six or seven hours of talking every day, letting the conversation wind its way across our differences, gradually quickening in pace as the end approached. Gregory brooded between sessions, but when we met he limited himself to a few guiding words at each beginning and an indication of the turn of people who had said they wanted to make presentations or speak at some length.

One of these was Peter Klopfer, who had been somewhat hesitant to rush into the argument when it was in full spate. Peter was soft-voiced and engaging, a long-limbed, gentle man who, in spite of his list of books and publications, looked hardly twenty years old. He seemed to find great pleasure in small symmetries and precise analogies, and spoke with care and precision. Starting out with a description of some of the shifts his own thinking had gone through in graduate school, he showed how several different lines of argument might also lead, as Tolly's presentation had led, to an understanding of the organism as a point in space where certain processes were taking place, rather than as a thing. "It's been suggested every once in a while here," he continued, "that some of the dissonances between ourselves and our environment might have been avoided had we all along been accustomed to looking at biological and other phenomena through the sort of spectacles that Tolly presented to us. What I would like to suggest is that, valuable as Tolly's model might be, it really doesn't do anything that other models, including verbal ones, couldn't do as well. This doesn't mean that it isn't very important, because the suggestion that I'd like to advance is that what is important for avoiding dissonances, which are the result of imperfect perception, is a constant change in the vantage point, a constant shift in the way we perceive. If I may use a crude analogy, it would be that, when we fix upon an object with our eyes, if we are to keep it clearly in focus, it is necessary that we continually shift our eyes; if these movements are in some way inhibited, our vision becomes blurred. It is by changing the vantage point, changing the perspective, that we avoid perceptual dissonances."

"Things disappear," Fred supplied.

"Yes. Literally disappear, if the gaze is really fixed for any period of time. So, in the field of visual perception, change in the angle is important. I'm suggesting this is true in the conceptual realm as well. Now, it is quite clear from the history of man that we tend to be very fearful of accepting new ways of looking at our environment and thus it appears to me that the critical question, both from the point of view of understanding how and why men behave, as well as from the point of view of a concern with political solutions, is how to make man less fearful of new perceptions. We need to know the basis for developing a willingness—indeed a need—for reappraising goals and attitudes."

Horst picked this up enthusiastically, pointing out that since the form of errors depends on the type of coding used, any second way of coding observations would slice right across the number of errors, reducing them to a fraction, rather than simply subtracting. "You might even optimize the procedure by having many ways of coding available to you. You might find so many beautiful models that if you check your deductive procedures with three or four of them, the error may be smaller and smaller."

"Yes," Gregory said, "and what was very important with

Tolly's presentation and with the whole didactic process that Gertrude was talking about, is that what Tolly did was to run simultaneously a cobbler shop and a diagram of a cobbler shop. What we were able to do was to achieve some degree of pre-verbal learning from the contrast between the two 'languages' which were presented to us."

After he had given a general argument for the advantages of perceptual and conceptual diversity, Peter went on to talk about imprinting, which gives an example of one kind of perceptual fixity that might be related to human resistance to new ways of seeing. He gave some examples from his own research of ways in which fixity is combined with diversity. In imprinting, a newly fledged bird is ready to learn to recognize its mother shortly after hatching: there is a fixed period of time during which any moving thing of approximately the right size can be accepted as a mother and call forth the appropriate behavior. After imprinting, the recognition or the visual preference is fixed. "If a particular preference is going to develop, the organism has to be exposed to that object or some representation of it within a particular period of time, which may be a few hours or weeks or just a matter of moments, and may occur at various stages of development. Alternatively, the sensory system may impose filters, so that only certain kinds of patterns can be learned, or there may be an overlapping of both kinds of constraints." Later, food, nesting sites, and mates may all be selected on the basis of an early-acquired preference pattern, and reflect differences in early environment in an adaptive way without genetic coding of the details.

"Now, I would like to suggest an evolutionary stratagem that we ought to consider, which can extend the effective elasticity of the species, particularly when we talk about the animal man. This is the stratagem we call polyethism, intra-specific behavior diversity. If a group of mallard ducklings are exposed,[1] twelve to twenty hours after hatching, to a moving, calling model of the mother duck, this initiates a following response in the whole group and they are imprinted to that particular model. Later, when the imprinting period is over, so that if the ducks have not yet learned to recognize and follow a particular Momma they never will, they can be tested individually and about half of them don't respond at all—they simply haven't been imprinted. Of the remaining half, it's quite clear that some have learned to define Momma only in terms of the sound; if you give them a choice between two silent models, they are simply confused, but if you give them the sound, they choose correctly every time. The remaining group respond purely to the visual pattern; they don't discriminate at all between the sound Momma makes and other sounds. A very small number are capable of responding to both visual and auditory cues."

This variability within the species was discovered by testing the ducklings individually, because ducklings under a week old stay very close together and there is a "social facilitation" of the following response, so that whenever a certain number of ducklings in a clutch set out after Momma, the others follow, head to tail. Subsequent experiments, however, tested the number of ducklings needed to bring all the others along and it turned out that the social facilitation works only so long as you have a ratio of at least one responder to three non-responders. At anything less than that ratio, you get ambivalence and the group may break up. Under normal conditions, where the mother duck is usually both seen and heard, about half the clutch will respond and easily bring the others along, but even in the special case where the mother was for some reason invisible or inaudible, those who responded to available cues would be enough. "The point is that the perception of mother duck in a group of ducklings is effectively doubled over what is possible for a single animal."

Peter had been very interested in Ted's descriptions of which members of Manus society became involved in the cult, and he had presented an analogy for thinking about the value for a group of having some members with apparently dysfunctional characteristics. "This is immediately very far-fetched and needs to be thought of literally as an analogue. In England, there are flat stones which are known as thrush anvils, because certain species of birds have the habit of collecting snails and smashing the shells on exposed rocks so they can eat them. Now, the snails range from yellow to pink, and some are quite striped while others are quite plain, but if you collect the broken shells at any particular time of year, you find a particular color pattern that predominates on the snail shell. The point is that this kind of a census made by the birds suggests that a particular color is vulnerable at a particular time of year. If you go back at a different time of year, when the color of the substrate is different (it's green and lush in the summer, you see, and brown and dry in the winter), the prevalent color pattern has changed. There is, in other words, a fluctuation in frequency of the different morphs at the thrush anvils, as a function of the time of year, because of a difference in selection pressure related to seasonal change. Do you see the point? By having a minority of individuals whose color pattern is highly maladaptive in the summer, because it makes them conspicuous to the thrushes, you preserve the genetic material which at another time of year becomes extremely important for the survival of the species. There is a value for the species in diversity, which makes it evolutionarily useful and desirable, however maladaptive it may be to the individual organism.

"In the case of the mallard ducks—which generally nest in open situations where the probability that the mother will be invisible but audible is very, very much lower than the reverse probability—it might be much better from the individual duckling's point of view to develop the visual capacity and forget about the acoustic capacity. But as far as the clutch is concerned, by gosh, the diversity is best. This is why, when we were listening to the Manus material, I got interested in the question of why the structure of the human mind should be such that it can contain such dissonances. Is it in fact the case, as Gertrude suggested, that the dissonance leads to inactivity, a breakdown of function? My own suspicion is that it can't, otherwise you wouldn't see it preserved time and time again in various cultures in various contexts."

Peter ended with the possibility of drawing further analogies from the necessity of there being a certain ratio of responders among the ducklings, which protects the whole group from dashing off when one of them goes after a fly. "I suggest this implies that to maintain certain kinds of world views as viable options among humans, it perhaps isn't enough to have just one or two people with that view. You have to preserve, perhaps, a certain percentage of the population with that view. I just put this out as a suggestion." Peter smiled shyly as he finished.

Gregory said, "There's a formally similar phenomenon in the genetics of domestic animals and crops. For example, cotton has wild stocks from which domestic cotton is a derivative. Now, when you domesticate an organism, you desire to have a uniform population, usually with some peculiar characteristics that suit your domestication: cotton has to have long fibers, beef has to have large deposits of muscle, and so on. Wild stocks in general are genotypically mixed, so the geneticists or the farmers go to work and do a selection job to make a pure line, which they then multiply into the thousands to make their domesticated stock. What happens then is that the domestic animal or plant is a creature that is almost totally unable to deal with complex change. A virus can come up and wipe them out and then somebody has to go and find the wild stock and breed a new line, which happens to be immune to the virus, if you're lucky, and you go on. But if your wild stocks are all destroyed in one way or another, as is happening to many organisms, you are stuck with this specialized object, which is unable to deal with the next emergency. The geneticists are getting on to this point and are now establishing wild stocks of a good many organisms under cultivated conditions."

"I think Peter's point is marvelously illustrated in every ecological system," said Barry. "Wherever a system becomes reduced in complexity, it loses its options and therefore becomes less and less stable. The easiest way to think of it is the business of how farmers keep cats. They don't really domesticate them; they just want them wandering around to eat the mice. Now, if you simply say, well, there are mice in the barn and we'll introduce some cats and an ecosystem will be established where the cats will eat the mice, that won't work. The cats will catch the mice and, having nothing else to eat, they'll wander off and the ecosystem will break down. On the other hand, if the farmer puts food out at the kitchen door every day, then there is an alternative to eating mice, so that when the mouse population has been brought down, the cat has a reason to remain. It's that alternative, it's the flexibility of the network that allows the network as a whole to remain. I think practically every ecosystem involves exactly that sort of thing."

Peter nodded. "If, for example, you have a food chain in which the grass is eaten by the mice, which are eaten by the foxes, so that each animal in the chain has *one* source of energy, then any perturbation anywhere along that particular line is going to wipe out the whole thing. But if you have a few alternative lines through which the energy can flow, the grass is eaten by mice *and* by rabbits, and these animals are preyed upon alternatively by foxes *and* owls, which can shift from one to the other, then when there is a perturbation which reduces or increases the numbers of organisms along one of these lines, why then the flow of energy can be shifted along another. In fact, these occurrence diagrams of Tolly's would represent ecologic food webs very neatly. If we define the difference between two species in terms of different ways of extracting energy from the environment, then the more of these you have, the greater the stability."

"When the system becomes simplified," Barry concluded, "first you begin to see oscillations—you know, the classical rabbit-wolf oscillations, when one population goes up and the other goes down. That is already a highly simplified ecosystem, and that's the last step, obviously, before an ecosystem collapses." The simplification of an ecosystem seemed to me formally similar to what we had spoken of earlier as vulgarization in human cultures.

Barry leaped to another level of systemic organization. "This is similar to the whole business of metabolic stability and toxicity we were talking about before, for different kinds of tissues. The brain is, relatively speaking, a simple metabolic system with all of its energy piped right through that one cytochrome system we were talking about—that's why it's so sensitive to cyanide. In contrast to that, the liver cell, for example, has got all of the metabolic cycles operating full blast, with alternative ways of getting the food in contact with the oxygen, and if you poison with cyanide the liver will continue to function pretty well. The brain is so specialized, so restricted in its metabolic pathways, that it is highly vulnerable to any intrusion."

Peter was wary of confusion developing. "The kind of flexibility that I'm meaning to focus on now is not so much the one that exists in complex ecological or metabolic systems, but flexibility in ways of looking at the world that will allow us to recognize the need for maintaining complexity in the environment. I think the critical problems are, first, to find out how the conditions of rearing can reduce the number of constraints that act upon us to limit our world view or reduce our willingness to try, in Tolly's terms, new kinds of spectacles. Second, I think we ought to be concerned with the reduction of diversity within the human population, reduction of the potential for generating new views, which may come about through increased uniformity in our environment. If I may put it very crudely, when all of North America is one big urban sprawl, I think there will be very few people still functioning who share my disposition, which is one that is congenitally incapable of coping with the stresses of city life. The kind of perceptive mass that I and my genes represent is clearly going to be lost; maybe this is good, maybe this is bad. I suggest, however, that the loss of any source of variety in kinds of perceptual mechanisms represents a serious matter."

Peter's caution served to underline for me the way in which we were leaping from analogy to analogy as we pursued the notion of diversity. Within a few minutes, the idea of diversity within a species—ducklings with different types of imprinting, the various banding patterns of the snails, mixed stocks of wild cattle or cotton—had been juxtaposed with diversity within an ecosystem and diversity of metabolic pathways within a cell, and all of these were being compared to diversity of perceptions or world views in human populations. Anyone in the room who could follow the details of one of these analogies, checking it against his own expertise, could immediately move to the others because of their formal similarity. As in the mathematical picture-making Tolly had spoken of, we had begun to share enough notions of how systems operate so that a particular pattern could be seen to represent a multitude of different examples.

Sitting there and shifting from one analogy to another, I could apply them to the human situation comfortably so long as world-view diversity was seen as producing a diversity of response among different people, but still in my mind I wrestled with the extent to which the analogy applied directly to dissonance or ambiguity in thought. Surely we could argue the need for a tolerance of diversity in society as a whole, and yet still look for the consistency within any individual's world view that would allow him to make transfers of learning. Yet there was a tension here: within an individual, inconsistency seemed to depend on blocked pathways, an incomplete annealing of new material into the net, while the advantage of diversity that we were speaking of was that it multiplied pathways.

Now Ted went further in applying the analogy to human cultures. "One of the reasons I went to Manus a second time was to study the order of diversity in this whole area. It fascinated me that, in such a small archipelago, you had some twenty languages spoken—an incredible number; that's an average of less than a thousand speakers per language, languages at least as different as Spanish and Italian, in spite of the fact that they live near each other, they intermarry, they make war, they take captives. There's a tremendous amount of multilingualism. Virtually every one of these linguistic groups has a different song style too, so it's almost like studying bird calls, or like Peter's different groups of ducks. One group has a type of music that is totally verbal, with absolutely no melodic variation, while another group has a type of music entirely melodic. The two have reached the extremes on this variation to such an extent that the verbal people mock the other people's music as a lot of *wah, wah, wah,* as they put it, and these other people reciprocate. The same with the other arts.

"One thing that helps in this is their attitude toward any variation as a form of property. You know the other man's thing, but that doesn't mean you do it; you recognize this as his property. Every single thing that was made there was made by only one or two out of some sixty villages and traded throughout the archipelago. They cherish difference and it's not a breakdown in communication.

"Now, however, as in the rest of the primitive world, it's all breaking down, even the valuation of difference—one of Paliau's main points was not to be different any more. I'm studying the convergence process—what's going to go first and how long the personality differences are going to survive. I think that all these cultures, if they were isolated, would be entirely different. Being a part of a cultural mosaic is responsible for their very openness to change and yet it's undoing them, in terms of their readiness to throw out whole blocks of things and to expect whole blocks of things to come in. They regard variations as property, but that also means that variations can be licensed, transferred; a woman marrying into a group can bring in pottery-making, for instance. So now all of this tremendous diversity is vanishing extraordinarily rapidly. I think if we take the whole picture of human evolution, what we find is a constant loss of small-group diversity and instead the only chance we have, really, is internalized diversity within large groups and perhaps even within individuals."

"The diversity business is quite complicated and has other aspects," said Gregory. "The moment you're dealing with communicational systems with multiple, alternative pathways, you do not get a subtractive budget, such as we're familiar with in economics of money or energy, but a multiplicative budget in which you fractionate sets of possible alternatives. If you add another set of stressful circumstances, you fractionate again, and you've fractionated the remaining set. This also makes for quite a different sort of feeling about quantity, and scale, and such things.

"The downs of England, on which I collected plants as a boy, had a turf about two inches high, which was a very complex botanical system with forty or fifty species of flowering plants in it. That turf was maintained partly by sheep and partly by rabbits. Then the automobile came and fencing the downs was a larger project than anybody wanted to undertake, so when the sheep went on the roads and were hit by the automobiles, they were taken off the downs. This left the rabbits in control, which they managed on the whole to do, but about fifteen years ago, the rabbits were murdered by bacterial warfare down to maybe 0.1 per cent of their population. The whole country, I may say to its credit, was deeply shocked when this happened, because there were dying rabbits everywhere around, but anyway, that didn't last long. From there on, the turf started to grow and when I saw it last summer, it was a botanical mess about three feet high, with small trees in it up to six feet high. Now what lived in the new botanical mess? A fraction of the original diversity: those plants that were able to survive when the turf was down to two inches and *still* able to survive when the turf was up to three feet. What you get with each change is a slicing down of the ecological diversity. This whole business is obviously a very complex function of rapidity of ecological change and rapidity of evolutionary change working against each other." The generation of new diversity by evolution, or even by diffusion, is necessarily much slower in comparison. "I leave it to the mathematicians to work out the relationship. A further change would probably reduce the list of survivors to our friends the weeds, these being the plants that can live anywhere and will no doubt outsurvive man. Was it Julian Huxley who said that the last organism left alive is going to be a dying insect eating a dead weed? This is possible. Let's break for some coffee."

"Gregory, Peter put some words in my mouth that I think I must spit out before I can drink anything," Gertrude broke in. "If what the Manus had in the cults was suspended judgment, that to me does not mean suspended activity; it may mean doubling or tripling activity, because it means getting ready for more than one eventuality."

Peter said, "I meant inconsistency, that which you say blocks activity. I was raising the question as to whether an inability to act as a result of a dissonance could not also under some circumstances be functional. Here's an animal; you train it to do this, you train it to do that; now you're demanding both actions simultaneously, he can't perform either. Granted this is dysfunctional for the individual; for the species, however, may not this perhaps be functional?"

After the coffee break, Ted picked up the thread again, this time talking about movements in the opposite direction. "Living in Los Angeles, where I went after having heard every sort of horror story, I'm very impressed with the amount of relatively new diversity that I see developing there. Mankind has gone through one enormous cycle of, first, great diversification and, now, great convergence, but this may not be the end of the story. We should be looking for the sources of new variation and seeing these as ways of controlling scale. Another thing that comes in is the contrast between a great primitive artist and a great artist in a complex civilization. In Manus, say, they've developed twenty distinctive art styles, but within each, a person works within a tradition. Our artists, on the other hand, have a tremendous eclecticism—there is a new kind of diversity and even a pressure toward diversity and originality. Some of it may be phony, but not all of it."

"It seems to me this question of variability is potentially very important to this conference, Peter, if we can have some assurance of the notion that variability is really a good thing," said Bert.

"Well, variability in ways of extracting energy is, I think, only analogically related to variability in ways of looking at the universe."

"Yes," said Bert, "but . . . is it possible to make a pronouncement that variability is important and the reduction of variability constitutes a danger?"

"There just can't be any argument."

"With respect to ecological systems, as Peter and I have been describing them, there is simply no question about it," said Barry.

The emphasis on ecological diversity in our discussion gave

me a clue to another problem of vocabulary that had been bothering me. Like the word "environment," the word "pollution" expresses a human-centered and non-cybernetic view of ecological deterioration. When we think of "polluting" a river, we think of the addition of substances that we find noxious, so that it stinks in summer and the few fish species that survive are dangerous to eat. But many of the ways in which ecosystems are destroyed do not fit this model: overfertilization or eutrophication of lakes, destruction of soil by irrigation, the elimination of predators as well as pests, and many others. Instead, we need to focus on the dangers of systemic degradation, reduction of complexity—which is equivalent in evolutionary terms to reduction of flexibility and responsiveness. Any intervention that reduces the ancient complexity of a system is a degradation of that system that deserves very careful consideration. What we call "pollution" is only a special case, and "pollution abatement" rarely provides a solution, except over long time periods, although it may prevent further deterioration.

"I think the significance of this is as an illustration," Barry said, "as a metaphor, if you like, of the flux involved in the real world, and of the consequences of the limitation of complexity. In a sense, the oscillations in an oversimplified ecology fit the way in which I've been thinking of the nouns. What you see in a complex ecosystem is just process. If it becomes simplified, then suddenly there are a lot of lemmings or a lot of rabbits and it is an object sort of thing. This is the importance that I attach to this particular notion. You will not be able to use ecology as the crutch on which to stand when you want to worry about the primacy of process. You can use ecology as an educational experience, but not as a scientific validation of some of the troublesome things that we're trying to say." Thinking back to Bernie's films, I began to wonder whether ecology was an appropriate educational experience for the first learning of these ideas, or primarily a remedial tool for adults.

Will was quick to see the relationship between Peter's remarks and his own position, maintained throughout the conference. "I don't think anyone would try to deduce the desirability of conceptual diversity from Peter's ecological systems, but it affords us an interesting analogy. Barry, you made a remark just now about the 'real world'; well, just suppose, for instance, that it turned out that reality was the sort of thing that couldn't be exhausted in any single conceptual system, however complex it was. Then it would turn out that it was desirable to have diverse conceptual systems. For instance, I think it might prove to be the case that it was better to have the diversity of two conceptual systems, one separating mind from matter and one merging them, than a single conceptual system."

"Sure," said Gregory, "one for Sundays, and the other for weekdays!"

"No," said Will. "The presence in the society of diverse value systems and diverse conceptual systems may be a good thing because it makes for some humility. I don't particularly like nouns, but I don't want to trample on them, Tolly. I think there is something to be said for diversity of world views in a culture, analogous to diversity of species. What has troubled me about the conference is that it seems to me to be content with a single world view which somehow . . . no?" Gregory and Barry were shaking their heads vehemently. "It didn't? I thought that was the tendency . . ."

"I don't think the conference has been content, period," said Barry.

"Happy, but not content," said Gregory. Certainly if I had tried to list the propositions on which we all agreed they would have been exceedingly few and it seemed to me doubtful that the people in that room could ever agree on a single world view.

It was during the discussion of diversity that I realized for the first time the formal basis for Gregory's objection to a public relations campaign. The topic was one that cropped up again and again in the stale last hour of afternoon discussions or over meals and cocktails, and each time I heard it I understood it a little bit differently. The first time, my worry was simply in terms of the difficulty of suggesting corrective measures, since, if these were devised with the same conceptual limitations as the original interventions, they would probably produce similar pathologies. This, I suppose, is the reason for the overwhelmingly negative tone of most ecological concern: we can only guard against irreversible losses by saying, don't build that highway, don't drain that swamp. Even if the necessary, positive, corrective measures were known, it would be impossible to advocate them in the oversimplified rhetoric of public debate. I find this still—that in a brief discussion of some ecological issue I often can counsel only non-intervention. It will take many, many people, thinking in a new way, to evolve an effective positive concern for the environment, to replace a haphazard plugging of holes in the dike; in order to do this they will have to share a new style of thought.

The next time we discussed public relations, I had the Manus story very fresh in my mind and I brooded on the complex feedback of hope and fear, and the danger of starting a movement or even a religion that would create its own opposition, as the cargo cults did in Manus, starting new waves of polarization in the society.

Now Peter's comments suddenly meshed with Gregory's comments about vulgarity and the maximization of values, and Tolly's impassioned declaration that what one strives for cannot be what one strives for. A monoculture—an environment containing only a single species, like a cotton field or a massive chicken farm—is always produced for the maximization of some good, some individual thing seen apart from its context within the whole. This is done with pesticides and herbicides and fences, as well as by genetic selection in the single species being preserved. Diversity is removed bit by bit, first because it seems harmful to the chickens or the cotton, later because it is unproductive, with no direct contribution to the maximization of the value—until finally the ideal single crop is achieved. Curiously, that ideal proves to be extremely precarious and unable to survive without massive protection and intervention; the level of needed intervention rises every year, as the users of pesticides have discovered. The same thing is true where the good is human health and comfort, as in those most gigantic of monocultures, our cities, and would be true in the fantasy world of some science fiction where we imagine man surviving the almost total destruction of the natural environment and achieving the incredible level of protection and intervention this would require. Yet this would be the logical result of an idolatry of man—of the human family.

In Peter's examples, the preservation of diversity required the preservation of traits that were dysfunctional for the individuals themselves—exactly the kind of traits that some visualize eliminating by genetic engineering. There is no doubt that the visually oriented duckling has singly a better chance of surviving than the aural one—but this would not be true in a population composed exclusively of visual ducklings; there is no doubt that the beautiful, strong, and healthy child has a better chance of a long and happy life—but would this be true in a world populated only with healthy, beautiful, and intelligent people? And surely it would become less and less true as the values being maximized were more and more carefully stated, refined in application and definition. Would the same apply, perhaps, to programs of education or mental health? To what extent is it good that society include in its number some members who are apparently unhappy and deluded, as it is necessary that man affirm the value of an environment that includes termites and mosquitoes and viruses fatal to himself? Then the coming of the cargo, the ending of all desire by a maximization of values, would be, quite literally, death. In this knowledge, the advocacy of any specifiable goal becomes dangerous, and broader and broader definitions are needed.

Early in the conference, after our resounding denunciations of atomism and reductionism, of apocalyptic value systems and of treating persons as machines, Gregory had offered the group a definition of love, suggesting that this might give us something to work toward. He was responding, I think, to the same kind of negative tone that pervades discussions of environmental pollution, and providing the first piece in a positive answer. He had said, "You could say that love is a rather difficult-to-define concept, related to things we have been discussing—systems.

At least a part of what we mean by the word could be covered by saying that 'I love X' could be spelled out as: 'I regard myself as a system, whatever that might mean, and I accept with positive valuation the fact that I am one, preferring to be one rather than fall to pieces and die; and I regard the person whom I love as systemic; and I regard my system and his or her system as together constituting a larger system with some degree of conformability within itself.' "

"How about *its* system?" Warren had asked.

"And its system, yes, oh certainly. I'm very willing to love animals, ships, and all sorts of quite inappropriate objects. Even, I suppose, a computer, if I had the care of one, because care and maintenance are in this picture too. Now if that be what we're at, this gives us, at least in a very abstract sort of way, some idea of what positive outcome we might get from our deliberations. And perhaps this carrot in front of us might help and might give us a little more wisdom than responding to the kick behind provided by the threat of atom bombs, pesticides, etc. to our survival. I don't know. Maybe everybody has thought of this before."

Fred had said once that a concern for survival was essentially negative, and now Gregory raised the question of the unit of "survival." "This might be the gene determining skin pigmentation or short-sightedness, or it might be the human individual. It might be the human species. It might be a much larger system involving the redwoods *and* the human beings."

"I know it hasn't been very many years since a phrase like 'kinship with all life' was shocking to a great many people," Gertrude said. "When I realized that shocked other people, I realized that I went farther than that, not just kinship with all life, but kinship with all that's around, including the chemical make-up of the soil, the air and the water and everything. I found out that I was completely alien to the views of my own parents and family. It's amazing, but it seems to me that there's a kind of freedom that comes with it, the sense of so many more outlets than there are with any other view. But I'm very, very conscious of how few, well, teachers in the public schools, for example, can face such a view. This is the first time in my life that I've been in a group where I could talk about the dynamic quality of the unverbalized state of learning, even if I haven't mentioned horses or dogs or cats, without having more than half of the people freeze up with distaste and dread. This is the first time in my life."

"I think this is a very crucial point you're making," Fred responded. "What is the class of objects with which a particular individual feels kinship? There's obviously a considerable amount of variability even within this group. I think we all feel kinship with other people? I haven't heard anybody exclude that as a possibility."

"There's a small question, there," said Gregory. "Kinship with other people, maybe so; kinship with the social system or the larger ecosystem, which threatens to run over the hill, we swing on that. We are, of course, part of it and our deliberations are part of it, but the degree to which we are sensible of the part-whole relationship between us and the thing we're looking at varies very much around this room."

Fred frowned slightly. "Yes, but on a rather more concrete level, I think we can still find variability. Some people obviously feel very strongly about whether it's permissible to feel kinship with a hypothetical machine—or can we go in the other direction and ask what animals or other living things we feel kinship with? I think almost all of us feel kinship with the primates and with dogs, to some degree; I don't think anybody in this room would want to see a dog tortured."

"Notice, when Marvin Minsky says he wants to create a race better than us, the issue is not kinship with anything," said Tolly bitterly.

"It would be for me, though," Fred said, resting his gaze on Tolly thoughtfully. "This could become a very important issue for me. How much I would want to create such a race would depend very much on how much kinship I could feel with these machines. Under some circumstances I could, under others I couldn't."

"It is unlikely they would regard you as kin."

"This depends on how they're constructed. They may have great sympathy and compassion for me. In fact, I think that would be one of my requirements."

"I am afraid I would feel no kinship for them," I said, "if Minsky's definition of what we're going to construct is that they have no suffering."

Fred nodded. "I would be inclined to agree that they would have to be able to feel pain. Whatever this is, and this is another very important question. I think it's very interesting to go down the animal scale and just ask yourself, what do you feel sympathy or kinship with? An amoeba? Well, I would say no. Worm? No. With a fish? Yes, I think it's about at the fish level that I start feeling some sort of kinship."

"What about the movement of the ocean?" asked Gregory.

"Or the nitrogen cycle?" Barry added.

"No, that's not what I . . ." Fred looked reproachfully at Gregory as if he were deliberately allowing the discussion to become confused.

"This is why we are in trouble," Barry said.

"I think you completely miss the flavor if you don't extend to inanimate objects, even where they're our own productions, our tools, if you don't want to call it sympathy, call it empathy," Warren said. "It hurts me when somebody picks up a sledging hammer or a blacksmith's hammer and uses it on a rock. I know what he's doing to the hammer. It's an extension to inanimate objects; I have it for ships, particularly small craft; I have it for airplanes; I have it for works of art; I have it for computing machines. But if you don't happen to have extended it, to feel as you would if you were it, then I say you've dehumanized the machine."

"There's an extension of another kind," said Gregory. "You can extend to human individuals; it is a little more difficult to extend to human families. You can extend to ships, computing machines, screwdrivers, I don't know what; it is a little more difficult to extend to the relationship between man and screwdriver. We are concerned here with an extension not to the creatures of nature, but to a total system of interrelationships involving the whole of nature."

"And us," Barry added.

"And us, even, yes. Because it's no good to say we want to preserve the parks, you know, because of the birds. No. That's just the same thing over again. You get into the same error as by separating nature from us, or by separating the components of nature, saying the seagulls are beautiful but the tapeworms are ugly." Focusing on the seagulls or the redwoods turns our relationship with nature into what Barry called "an object sort of thing," a focus on nouns rather than on process.

For understanding the integration of nature we are infinitely richer in our perceptions than our ancestors, yet our attitudes go back to a time before the microscope made it possible to see complete cycles. From earliest childhood, the larger animals and the birds are romanticized and we learn a kind of identification with them through the anthropomorphizing in children's stories, but the microscopic life in the waters and the soil and in our own intestines remains estranged from our imagination. Insensitive to these essential links in natural systems, we walk through the woods or by the seashore unable to understand the similarities between their life and our own life processes, feeling perhaps an unexplained recognition. Perhaps in response to the form of a tree or the twist of a leaf, each one bearing evidence of growth and adaptation, aesthetic insight achieves a recognition and a kinship, which science now allows us to understand. Ancient religions symbolized that recognition in animism, but now our new techniques of recording and looking give us the structure of a new animism, an informed affirmation that, yes, each of us, in the rhythms of his or her body, is like a bird or beast—but also like a pond or a forest or the vast single life of the seas.

# Our Own Metaphor

THE LAST DAY. One person after another had spoken, and we had moved into an increasing sense of closeness. The questions we had posed and the contradictory positions we had taken worked in each of us, crying out for some resolution. We were engaged and yet wary of each other, braced against the challenges to our habits of thought. Gertrude had described the paralysis of an animal confronted with a contradiction, unable to articulate and resolve it, and for all our verbiage, the endless hours of talk going into the microphone, we had talked ourselves into paradoxes we could not yet clearly state.

We had struggled for hours over the relationship between man and the rest of nature, realizing more and more that man needs a deeper sense of himself as a part of natural processes than has existed since the beginning of civilization, and yet must keep sufficient distance to take responsibility, must feel a kinship of care and fostering, like the child who learns to build peace between his quarreling parents. We had been told that compassion for the hungry, medicine, and even the effort to keep the newborn from dying could be fatal to man's life on this planet, and yet none of us would want a society, surely, which fostered a habitual callousness to starvation. Tolly had reminded us of death, a reminder that called up my own grief and called

284

up in each of us, young or old, parent or child, the paradox of mortality. For myself, my mind was laboring with the realization that all of the religion I knew had historically fostered false and dangerous epistemologies, with notions of transcendence and apocalyptic hopes, and yet the wholeness I had felt sometimes in worship and celebration was the best model I knew for what I had spoken of as cybernetic peace.

Others had the experience of synthesis in the last days of the conference, but they must have followed different paths through our debates, each to his own sense of insight. Looking back, I felt that the whole conference converged on my own resolution and that what was said afterwards had the effect of taking it up and reinterpreting it so it would apply more widely, but this is surely the illusion of my own vantage point.

We had been moving in many ways toward a sense that a solution to the ecological crisis would demand a new definition of the individual, a definition by which the arguments of "economic man" would cease to be relevant, one that would retain a sense of the vividness of persons and at the same time allow each person to identify with natural process. To learn to love, we would need to recognize ourselves as systems, the beloved as systemic, similar and lovely in complexity, and to see ourselves at the same time as merged in a single system with the beloved. I thought of a sentence and, in a trance of thought and feeling combined, I found in it a range of meanings and an interlocking of different levels.

"I want to say a sentence to you and then I want to interpret that sentence in about four very different ways, all of which are related to what we're talking about. And the sentence is, 'Each person is his own central metaphor.' *Each person is his own central metaphor.*

"The first thing that I want to mean by that has to do with perception and coding. Any kind of representation within a person of something outside depends on there being sufficient diversity within him to reflect the relationships in what he perceives, as it depends on coding of some kind. The possibility of seeing something, the possibility of talking about it, and probably the possibility of loving, depend in every case on arriving in yourself at a comparable complexity, which depends in turn on the kind of diversity existing within yourself. Another way to put that would be to say that if human beings were totally non-comparable in the degree of their internal complexity to what's outside, then there would be no chance of any kind of valid internal representation of what lies outside them.

"Now, we've talked here about the fact that there are lots of different kinds of representations—that is, the relationships within this system that is me can be used to reflect or to map other relationships in a very large number of ways. At this level of abstraction, to the extent that the two relationships are the same, there are not two different things in two places. There's only one relationship and they're both it. If we're going to talk about relationships instead of about things, then all our talk about what exists, what's prior to what, and so on, just has to be rethought completely. I mean this first interpretation of that statement of mine to relate to many of the things we've said about how errors get in, since the way in which something is coded determines the kind of errors you can get. We can't relate to anything unless we can express its complexity through the diversity that is ourselves." We err through a mismatch between ourselves and the other, and all our falsehoods are falsehoods about ourselves as well.

"Okay, the second thing that I want to mean by my sentence," I went on, "brings us to the edge of a lot of more anthropological and psychoanalytic ideas. See, most of the ways in which we mutilate the environment and muck up systems have to do with things that we dislike about ourselves. Like death. Yesterday, we asked Bert what there is that one might worship. Now I've tried to say that the whole possibility of our dealing with complexity at all has to do with the complexity that is within ourselves. We are extraordinarily beautiful and intricate beings, sets of relationships. If we could see ourselves in the intricacy that we are, not just the little bit that comes into consciousness, we would be, I think, worthy of that worship, because that's the only way we can love or worship anything else. This is different from the idea of Renaissance man or of Superman or all the other ways in which people have made an idolatry of themselves, ways that don't include all of the complexity. But, if we include, about ourselves, all of the intricacy, all of the cycling, all of the being born and dying on various scales, right down to the processes Barry has described in our cells, we have a position from which to love other persons equally complicated, or an ecosystem, or anything else.

"I'd like just to refer here, without spelling it all out, to a whole lot of stuff about the relationship between body image and the way you see the world, the relationship between the rhythms in our bodies and the way we deal with the world. This is partly where Bernie's stuff comes in, because his films of mothers and babies in the Azores have to do with how a sense of oneself and very often dislikes of bits of oneself are built up and mapped out on the rest of the world. I mean—this is now to move to a very crude example—if we learn as tiny infants to hate the fact that we defecate, we're going to set up 'Eradicate Stinkbugs' campaigns when we grow up. Then a great many of our machines reflect the dislike of ourselves that we learned: if we invent a machine that will play chess better, we are making a judgment back on what we are for and what we don't like about the way we live up to it. Another example: Peter and I were talking the other day about what it might mean for human adaptation if you blotted out the emotional irregularities that go with the female menstrual cycle, changing the experience women have of their bodies; one of the things that you would be blotting out is a diversity that may be the basis of responding to some other kind of diversity. Most important, I keep feeling that one of the crucial moral questions that is around, made more urgent because of medical developments, is the question of willingness to die. The human willingness or unwillingness to die has a tremendous amount to do with how we define life and where we feel we can cut into natural cycles. All right—so that, very blurred, very allusive, is my second meaning of 'Each person is his own central metaphor.' " Of all the cycles we deny and distort, the denial of our own return to the soil, when we extrapolate ourselves into eternity, sets us most at odds with our turning world.

"All right. Then the third thing that I mean by 'Each person is his own central metaphor' is theological. I object passionately to a representation of the Christian view that says that at a *point* in time something happened, that the Christ event is a point. The life of a person is a process; Jesus lived a life that had birth at the beginning and death at the end of it. The potential usefulness of talking about that person—the way in which our feelings about that person can influence the way we treat other persons or the ecosystem or society—has to do with how much person we are willing to let into our metaphor, because we need religion to make us aware of process. If we can tolerate our humanness, we can tolerate his humanness, and vice versa. (Hardly anyone does, they paint pictures which imply that he didn't sweat. If he didn't sweat, he's no use to us!) He can become a projection of the degree to which we refuse to look at our own humanness as a way of relating, or he can become an insistent parable that says to me that the only thing that I am is my whole life, a person—that directs me to go on looking back at the whole life of persons, including the motions of the cells. So this is the third thing that I want to mean when I say that 'Each person is his own central metaphor,' as giving us a basis for extending that metaphor in wider and wider ways.

"Now, the question of consciousness brings up the fact that we have incomplete access to the complexity that we are. We've blocked a great deal of it out. In a Freudian sense, we've blocked it out by rejecting it. We also—it eludes us, it's too fine-grained, we're just not organized to be aware of it. One reason why poetry is important for finding out about the world is because in poetry a set of relationships get mapped onto a level of diversity in us that we don't ordinarily have access to. We bring it out in poetry. We can give to each other in poetry the access to a set of relationships in the other person and in the world that we're not usually conscious of in ourselves. So we need poetry as knowledge about the world and about ourselves, because of this mapping from complexity to complexity."

"May I ask a question out of ignorance as to exactly what you mean?" said Warren. "In a certain sense, Socrates began as a zygote and ended as a corpse. In another sense, somebody says something and I say, 'Aha, Socrates!' Right? Now, when I say 'Aha, Socrates!' I'm referring to the relations among the events that began as that zygote and ended as that corpse. Is that right?"

"Yes."

"Now you say it takes poetry to bring it out. It certainly does."

"I want to add another thing that has to do with this business about poetry," I said. "Daddy, you talked about seeing an ecosystem as beautiful. Now, when we say we can see it as beautiful, that may be the only way that we can talk about the fact that we've perceived a set of relationships in it."

"And in ourselves."

"And in ourselves. That's the point. They have to be in ourselves to see them in it."

"Now I'm not sure if I understand how a relationship that's *here* comes to be a relationship that's *there* as well," said Bert. "It doesn't start that way. We take something that belongs to nature and we open ourselves to it. It comes to us. Or are you suggesting that it is in both places?"

"No, we don't *take* it."

Bert set out to explain what he felt was a more usual theological understanding. He drew two lines on the board and then amended the diagram so that one would be larger than the other, God and Man. (Barry suggested that Bert put whiskers on God.) Bert proceeded to define his concept of God as "a way of saying nature, all nature, or rather all being and the possibilities of all being. God is simply the largest and most embracing idea that's possible for human beings." It seemed to me that in saying that God was nature, Bert was invoking a somewhat different concept of nature from the one he had used in speaking of the man-nature dichotomy.

"Now, the Christian theological notion is that man is finite.

He's small and he's humble. He and God aren't partners in the universe, and all learning goes from God to man. All we've got is a capacity to be open, to see there's a light that we can receive, something that is not ourselves, so that there is a meeting between a finite human existence and an infinite universal one."

Gregory said, "Bert, I think these entities of yours are a little lonely. Could you give them a tree?"

"Now I'm not sure I know what you mean; where does that come from?"

"Well, there seem to be trees around, you know, and I want to know what God has to do with how man sees the tree or how the tree sees the man." To see the tree as a god or as a woman, as a dryad, is a more accurate way of looking at a tree than our usual casual attitude that treats it as a separate and static object. Like a woman, a tree grows, interacts with its environment, and dies. To anthropomorphize the tree gives us access to a certain truth about it, and the same is true when we anthropomorphize the orderly and unfolding process of the universe.

"Well," said Bert with forbearance, "if you think of man, we understand fairly well; then we think of everything else, everything that's other than ourselves, as God."

"The tree is God, but man is not?"

"God is the tree, other people, everything. As far as we're concerned, this is the situation of ourselves facing that which is not ourselves. Now in Catherine's image, the self looks out and what it sees is something like itself. That seems to me—well, it's out of line with my theological understanding. Kierkegaard talks at one point of the King—that's God—and the humble maiden. The humble maiden of herself can't do anything, but the King looks at her and loves her, He really does. He's a very nice king and what He does is He decides that she should choose Him freely, so he takes off His kingly clothes and He presents himself in the aspect of a humble young man. What He really wants is to give her a chance out of her own will to choose Him, rather than sort of appearing in a blinding flash."

"Would you choose yourself?" I asked. "I mean—well,

that's exactly what I mean. I think a great deal of what faith is about is being able to choose yourself."

"Well, the only point I wanted to make is that there is a theological understanding that isn't what you said. Now I don't know who has the superior claim, but, at least in Kierkegaard's terms, the religious act is to choose God, not self."

"They're not necessarily different, because relationships aren't in one place rather than another. The religious act is choosing self *and* God rather than a part of self. If God's a 'thing,' and you're a 'thing,' you can have competition, you can choose one or the other. But we don't deal with 'things,' whether tables or God, but with relationships. Now lots of people want to stop saying God is a thing and say God is a metaphor and we'll be things. I won't go along with that either."

"Well, okay, the other sort of notion that appeared in the nineteenth century was that God was the human being's idea."

"That's the other thing I'm not saying. Now you've said both the things I'm not saying!"

"I insist that your view of Christianity, Bert, is rapidly disappearing from the face of the earth," Barry declared.

"Look," I said, "you have a set of events and relationships and so on, which are Christian, they've been called that historically?"

"Christ's life," said Barry.

"Christ's life. Yes, okay. And the process things, like the life of the Church and the sacraments and so on. And then you make up various theologies about them, phrased in the language of your time. Now this is all a matter of language change. Around this table, we've talked about having a language of relationship. How am I going to express what there is in Kierkegaard, what there is in Augustine, and so on, in this relationship language? Not talking about ourselves *or* God as things? Whenever you say one aspect of human life is 'thing,' and something else is 'not thing,' you get nonsense."

Tolly drew himself up. "Ladies and gentlemen, it's getting very late and the nineteenth century is very long ago. I don't myself think in Christian terms, but I would anyhow say, listen to Catherine. We are in desperate need, it seems to me, of a rhetoric of human freedom. I mean, it's apparently been adaptive for mankind to live with very rigid systems. It has been necessary, for people to survive, evidently, to be bound by rigid rituals and conceptions, to have very strict ways of interpreting the signs from heaven, and so on, whether in great empires or in primitive tribes. I think freedom is an extraordinarily complex and relatively new idea on the face of the earth, anyhow. We have slipped to new kinds of mental bondage, you know, science and systems thinking, and 'the efficient,' and the various settings of parameters by which we decide on governmental policies and decide on matters of peace and war—all the rules by which people in the technological society decide how to run their lives and run their committees. And clearly something very, very different from this is desperately needed, and that something-very-different just cannot be what the nineteenth century said; the world has changed."

"May I add a little note on that, Gregory?" said Ted. "With all these statements of theology, I think to respect the diversity of this table, I might make a statement too. It seems to me, in all the talk about humanness and what is dehumanization, that it is very relevant to say 'nothing human is alien to me,' to which we might add, 'or to nature.' By this I mean that I accept within myself everything that we have seen that we're blaming the present mess on. I'm part of it. I can study it in myself. I can study it among all of us and I don't mean that any of us are exempt. I think we have to consider human nature as generating everything that humans have ever done, whether it's cannibalism, perversion, beauty, liberality, racism, or anything else. All these things are human. Perhaps humanization is a continuing process and what we're really doing is looking ahead of ourselves. We haven't yet created, in any thorough or consistent or reliable way, the kind of humanness that we're using as our standard. I for one vote on this humanness-dehumanization business that it had better be a pretty eclectic view, based on the whole repertoire of human behavior—destructive, murderous, spoiling, all the rest of it—and at the same time, project ahead of us what we hope we might be able to do.

"We take a tone very often, I think, of moral distanciation, putting these things apart from ourselves and looking at them, when in fact we could probably find all of the difficulties that have led us to the crisis that this conference is about if we analyzed the conference itself. But we have all agreed on an objective situation. No matter what we do at this conference, it still confronts us. If we decide to be methodological, epistemological, or theological, it's still there confronting us. It's in the air we breathe and the earth we walk on. The fact is that we keep lunging away from this; somebody brings us back to it, and we get away from it again. All of the errors, all of the mechanisms that we have been discussing are operating right here, and we can study them among ourselves."

"Yes," Gregory said, thoughtfully, looking at Ted, "I think it's true that most of what we are talking about on the grand scale involving the whole of nature and the whole of man has been exemplified around this table. I've had a job—sometimes it worked well, sometimes it didn't—of trying to weave the . . . no, trying to *let* weave the fabric of our conversation, so that it would be a small model of the larger thing we're concerned about. Rather frequently, it's become a model of all the false epistemologies we've been talking about; once in a while it's transcended that and got halfway across.

"Now, I think it's worth trying to think about what I would mean if I said, 'Gee, when I gave so-and-so the floor, I made a mistake.' Let us suppose that when so-and-so takes the floor, he tears what a minute previously I had thought was the fabric of our interaction. It's too bad, *but*. The fabrics of interaction are going to be torn and they're going to mend. And after all, we are only a model of what we are trying to talk about, and it would be absolute nonsense to try to construct that model as though it did not contain the tearings of fabric.

"Now the other side of this is the aesthetic problem. By fabric I don't mean just intellectual coherence or something like that, though this is always nice when it happens . . . I had a fantasy once under LSD. I got into LSD research with the intention of thinking about the problems of aesthetic order, as distinct from other sorts of order that we in science are more familiar with. And it took roughly this shape: that the human body is a beautiful thing; in fact, remarkable. I had, I might say, been listening in the same LSD session to *Goldberg Variations* and to other Bach, so this influenced my theory of aesthetics. I said the human body is a beautiful thing, because after all it's a product of evolution. But—wait a moment—it's the genome and not the body that is the product of evolution, and this genome has been subject to millions of reproductive generations in which the organisms did not replicate themselves perfectly, but in which, in fact, they underwent various sorts of transform from this pattern to the next evolutionary pattern, which is a transform of the previous one, and you get transforms of transforms and transforms of transforms superposed. And the organism, after all, is only a transform of its genome. Then it seemed to me that aesthetics has something to do with the superposition of multiple transforms.

"Now what would be the opposite of 'the beautiful'? Under LSD, I took as my paradigm for the opposite of 'the beautiful' what is called Still's Lesion. This is the central myth of osteopathy: when the osteopath runs his finger up your spine, he finds a tense point in the successive series of transforms, either in muscular tension or in the anatomical segmentation from vertebra to vertebra or homogeneous muscle set to the next homogeneous muscle set. It is a point at which the gradient of successive transformation is in some way interrupted. He then takes you by the shoulder, puts his foot on your hipbone, and gives a sudden wrench in order to reduce that non-conformity in the series. I took Still's Lesion as the anti-aesthetic thing that disrupts transformational process, communicational process— in this case down a segmental series, because we are segmented animals.

"But then, of course, it's still very mysterious how we manage to perceive beauty. I mean, granted that I had in the abstract accounted for a certain state of the human organism or of other organisms, but still, why do they notice it? And, like Catherine, I took the view that you could represent in your 'think-mechanisms' only that for which you have not merely the appropriate diversity but also the appropriate patterning to receive the representation—so I observed that man himself is a segmented organism. (This doesn't quite make sense; you've got to remember I was under LSD the whole time, and I'm really only giving you a parable of a parable.) Man being a segmented organism, and the segmentation series being itself a successive transform of transforms of transforms running down the series, this made it perfectly reasonable to expect that this organism, which had these transform complexes and series embodied in its segmentation, would therefore be an appropriate organism to receive the information that another organism was beautiful.

"I then proceeded to consider what controls we might get on this theory and raised the question, well now, what about the unsegmented organisms? The principal group of course is the mollusca. When you begin to consider the mollusca, you observe that they do not have secondary sex characters, with the exception of the cephalopods, which perhaps we could say are repetitive creatures—that's the cuttlefish and some others. That is, the unsegmented organisms are not able to use beauty as a mechanism for sexual attraction. Well, I leave the theory with you. There are some objections to the end of it, because of course almost all the gasteropods are hermaphrodite, and . . . their eyes are very poor."

We laughed, but Gertrude was looking very perplexed. "May I present a communication-block problem? It's about this word 'metaphor.' Up to about twenty years ago, I had a pretty clear referent for it, but when I come to 'Each person is his own central metaphor,' I want to know if the word 'metaphor' is a metaphor."

"Yes. Yes and no."

"Well, are we throwing away the use of the word that refers to using some kind of symbolic representation of similarity by referring to one as if it were the other? When I said the other day that Peter had put words into my mouth that I must spit out before I had coffee, I was talking in metaphorical language, is that right? The whole thing is a metaphor. Now, 'I am my own central metaphor'—I'm completely blocked to get to that. I've been running into that word in contexts that confused me now for the last twenty years."

Gregory set out to try and explain his understanding of the notion of metaphor to Gertrude, set in the context of a theory of the natural history of the human mind. It was curious to hear him explaining to her in particular, since what he was describing was the general case of her own work and of Bernie's, the establishment of contextual regularities at a very deep level of the mind, patterns that are then applied to new items as they occur in life, as the mathematical operation of squaring, say, can be applied to new operands. "You have experiences of one kind or another, and certain regularities in the experiences get pickled in your brain and probably other parts. You do not merely aggregate the detailed information. You have not only learned that on Monday the cigarettes were there and on Tuesday there were some matches there and on Wednesday there was something else there, but you've also learned some rather complex generalizations about the position of things in the universe; you organize this information, so that propositions about patterns get recorded. Now, some propositions about patterns of experience, often experiences involving your own action, such as 'Dependency pays off' or 'Greed pays off,' quite obviously get pickled at a new level, different from where you handle propositions about detail. Warren the other day was talking about context being an operator. Now, I think what I'm trying to say is that while the operands get stored in one place, the operators get stored somewhere else. Their kind of truth, you see, is much longer enduring than the operands, because they are generalizations of some kind.

"When, for example, you dream, what actually happens is that you drop out the functioning of the apparatus that handled the operands and leave in the functioning of the apparatus that handled the operators. Therefore, you construct patterns of dependency, or whatever it is, in dreams, and fill the slots in those patterns with what would, in the first instance, look like inappropriate operands—in other words, you construct metaphors, the metaphor being a chunk with a certain structure inside it, corresponding, we'll say, to a chunk of nature. You can dream, let us say, about the matches in the ashtray as a metaphoric representation of a baby at mother's breast. Now the gimmick about metaphors, of course, is that although you don't have to be asleep to produce metaphors, when you are asleep you can produce practically nothing else, and this was Freud's central discovery. This leads to the curious situation that, in waking life, you've got to represent somehow not just your top levels of thinking and perception, but also rather deeper things, less 'conscious' things—and what happens is that items of your daily life become outward and visible metaphors of the patterns of deep traumata in the past."

Gregory often quotes Pascal's aphorism, *"Le cœur a ses raisons que la raison ne connaît point."* There is a tendency to oppose the structures of conscious—even verbal—thought to the processes of other parts of the mind, particularly the emotions, and yet the entire nervous system, the hormonal system, and in fact the entire body can be said to think: these complex systemic organizations pursue goals, respond adaptively to differences, and transform inputs into new forms. Freud argued that conscious behavior is constantly being influenced by a deeper thought; when we wish to explore the relationship between conscious thought and other processes of computation, the deep reasoning of the body or of an ecosystem, we need to know the differences between the ways they compute. Biological systems in general compute analogically, with pattern, while the conscious mind has access to digital processes, including the possibility of negation. "At whatever level it is in your mind that the operators are stored," Gregory continued, "at that level there is no *not*, there is what's called primary-process thinking, so that if you represent the Body and Blood with the bread and the wine, that level of your brain is just not concerned with saying that wine is wine and blood is blood, but the wine is not the Blood. The Catholic view of the sacrament, which asserts an identity between the wine and the Blood, is the way that level of your mind functions. If you become a Protestant and protest that the wine has no corpuscles in it, you are talking, from a Catholic point of view, complete nonsense. On the other hand, you are making a wide general statement about the nature of man and about yourself—namely, you are asserting, as a Protestant, 'I am going to handle my religion totally at a conscious level.' This excludes from your religion about three-quarters of yourself, because you aren't all at the conscious level, and you create, in fact, a secular religion."

Gertrude was still bewildered. Horst explained, "See, the sacrament is a simile in the Protestant—or rather the Calvinist —tradition, not a metaphor."

"But they still use the same words. There's just an agreement among the sects that this is not the Body."

"If you dream of having words put into your mouth, there will be no agreement that you didn't spit."

"For years and years I haven't been able to remember any of the dreams I have, so that doesn't help me either. But I don't see how this hooks up with what Catherine was talking about when she was talking about a relationship being in two places. Now that makes no sense to me. A relationship between two things requires both of these things together and also my awareness of it."

Gregory held up two match boxes, slightly different shades of blue. "Gertrude, can you see the difference between those two boxes?"

"Yes."

"Where is the difference?"

"Well, I think it's there as well as in my perception of them, of course."

"You can say it is both in your perception and there. But of course it's not localized over here?"

"It's not in the one box," Gertrude sang. "It's not in the other box."

"If I bring them together I should be able to pinch it?"

"No . . . the relation is there even when the boxes are apart."

"Agreed."

"Well, the relation exists," Gertrude affirmed. "That's my view. And I keep slipping off the communication track of this. If it does exist, if there is a mirror of it of some kind up here that I have, and if my awareness of it is *it*, that's one view. If I'm talking like the mathematician Hardy about the world, why, I think the thing's there for me to become aware of."

"I was just going to add, keep in mind that the *box* isn't in the box either," said Tolly.

"Quite. Quite."

Tolly stretched way back in his chair and grinned. "Yeah. And I feel that there's been a noticeable reduction in the rate of word production today, which has been connected with a notable increase in the rate of meaning production. Ted and some others perhaps feel a certain impatience with the area that we've drifted into. We're rather far removed from the comfortable home ground of analyzing and 'understanding' in the way in which scientists always understand, but I feel it's really a good thing that the conference has been focusing attention on these very delicate religious or quasi-religious areas, in addition to looking at what is happening with the nitrogen cycle and what is true about ecologies and what messages should be broadcast to the people of the United States or the people of the world, so as to arouse their concern over the imminent destruction of themselves. In a way I feel as if the paper that I didn't write, a portion of which I read the first day, is a kind of prophecy for the conference.

"At the risk of trying your patience, I just want to make one more remark which may seem all but totally unrelated. I've had a sort of funny image of a new kind of music that could be produced in the world, which of course has to do with occurrence systems, as very much that I do does. You know, occurrence systems are another way of creating pictures and patterns and these, in a funny way, are related to music.

"In any case, I have the image of a kind of music with a lot of concurrence in it, relative to one or perhaps some larger number of observers. Now, you know, we have an audience that sits in a concert hall and up front is an orchestra. There are plenty of acoustical effects whereby what a guy hears in one corner of a room is not quite the same as what somebody in another corner of the room hears, but you generally try to even things out. In concept, the idea is that everybody hears the same thing and all the parts are progressing synchronously. Anyway, can you imagine a kind of music that really has concurrence? Where there is a whole lot going on concurrently, which nevertheless is aesthetic and has musical relation, but no one observer can hear it all at once? Right? I mean, if he could, it wouldn't be concurrence. And all you can do at any one time is to focus on some part. Perhaps you can imagine being able to wander in this musical web. You could turn knobs or something to move about in this space. And indeed, a number of different people could wander about in this space and perhaps even meet each other there. Well, that's about all."

Gregory asked, "That with music was a metaphor about this conference? Or about the world in which we live? Or both?"

"In my mind, anyhow, it relates to the remark that I made about the need for a new kind of rhetoric of freedom. It's an extraordinary fact in my mind that this whole idea of concurrence is so totally new and unaccustomed. I'm once more trying to ring a gong, which will no doubt reverberate differently in different heads."

We talked about some experiments similar to this in music or with lights, where no one person can experience the whole at once. Barry said, "There ought to be some kind of contrapuntal relationship between the singing, the nitrogen cycle, and the cargo cults, and the stuff going on in somebody's head. Perhaps the only way that you can become convinced of the importance of this kind of complexity that we've all been grappling with is to learn how to move in that landscape, so that you sense what I at least have sensed in this conference, that there is a common song being sung. Even the striking differences are common. I don't know whether you'd call this music or religion or science. This is the music that's required for social reform."

"It can work the other way too," Ted warned. "The Manus tried to explain to themselves why there were fifty-seven missionary orders and sects that had come to New Guinea to proselytize them. Well, not exactly fifty-seven, that's Heinz's varieties, but it was something like that. Their explanation is that this was a conspiracy to divide the truth, that is, to put it into concurrence, so that no matter which sect you joined, you only got a part of it. Concurrence can mean, in fact, that many of us will have too partial views of things. I think one of the things you're offering, Tolly, is a music in which we're not stuck in one of those concurrent strands, so that we can move back and forth.''

That afternoon, in the last hours of the conference, with the question of a final harmony still unanswered, Gregory agreed to open. "We all knew it before we came, but one of the most impressive things that has been explored here is the long historic roots of these pathologies. It came out very clearly, in the conversation between Bert and Barry, that at one of the highest moments of European civilization, in Leonardo, the premises related to what is bothering us were rather clearly crystallized. That moment of crystallization may even be historically related to the enormous efflorescence of civilization at that time. God knows. Obviously the stuff goes back a great deal further than that. There has been a long, progressive increase in complexity, an interweaving of mutual dependencies, values that it was thought good to maximize, various sorts of caution and tact that were thought good to preserve, weaving along to the situation we now see. Now there are certain things—the atom bomb, the destruction of the soil, the population explosion—we can run down half a dozen more, no doubt—that seem to push us toward immediate action at the panic points; by 'us,' I mean partly this group here in this room, partly all men of good will throughout the world.

"You know, good will is an awfully dangerous thing to have. I'm terrified of it. I think one of the things that has come out most clearly in our deliberations has been that, while these particular points are legitimate points of crisis and panic and all that, the etiology of the condition has nothing in particular to do with them. If a steam engine with a governor goes off on a runaway, it may blow the flywheel to pieces. But if the engineer looks at it and says, 'Gee, that flywheel isn't strong enough, we ought to strengthen it,' this is poor and temporary therapy. The problem is to change the sign of the gain in the system, whatever formal phrasings you may want for that.

"It is in that position that we face a problem of the status and functions of this conference. I would go on very determinedly, or perhaps I should say stubbornly, in favor of making more, as may be possible, of the sort of advances which we have made in this room. I feel personally that if my 'understanding' were evaluated at about 10 per cent before I came to Burg Wartenstein, I may have doubled my understanding of something which in general remains almost totally mysterious. There's a well-known story of Bertrand Russell and Whitehead, which I think is related to the thing that Tolly referred to, this tragic desire of man to think he understands things. Russell had been Whitehead's student and collaborator on the *Principia* and, when Whitehead had gone to Harvard, Russell came to give a lecture in one of the big auditoria, on a hot August night, and all the professors and the professors' wives turned out to hear the great man. The great man lectured on the quantum theory, which has never been a very easy subject and in its early stages was probably more difficult even than it is now."

Warren shook his head. "It's getting worse."

"All right, that does happen in civilizations. Russell labored to make the matter clear to the wives and the professors and finally sat down sweating. Then little Whitehead rose to his feet, with his falsetto voice, 'to thank Professor Russell,' he squeaked, 'for his brilliant exposition and especially . . . for leaving unobscured . . . the vast darkness of the subject.' Now, the temptation in our position at the present time, vis-à-vis this enormously complex set of problems, is to grab quick, quick, but *quick*, at anything that will obscure the darkness of the subject and, above all, give us something to do, preferably with our larger muscles. There's a very high probability that we will walk precisely into just those operations that fall into place as part of this whole system and increase by a negligible fraction the rate at which the world is approaching hell.

"I think, on the other hand, that in this group we have developed certain ideas which are of first-class importance. Several of these come out of Barry's analyses. Much of it comes out of Tolly, both his formal analyses and his passionate statements. Others have come out of, oh, one thinks of 'the person as his own central metaphor,' Attneave's presentation of the interlocking factors going toward hell, and so on. I think our achievement is perhaps not so much any one of the points that stand out, but their juxtaposition in our conversation. I blew my top a little when Ted and Barry wanted to go toward action (or whatever they wanted to go toward, which I didn't really understand anyway). I think the thing that most frightened me was the feeling that, as you go toward action, what you in fact do is lose the understanding gained from the interlocking of the various things that have been said, the extra value that those things had by virtue of being said in the same conversation with each other. I would hope that we might somehow preserve that. As you précis, as you make policy and such things, you obscure the vast darkness of the subject and you obscure the very real elegance and significance of the interlocking plexus. I think the first value that I would want to maximize (if maximization of values is not always immoral—I don't know) would be the preservation of that in our deliberations.

"I think I've said what I want to say as an opening statement about us. Will Jones has asked to speak about the status and nature of our conference, so let me ask him to start."

"Well, I'm really not sure whether what I'm going to say will be disruptive."

"It doesn't matter," said Gregory, "we can stand it."

"Yes, I know, but I'd rather it weren't. You see, I've made a discovery about what I think the conference is about. When I came, I remarked that I was puzzled about why I was here. I've remained puzzled, in a way increasingly puzzled and uncomfortable. Then suddenly, as a result of some talk yesterday evening with Catherine and with Bernie, it occurred to me what the conference is about, and this was kind of a new light to me. This conference is different from any conference I've been to before, but I've tended to try and see it in terms of the con-

ceptual framework in which I've perceived other conferences."
Will smiled apologetically.

Gregory laughed. "Poor man!"

"Well, you see, Gregory, I think the conference isn't about
any particular thing. It isn't about Barry's nitrogen cycle which
I thought it was about for a while, it isn't about cybernetics, or
about Gertrude's non-verbal learning . . . these were all pen-
nants, banners that I saw displayed. It's about the effects of
consciousness on purposive behavior!" We roared with laughter.
"Well, that's what it says it's about, but it's about it in a different sort of way. What this wretched man has done is to put us
here, a set of conscious people with their own purposes, and
seen whether these wretched, rather hard-programmed pieces of
hardware were going to get together in some sort of system with
relatively little pathology. So it didn't matter so much to you,
Gregory, where it came out, or which hill it charged up. So you
see, just on the eve of the disappearance of the whole thing, I've
had this sudden revelation."

"We are our own metaphor," Gregory nodded.

"Um. Well, so I too have a banner, and the device on my
banner, I think, is not too much overcommitment. I think a
certain amount of detachment . . ."

Very softly, "No," said Gregory.

"Oh. Well. May I?"

"Yes, I'm sorry. I was just thinking about how much passion
there has been in this room. I think the passion has been one of
the major things that's contributed."

"I quite agree. But you see I think that I'm probably as
committed to detachment as you all are committed to overcommitment. I associate detachment, you see, with consciousness. I don't know just where the balance is, but some sort of
detachment seems to be desirable, because it prevents the kind
of closure and fixation on a particular version of a situation
that is likely to get one into trouble. This is precisely what happened with my view of the conference: I was overcommitted,
you see, to my original notion of what conferences ought to be.
I may be quite wrong about this, but this is the way I perceive

some of what's been going on in the conference—overcommitment, I guess by all of us, to different metaphysical realisms.
I think this explains why, as I think, Bert was systematically
misunderstood by quite a number of people. And so this is my,
this is my banner—less overcommitment, some detachment.
With it, I will follow along, grumbling all the while."

Barry plunged in. "I think I agree with everything you said
as it refers to an individual consciousness cum behavior. But
I do not agree that the consciousness of this system, the conference, is any kind of sum of the individual consciousness.
You ask for something that's impossible, in any individual:
commitment with the detachment that will provide the correctives on one's view. I don't think it's possible. I do think it is
possible to build the correctives that lead to the detachment into
a system of this sort, so that this group is then a synthetic
entity, a system capable of both commitment and detachment."

"That's what I meant by saying I would come along behind."

We had spoken about the relationship between individual
consciousness and membership in larger groups in several different contexts. There was Gregory's indictment of the kind of
groups in which people participate as part-persons, either as
members of the board, with their heads sticking up above the
boardroom table and their feet blurred beneath; or in encounter
groups, in which clarity and the capacity for self-criticism are
lost in the search for emotional communion. Groups of these
kinds, including most conferences, make the kind of decisions or
elaborate the kind of epistemologies that endanger the world.
In the last few days, out of the depth of our commitment and
the love or anger we felt toward each other, we had begun to
be a group of whole persons, some plunging in fully with full
feeling and thought, while others still moved gingerly in this
new kind of environment.

Here was a partial answer to the problem posed in Fred's
presentation, when he had asserted that man's failure to limit
his reproduction is due to the fact that mankind is not conscious,
only individuals are conscious. A sense of shared consciousness
in a small group might be the beginning of a model for patterns

of communication that will one day allow us to speak of mankind as a whole as conscious, patterns for which we already have many of the tools.

Barry went on elaborating the meaning he saw in our increasing convergence: "It's the emergence of this entity that to me provides the foundation for realism. To me, something can be defended as 'real' if it withstands or interacts effectively with some other individual view. This suggests that we ought to look toward our willingness to enter our individual consciousness into the system comprised by this new kind of organism. We have to ask ourselves whether in some way we can understand the world and act on it better, with passion and commitment, through becoming an organ in such an organism, if you like, than we can by ourselves. I think the brilliance of Gregory's move is that he sensed the need of a new kind of 'thinking beast' in order to cope with the crisis that the world is in."

"We're awfully close to the things Pask wants to talk about," said Gregory.

I was full of misgivings as Gordon pursed his lips, straightened the papers in front of him on the table and began to speak, with a small precise cough. It seemed to me that we had passed the time for presentations and should be evaluating our results and preparing for our farewells. We already shared a feeling of poignancy, expecting to end in a few hours and scatter across Europe and back to the United States, and yet Gordon, who had had to be absent from some of our most crucial sessions, was not fully a part of that feeling. Yet when Gordon finished, I felt that he had provided a final essential link in our discussion. He started out by re-emphasizing the exponential nature of population growth.

"Now, the point I want to make is this," he continued. "I don't think that you could ever say that individuals should not reproduce. It would seem to me an essential part of the notion 'consciousness' that an individual is that which wants to reproduce or perpetuate itself, and yet, in the naive interpretation, the only way for an individual to reproduce is to go out, be fertile, and have children. I don't think we can say 'thou shalt not want to go on,' but it is evident that we have somehow to persuade people not to do it in this way. In other words, I think it inevitable that we have got to persuade them to think of individuality as something distinct from the biological head to which it is attached. This is why I think it is important to consider an alternative interpretation of the notion of individual. It could be phrased in a variety of ways. I phrase it from the point of view of a 'philosophical mechanic'; that is to say . . ."

"A philosophical . . . ?"

"Mechanic. You see," said Gordon fiercely, wheeling toward Tolly, "I am a mechanic. Whether you like it or not, Tolly, I am a mechanic, and I'll tell you why. I used to go around speaking at conferences and things, and because I'm a very bad mathematician, in order to support my point of view, I used to make a machine that embodied it and take it with me.

"Now, if you think in mechanical terms, you can think of a population of general-purpose computers called 'brains,' in which, given a suitable programming language (perhaps a system very similar to the one you have described, Tolly), it is possible to run classes of programs. Now, we are at liberty to redefine an individual, looking from this sort of mechanical point of view, as being not one head, one particular general-purpose computing machine, but one named class of programs. And we can interpret the reproduction of this named class of programs, not at all in a biological sense, but in the sense of reproducing and perhaps evolving a class of programs bearing the same name. This is consonant with the motive of the individual to reproduce himself, it does not introduce the problem of overpopulating the world with general-purpose machines, and it does allow for the perpetuation of the individual and the proper interpretation of the term 'consciousness,' as an in-built wish to reproduce that which specifies *me*.

"This isn't, of course, such a strange point of view, because although you may be offended, mildly, if I call you a class of programs, you would really be equally offended if I insisted that you lived inside your heads, at least you should be. Isn't it evident that you are distributed through a lot of these general-purpose machines? Don't you love? Don't you dislike? Don't you take part in the self-images of other people? Don't you interact in this unity we were talking about a moment ago, which weds the consciousness together? If you do, you are saying that you partake of the nature of a class of programs. This is simply a statement of that fact."

"Did you want to say something, Peter?" asked Gregory, noticing Peter suddenly and urgently leaning forward.

"Yes. This is one of the most elegant statements I've heard yet of the way in which the system we call 'natural selection' defines the individual. This was alluded to in a little section on altruism in my preprint, but until this moment I thought it was totally irrelevant. I had raised the question of how natural selection can allow the development of a trait, like altruism, that leads to what we would say, in our usual language, involves the self-destruction of the individual. Well, in point of fact, if that self-destruction, say of a mother, allows for the survival of more than one of her offspring, from the standpoint of her genotype, which is that program that you referred to, her fitness has been increased. So since natural selection is working in this way, obviously the individual in evolutionary terms is not the corporeal entity of the head; it's the genotype. The work that's been done on the evolution of altruism, I think, is the nicest empirical support for your statement that I know."

Bert was perplexed and turned again to Gordon. "I'm not sure . . . what are these individuals?"

"Classes of programs."

"Now just say one or two more words about examples of that?"

"Well, I use the word program to designate any well-defined 'formula for' or class of 'formulae for,' with the possibility of having underspecified goals in it; in other words, it's a heuristic procedure. I refer to the individual as a class of 'formulae for . . . me,' where 'me' is my name. And the important point about this is that these 'formulae for' might be run in any convenient machine, including the brain . . . including *your* brain. In a sense there are two parallel sorts of evolution: there is

biological evolution going on, and then, because of this interpretation of the individual, one can perceive a separate sort of
evolution that I refer to as 'symbolic evolution,' which is perhaps exemplified by this conference. To avoid overpopulating
the world with general-purpose machines, what we have to do
is to control the symbolic evolution process. To do so, I believe
that the first thing we must do is redefine what we mean by an
individual, get away from this idea of individuals as heads. We
can't get away—I don't want to get away—from the idea *I*,
my class of programs. We've got somehow to get away from
the idea that that class is in one-to-one correspondence with this
apparatus on my shoulders and the apparatus attached to it."

"Gordon, I agree with you entirely in principle on your
major point here," said Fred. "I would like to haul you back a
little bit to the earlier point that you can't tell people not to
reproduce. I don't think that's been proposed by anybody—
rather, telling them, 'Don't reproduce so much.' Isn't that an
important distinction?"

"It's quite an important one, but I think it would be equally
difficult to tell them this. Why do people reproduce? Well, they
reproduce because they wish to secure themselves a footing in
the world of images and symbols in which they primarily live,
and people will produce as many children as they feel will give
them this footing, will perpetuate them. Now I submit that they
don't need to produce any children at all; they might think they
do, but they don't, in order to do just that. And of course, there
are certain types of psyche who feel this anyhow, who feel sure
of their footing in history by creative activity."

Gregory quoted Samuel Butler:

> Not on sad Stygian shore, nor in clear sheen
> Of far Elysian plain, shall we meet those
> Among the dead whose pupils we have been . . .
> Yet meet we shall, and part, and meet again,
> Where dead men meet, on lips of living men.[1]

Tolly had been waiting for a chance to comment. "I have
quite a lot of respect for what Gordon has said, since it seems
to me to reflect what most of us think and what most cultures

have stood for as well, although I have to register my own divergence from it. All of you will probably remember the disaster that took place in Florence with the floods and the great damage that was done to those stored artworks. I had very mixed feelings about it. I thought, from a certain point of view, that it could well be regarded as good rather than bad; that is—yes, it's an occasion for mourning, but on the other hand, it also makes room. You know, there can be only so many masterpieces in the world, quite apart from the physical space in which they're stored, and new masterpieces must be produced, ones whose relations to your old masterpieces are perhaps hard to understand."

Gregory lifted up the blackboard eraser. "You can't live without this."

"Yes, that's right."

"Which is death."

"That's right. You know, the Hapsburgs, for example, accumulated their bodies in a crypt in order at a certain level to insure the continuity of them. You might argue it was a sort of primitive way of doing it. Given Gordon's idea and given that everyone would see his individuality that way, there would be better and cleverer ways of doing it. I don't see my own progeny as the perpetuation of me, at least I don't believe I do."

"I wouldn't swear to that," Gregory muttered.

"I won't swear, but I have to speak what I think anyway. I see it as connected with me, but I see it as a step in my own death and I see what comes out of it as something really different. I think I'm being altogether honest when I say, profound as is my personal commitment to occurrence systems, let us say, I recognize that they must die. They should not survive forever, even if you relativize forever to some sort of practical forever, like as long as our earth rotates around the sun. They too must make way for something else.

"There are perhaps several different directions philosophically in which one could go. One could become more sophisticated in the way Gordon suggests, about what it means for me to continue, so that I don't build vaults any more, or pyramids. But perhaps there is a way of understanding life as in its nature transitory, just as in my theory an arrow is the pairing of a beginning and an end. And since I have the floor, I just want to add one more remark. This is not absolutely in line with what we're now saying, but I was brought to think a little bit, while Gordon was talking, about my comment of yesterday about people's passion for cosmic certainty. They are not satisfied with evincing cosmic certainty. They have to have it!"

We laughed. Gregory leaned forward. "May I make a personal remark, Tolly?" he said. "I think, of all the people that I know, you are the most reproductive in the particular sense that Pask is talking about. Right at the core of your love, not only for your children but also for other people, is the desire to transmit . . . programs. What have you been doing around here, teaching us your games?"

"No doubt. Absolutely no doubt. I mean, that's biology. That's perfectly true."

"Love in your life means the transmission of programs."

"I want in, Gregory," said Warren.

"All right."

Warren was speaking very slowly. "I am by nature a warrior and wars don't make any sense anymore. I am a king, but I'm an anarchist, and in my country, there are simply no laws, not even this one. I went to work modeling the structure of water in tendon. We went out and bought a bunch of jellybeans and toothpicks and modeled the water. And then I found that I had to write on the blackboard, 'The jellybeans are not to be eaten,' and it wasn't until then that I understood why the Pythagorians had a law against eating beans. Now, the difficulty is that we, who are not single-cell organisms, cannot simply divide and pass on our programs. We have to couple and there is behind this a second requirement." Warren began to weep. "We learn . . . that there's a utility in death because . . . the world goes on changing and we can't keep up with it. If I have any disciples, you can say this of every one of them, they think for themselves."

Very softly Gregory said, "Sure, Warren."

"Freedom from and freedom for." We sat in silence for a long pause. "Coffee?" said Warren.

# AFTERWORD 1991

Participants in conferences commonly want to meet again. When our group began to talk about doing so, Lita Osmundsen agreed to support a new conference in 1969 with the title "The Moral and Aesthetic Structure of Human Adaptation." For although Gregory had been pessimistic about the usefulness of political action, he had considered other possible kinds of correctives. He had written to us before the first meeting in Martin Buber's terms of the possibility of love—of "I-Thou" rather than "I-It" relations, not only between persons but also between persons and a society or an ecosystem. "The arts, poetry, music, and the humanities," he went on, "similarly are areas in which more of the mind is active than mere consciousness would admit. *'Le coeur a ses raisons que la raison ne connait point'*. . . . Contact between man and animals and between man and the natural world breeds, perhaps— sometimes—wisdom. . . . [and] There is religion." All of these ideas are reflected in the quotation from the Book of Job with which he had concluded his charge to us.

The second conference when it was convened, however, had a rather different membership and was not really a continuation of the first.* Thus, many of the questions posed

*Gregory's paper setting the theme for that second conference is anthologized in *Further Steps to an Ecology of Mind,* edited by Rodney Donaldson (Harper,

313

at Burg Wartenstein and reflected in this volume remain with us unresolved, above all the questions of how human patterns of perception and decision might incorporate an understanding of the intricate interdependence of natural systems, and of how to bring about this shift so that what I referred to as cybernetic peace would strike people not as an oxymoron but as a new level of coherence in their thinking.

Over and over again at Burg Wartenstein we implied the need for a unified and widely shared vision, a vision that would be persuasive both intellectually and emotionally, to provide the context for action. But today I wonder whether such an epistemological unification could come about and whether it would not be a denial of the adaptive value of diversity. It was not clear whether new patterns of thought would look more like science or more like religion, or, as I increasingly believe, like a new pattern of inherently diverse information exchange and decision making, a new mode of conversation toward which we were feeling our way when we met.

The idea of paradigm shift has been important in the last two decades and has sometimes been seen as a solution. It came out of Thomas Kuhn's 1962 book, *The Structure of Scientific Revolutions*, which describes how one paradigm gradually becomes tattered while scientists still cling to it and then very rapidly is replaced by the simplifying power of a new synthesis. In popular thinking, paradigm shift, a concept developed to describe the history of science, has become curiously entangled with notions of enlightenment or conversion. Someday, according to this view, we will achieve some-

1991), along with a draft afterword by Gregory for a new edition of this book proposed some years ago. Some of the discussions of religion and aesthetics planned for the second conference are picked up, after long delay, in *Angels Fear,* jointly authored by Gregory and myself and published in 1987. In terms of Gregory's intellectual development, the most immediate outgrowth of the conference on conscious purpose and human adaptation was his paper "The Cybernetics of 'Self': A Theory of Alcoholism," which came out of our post-conference conversations. The period from 1968 to 1971 allowed Gregory to crystallize his sense that his work was basically epistemological, expressed in the Korzybski lecture, "Form, Substance and Difference," and the publication of *Steps to an Ecology of Mind* and *Mind and Nature.*

thing like perfect pitch in our actions in the world, and this wisdom will somehow be recognizable and acknowledged. Such ideas carry considerable retrospective validity, but looked at prospectively they resemble the cargo cult: a trumpet shall sound and we shall be changed in an instant. Implicit in the belief that a new vision will suddenly fall into focus is the assertion, you cannot set a course to there from here, but when you get there you will know the place. We may someday look backward and see that we have arrived; but in the meantime, our faith in paradigm shift, like any apocalyptic hope, may be more of a distraction than a program.

Some members of the conference seemed to feel that the formal analyses of cybernetics would provide a new paradigm, yet the traditional human way of transmitting a unitary vision has in fact been through religion. Early on in our meeting, Warren described our situation as one of those moments when society generates new religions—which Gregory in turn defined as new solutions to the mind-body problem. There has been a great deal of religious search and experimentation since then, yet the different religions remain at odds, while many thoughtful people reject all religious metaphors for describing the world in the conviction that we have available in science a reliable and testable knowledge that can serve that purpose.

To substitute scientific knowledge for religious understanding is, however, to ask more of the discourse of science than it can offer. No individual has what might be called a scientific view of the whole world, only of portions of it; and these, too, are always incomplete. Barry could talk of molecular structure, but he was a stranger in the woods. Those with the greatest reliance on science must take on faith both the knowledge they believe to be vested in other experts, none of them with a complete picture, and the knowledge that will be achieved tomorrow. When it comes to action, we draw only on those areas of science that seem relevant, so science is translated into technology—the fragments of the whole that serve conscious purpose. When we suspect some threat from technology, we can dip into science for counterarguments, but we seem unable to draw from science that unifying vision that must underlie sound decisions. One of the positions taken by the Scientists' Institute for Public Information that Barry described has been that scientists distinguish the limited task of making their particular fragments of knowledge available to the public from advocacy, recognizing that they, like other voters, have only a partial understanding of the whole. The day-to-day work of science, like conscious purpose, depends on highly selective attention.

Religion does offer unifying metaphors, but it is difficult to imagine any particular religion serving as a basis for a world-wide consensus on human responsibility to the planet. Some look back at the religions of small subsistence communities before the advent of literacy and systematic scientific knowledge, when intimacy with the earth and natural forces was necessarily greater and the earth was still enchanted. There is no doubt, for instance, that women today can find in revivals of the Goddess tradition ways to celebrate the earth, or that the poetry and myths of Native Americans can deeply affect the attitudes of seekers from other cultural backgrounds. But this does not mean that, if the communities that developed those ideas had had the practical power and technological capability to abandon them in favor of greater short-term prosperity, they would not have done so. The history of hunting peoples, going back to the Stone Age, suggests that those same preliterate people who lovingly invoke the game, thank the earth for producing it, and ritually welcome its spirits into themselves are nevertheless quite capable, given more powerful technology, of hunting it to extinction. It is not clear that these traditions are sufficient paths today to new understanding. Rather, I believe that their effect depends on contrast, on the impact of exposure to alternative visions.

A very large proportion of humanity identifies itself with one or another of the great universal religions. Where so many have passed, paths are there to be found, and strands of humility and recognition of the sacred immanent throughout the natural world can be discovered even in the most arrogant and other-worldly of religions. In general, however, such visions are to be found not in the popular versions of a given religion like Buddhism or Christianity and not in every experience of them, but in particular, specialized communities. Because each of these traditions provides a model of a unified cosmos, a metaphor of wholeness, a long and intimate experience of one of them may lead to transforming insight. Thus, it is critical that those who know these religions best and believe most deeply search for the elements in their own traditions that sanctify the ongoing life of our earth. Still, no one of these metaphors will serve for all.

There have also been proposals for somehow designing and propagating a new religion, founded perhaps on deep ecology, that provides the right metaphor and the right commandments, inculcates the right humility and respect; but no social engineer can create a religion that will satisfy the range of human needs and individual variations and lead to right action for all. Here, surely, conscious purpose cannot do the job. Indeed, the purposive use of religion is a tool that can turn in the hand.

In recent years, we have seen an effort at synthesis of scientific and poetic formulations in the development of the Gaia Hypothesis that looks at the planet cybernetically as a living—that is, self-regulating—organism. Yet the Gaia Hypothesis has been separated into two streams, a "strong" version that makes scientists nervous because it seems to them to be teleological and a "weak" version that notes various constancies, but treats them piecemeal. There is actually also a third stream in the influence of the hypothesis in which the metaphor of earth as woman infuses perceptions of the planet with attitudes toward actual women, with all the mixture of insight and error this may bring. The development of the Gaia Hypothesis, while it is surely a contribution in each of its three aspects, exemplifies their continuing separation. To do good, detailed work on the biochemistry of algae it may indeed be necessary to separate that work from the imagery of maternity. Yet the juxtapositions are crucial. I would still argue, as I did in my memoir of my parents, that "cybernetics

makes poets of us" by allowing the recognition of formal
similarities, not only from one living system to another but
from ourselves to other living systems. Cybernetics provides
the intellectual basis for empathy, for "I-Thou" relations
between humans and other organisms and systems.

Gregory believed that consciousness filtered out necessary
kinds of knowledge and that wisdom would come from the
unconscious: that love and religion, natural history and the
arts were all ways to tap into it. He also believed that the
effort to control that process or to bring it into consciousness
would necessarily corrupt it. But however valuable the wisdom
that is in the individual who acts on it without being able to
express it, we are in search of wisdom that can be embedded
in communities and social processes and transmitted from
generation to generation. Here the question of whether understanding needs to be verbalized becomes critical, and
Gertrude's comments on the subject are central. Ideally,
respect for natural systems should be so deeply embedded in
individuals that it guides their behavior without conscious
inspection—but as Gertrude showed us, if you want to change
a pattern of thought, you may need to bring it into consciousness. Today, I would argue that individuals have multiple
modes of consciousness and that our various patterns of
attention and inattention are learned and can be changed.

In fact, perception and attention are similar to other adaptive
mechanisms in human beings, depending on a high degree of
biological flexibility and culturally shaped learning. What the
frog's eye tells the frog's brain, what the bat's sonar tells the
bat, these are very closely tailored to the rather rigidly specified
patterns of adaptation of frog and bat. Human beings have the
illusion that their senses tell them about the natural world, and
this must be corrected by the realization that what we think
we know through the senses is in fact a construction. Much
of that construction seems to be shared cross-culturally, but
just as patterns of human subsistence are learned and changeable, so also are many aspects of perception. Attention is even

more malleable. The more plastic aspects of perception are governed by culturally transmitted patterns of attention and concepts of relevance, by the questions we learn to ask. Where the detergent goes after it goes down the drain is not knowledge inaccessible to human beings—but until recently the chemists who made detergents did not pay attention to that question, did not, in the context of their conscious purposes, regard it as relevant or allow it to affect their decisions. Today they do regard it as relevant, and today tuna fishers are beginning to regard the deaths of porpoises as relevant also, because of changes in public knowledge and in legal structures. Once we understood that the filtering mechanisms of consciousness are partly cultural their study acquired a new urgency. We can now look for systematic ways of thinking about attention.

Beyond the issue of new patterns of thought, the other fundamental question is whether Gregory was right in his rejection of action to bring about change. I believe he was not, although clearly he was correct in arguing that we might find ourselves increasing the very pathologies we were trying to cure. The campaigns Barry and Ted seemed to be suggesting were by definition purposive, and each would entail its own blind spots and unintended side effects. An interesting example of this today is the development of "green advertising," much of it deceptive. Yet I suspect that Gregory rejected these ideas because he was caught in the contradiction between inherited models of political process, tending toward ideological mono-culture, and the model implied in our discussions, which is genuinely ecological.

I believe that Gregory's rejection of political action came out of his World War II experiences, when politics were directed toward the defeat of an enemy, and Gregory's own role in psychological warfare involved the deliberate corruption of communication. Thus, I see him rejecting an action program that, by defining purposes and particularly the purpose of victory, would embrace a deliberate blindness. We have, however, in our heritage from the Greeks, side by side with the idea that politics are about domination and power over the other, the idea that politics are about conversation—that the process benefits from disagreement and difference.

We are mistaken, I believe, if we search for a single way of seeing the human condition that might be adopted worldwide, that everyone might be persuaded (or coerced) to accept. We do well if we promote in human institutions that essentially ecological pattern that has been called pluralism. Perhaps there is no single vision that everyone should agree on; perhaps the essential wisdom will be woven through the discourse of diverse communities. Perhaps I am right only by virtue of being contradicted, but whoever drowns out my words, for whatever reason, is surely wrong. Even religions may someday be recognized as contributing to understanding that is intrinsically multiple. The central achievement of political action and education may be the broadening of political agendas, the acceptance of new patterns of relevance.

I do not think it was an accident that 1990 saw an upsurge of environmentalism, for as long as the planet was sharply polarized politically, it was almost impossible for many people to see either its unity or its diversity—and equally difficult to achieve joint responses to problems. That year did not see the end of history, but it did see the decline, I hope forever, of a certain kind of "us-against-them" view of the world. We need to move on from an adversarial view of truth. Whatever conflicts and antagonisms the future brings, whatever the local polarizations between Arab and Israeli, Sikh and Hindu, Xhosa and Zulu, we may be able now to work toward the health of the planet without seeing it as divided between two monolithic views, one politically right and the other wrong, one of which should dominate or replace the other. Not every participant will visualize the health of the larger whole, so that health is best achieved by preserving multiple voices.

Similarly, we have not seen the end of nature, but we have perhaps seen the end of a picture of nature as separate, teaching us that the life of our species is intermeshed with all others, that nature includes us. A sentimental image, a form of romanticism, has been lost; but romanticism can coexist with exploitation. Nature is not an object that we can dominate or that we can decide to protect, as labor laws have sometimes pretended to protect women, while actually setting them aside. Nature is simply not separate: we do not defeat, exploit, pollute—or even protect—it without doing the same thing to ourselves. Any game we play with nature is either win-win or lose-lose.

I believe that the emerging ecological awareness is necessarily multistranded. There is no single metaphor that can be used to evoke in all human beings a commitment to protecting life on earth. I chafe sometimes at those who are so focused on cetaceans that they are careless of smaller species, yet clearly for some people the sight and songs of whales at sea has opened their imaginations to the value of other forms of life. For others, a first glance through a microscope at the teeming life in a drop of pond water can be equally revelatory. It would be disastrous for this planet if all of its human population lived the current wasteful lifestyle of the West, but even as we try to simplify we cannot regard those working to improve standards in other human communities as the enemy, for they too are responding to a vision of wholeness. What we can do is work to make sure that the perception of living communities of many kinds is widely and repeatedly available to people from early childhood, scattering the seeds of respect throughout human consciousness.

The rise of feminism and other liberation movements has changed the way we think because it has made us more sensitive to the necessity for multiple voices. Taking the questions discussed at Burg Wartenstein up today, we bring what has been learned in the interval to the discussion. We are sensitive now to the fact that phrasing the need to move away from exploitation in terms of "man" retains the assumptions of dominance that led to that exploitation—or to the enforcement of a single point of view. Thus Gregory's own ambivalence about political action may be connected to the flaws of the institutions in which he matured. Today we can affirm the possibility of acting to influence without attempting to dominate. Speaking of love or religion or engineering today may lead in new directions if we do not lock ourselves into authoritarian assumptions, even those of "political correctness." Indeed, the focus on narrowly defined purposes may be related to institutionalized divisions of labor, above all gender-based divisions of labor that have allowed individuals to respond to only a fraction of the context in which they act. A vision of the world that can allow us to live in it in sustainable interdependence will surely reflect some unifying truth; yet our discussion should always be multiple, just as our discussion at the conference had many different bits and pieces. The question is how fragmented knowledge and blinkered, goal-directed visions can lead to integrated action and how half-truths may be prevented from dominating.

When I went to Burg Wartenstein, I had just had an intense experience of pregnancy and of death. I felt then and continue to believe that the human body, with all we are still learning about it, is an ideal model for thinking about systems. For some that model will have intuitive and emotional immediacy while for others it will be largely intellectual. But there are different metaphors; I had never trained a horse or programmed a computer or brooded over the reflexes of a praying mantis. Growing up female in a society still heavily gendered did mean that I had learned, as women have traditionally learned, to attend to multiple tasks and to be concerned with process, as well as with achieving goals. We can hope that with a more equitable division of labor, these kinds of awareness will increasingly be shared by men.

The perverse and difficult process we call democracy—particularly in the American form with its separation of powers, its deliberate undermining of any single locus of authority, that seems so often to paralyze decision—has certainly been less destructive of the natural environment than state socialism, with its narrowly defined and narrowly pursued goals. Democracies, accustomed to internal compromise, are less inclined to warfare, especially with each other. Democracy requires an attention to alternative points of view, and only democracy allows the emergence of lobbies for the snail darter and the red squirrel. When decisions are being made it is essential to have some who speak for specific purposes, some who are concerned for the integrity of the process and the quality of the interaction, and some who keep their eyes open for issues that may not immediately appear relevant. The inclusion of women in decision-making bodies has tended to legitimate these different kinds of concern for both men and women, as it has tended to legitimate the use of empathy as a mode of knowing. Because women have lived contingent lives, they have had to learn to deal with context; because they have often been precluded from focus on single goals, they have learned a wide-ranging responsiveness.

Gregory's distaste for politics came from a deep unwillingness to determine the lives of other beings or to let others try to do so; he would have made a terrible philosopher king, and he was an extraordinarily reluctant therapist. For us this created a dilemma, a double bind in fact. We knew that there were insights that needed to be passed on but were warned against doing so. Two decades later, I can see the fallacy in Gregory's argument: refusing to dominate, he extended his objections to the act of persuasion; intellectually repelled by inconsistency, he was loath to send his ideas into a marketplace. Yet the political effort of persuasion is what brings ideas into interaction with one another. All of our ideas, Gertrude's, Tolly's, Bert's, and the rest, participate in an ecological process in which various and impassioned debate may be the closest we can come to truth. Each idea must be spoken but none is meant to prevail. Even religions can be seen not as exclusive truths but as alternative versions that may make their greatest contributions when seen—and accepted—as multiple. If you are a single species in a mixed community, you do indeed, as Darwin taught us, play to win; but if you win, thereby destroying the environmental weave with its multiple cross-purposes, you lose. Constitutional democracy is a way of assuring that no one wins too much for too long. As in a group of contentious people around a table on an Austrian mountaintop, all of them often wrong-headed but sometimes right, the fundamental error in a democracy is failure to listen, but failure to speak is also an error. It is very important to speak, to publicize, to broaden the political agenda and offer to others those systems of metaphor that may change their understanding, all the while keeping those understandings diverse, for that very diversity is the health of the system.

Two decades after Burg Wartenstein it is clear to me that the human species will not suddenly achieve ecological responsibility and that we and the other species we live with will suffer as a result. But we are moving. I begin to believe that the voices that call for new patterns, the various advocates of cybernetic peace—impassioned, despairing, but also visionary—have become part of the process. If we are ecological thinkers this is the most we should expect.

M. C. B.

*Fairfax, Virginia*

# THE MEMBERS
## OF THE CONFERENCE

THE FOLLOWING DESCRIPTIONS apply to the participants as they were in 1968, when the conference was held, and the only later information which has been added is publication dates for books that were then already in press. Further, to avoid long bibliographies, only *books* have been listed and only those that the participants themselves mentioned as relevant to the conference. For readers who might want to look up the contributions of single individuals, references are given to some of the more extended presentations made by them.

FREDERICK ATTNEAVE (Ph.D., Stanford, 1950). A psychologist with a special interest in problems of perception, who had taught at Mississippi and Berkeley before becoming a professor at the University of Oregon. Author of *Application of Information Theory to Psychology: A Summary of Basic Concepts, Methods and Results* (New York: Henry Holt & Co.; 1959). Fred's presentation on population increase, as a cybernetic system, and impediments to correction is on pp. 121–6.

GREGORY BATESON (M.A., Cambridge University, 1930). A British-born anthropologist who has done field work in New Guinea and Bali, followed by research on communicational and organizational aspects of schizophrenia, and then by a research appointment at the Oceanic Institute in Hawaii. Author of *Naven*

327

(Cambridge, Eng.: Cambridge University Press; 1936); *Balinese Character* (with M. Mead) (New York: N.Y. Academy of Sciences; 1942); and *Communication: The Social Matrix of Psychiatry* (with Jurgen Ruesch) (New York: W. W. Norton & Co.; 1951). Gregory was the organizer of the conference; his formative Memorandum, "Effects of Conscious Purpose On Human Adaptation" is on pp. 13–17. Other key statements by him were on the concepts of Creatura and Pleroma (pp. 69–70), love (pp. 279–80), and aesthetics (pp. 293–5).

MARY CATHERINE BATESON (Ph.D., Harvard, 1963). I came to the conference from the Philippines, where I had done research and teaching in linguistics and anthropology, and was on my way to begin a one-year NSF fellowship at Brandeis University. Editor of *Approaches to Semiotics* (with T. A. Sebeok and A. S. Hayes) (The Hague: Mouton & Co.; 1964) and author of *Structural Continuity in Poetry* (Paris: Ecole des Hautes Etudes; 1970). I made extended statements on conceptual dichotomies in our discussions (pp. 233–5) and on the thesis that "each person is his own central metaphor" (pp. 284–9).

BARRY COMMONER (Ph.D., Harvard, 1941). A biologist investigating problems of the physiochemical basis of biological processes, director of the Center for the Biology of Natural Systems at Washington University in St. Louis. He was one of the founders of the Scientists' Institute for Public Information. Author of *Science and Survival* (New York: Viking Press; 1966). Barry made presentations on nitrate pollution as an example of systemic disruption (pp. 36–43) and DNA theory as an example of scientific reductionism (pp. 55–61). His description of the information movement is on pp. 140–1.

GERTRUDE HENDRIX (M.S., University of Illinois, 1930 and 1935). A mathematician and educator who had retired from a research associate professorship of education at Illinois in 1966 to continue as a consultant in mathematics teaching to a local school system and to DePauw University M.A.T. program. Gertrude had written a number of papers on mathematical learning and participated in developing several teaching programs. She presented a theory of unverbalized awareness to be found on pp. 106–13.

ANATOL W. HOLT (Ph.D., University of Pennsylvania, 1963). A mathematician and programming systems designer, then director of Advance Systems at Applied Data Research in Princeton, N.J., and teaching part-time at Harvard. Author of numerous papers on computer theory. Tolly presented a theory of system description which is described in Chapters 9 and 10. Other key statements by him were on the nature of symbols (pp. 153–7), on man-machine interactions (pp. 215–16, 220–2), and on man's relationship to nature (pp. 248–50).

W. T. JONES (Ph.D., Princeton, 1937). A philosopher concerned with the relationship between philosophical positions and the culture of an epoch, now professor at Pomona College in Claremont, California. Author of *The Romantic Syndrome: Toward a New Method in Cultural Anthropology and the History of Ideas* (New York: Humanities Press; 1961) and *The Sciences and the Humanities* (University of California Press; 1965). Will had prepared a paper for the conference on Cartesian dualism (pp. 26–7) and spoke on the last day about the nature of the conference and the importance of detachment (pp. 303–5).

BERT KAPLAN (Ph.D., Harvard, 1949). A psychologist in the field of personality theory and chairman of the History of Consciousness Program at the University of California in Santa Cruz. Author of *Personality in a Communal Society* (Lawrence: University of Kansas Press; 1956); *Studying Personality Cross-Culturally* (New York: Harper & Row; 1961); and *The Inner World of Mental Illness* (New York: Harper and Row; 1964). Bert spoke on apocalyptic visions (pp. 87–91), conversion (pp. 128–31), and history as a human phenomenon (pp. 241–7).

PETER H. KLOPFER (Ph.D., Yale, 1958). An ecologist and ethologist concerned with parent–offspring ties, species distribution, and use of space, teaching and researching at Duke University in Durham, North Carolina. Author of *Behavioral Aspects of Ecology* (Englewood Cliffs, N.J.: Prentice-Hall; 1962); *An Introduction to Animal Behavior* (with J. Hailman) (Englewood Cliffs, N.J.: Prentice-Hall; 1967); and *Habitats and Territories* (New York: Basic Books; 1969). Peter discussed the regulation of animal populations (pp. 133–5) and the importance of perceptual and ecological diversity (pp. 264–71).

WARREN S. McCULLOCH (M.D., Columbia, 1927). A neurologist and early leader of the cybernetics movement, who was then a staff member at the Research Laboratory of Electronics at M.I.T., studying the functional organization of the nervous system. Author of *Embodiments of Mind* (Cambridge: M.I.T. Press; 1965). Warren discussed toxicity (p. 51) and holism (pp. 64–7).

HORST MITTELSTAEDT (D.Phil.Nat., Heidelberg, 1949). A zoocyberneticist concerned with problems of orientational homeostasis and control, now director of an independent division at the Max-Planck Institute in Germany. Author of *Basic Solutions to a Problem of Angular Orientation* (Stanford: Stanford University Press; 1964). Horst's discussion of the difference between feedback and feed-forward control is on pp. 135–6.

GORDON PASK (Ph.D., University of London, 1963). A cyberneticist, now director of research at Systems Research Ltd. and Chairman of Cybernetic Developments Ltd., both in London. Author of *An Approach to Cybernetics* (London: Hutchinson; 1961) and many technical papers. Gordon's presentations on control and on types of goals occupy most of Chapter 11, and his discussion of symbolic evolution is on pp. 306–9.

BERNARD RAXLEN (M.D., University of Toronto, 1965). After spending a year's psychiatric residency in Brazil, he was then just completing a period in Hawaii, where he became interested in mental patients of Portuguese origin—an interest which led him to do field work in the Azores. Bernie presented his findings, which are described on pp. 115–18.

THEODORE SCHWARTZ (Ph.D., University of Pennsylvania, 1958). An anthropologist who has done field work in Melanesia and Mexico and was then teaching at UCLA. Author of *The Paliau Movement in the Admiralty Islands, 1946–54*, in *Anthropological Papers of the American Museum of Natural History*, Vol. 49, Pt. 2 (New York 1962). Ted's presentation on Melanesian cargo cults and the problem of using cybernetic descriptions on societies—which can formulate new goals—makes up Chapter 4.

# NOTES

1. Gregory Bateson: *Naven* (Cambridge: Cambridge University Press; 1936); 2nd edn. (Stanford: Stanford University Press; 1958).
2. Norbert Wiener: *Cybernetics* (New York: Wiley; 1948); 2nd edn. (Cambridge: M.I.T. Press; 1961).
3. Josiah Macy, Jr., Foundation: *A Review of Activities 1930–1955* (New York: Josiah Macy, Jr., Foundation; 1955); and Heinz von Foerster, ed.: *Cybernetics* (New York: Josiah Macy, Jr., Foundation; 1950–6), 5 vols.
4. Condensed passage from Gregory Bateson: "Daddy, What Is an Instinct?" in T. A. Sebeok and A. Ramsay, eds.: *Approaches to Animal Communication* (The Hague: Mouton; 1969).
5. William Blake: *Europe, A Prophecy* (Lambeth: printed and published by the author; 1794).
6. Prepared under Career Development Award MH–21, 931–02, of the National Institute of Mental Health. The full text of the Memorandum, which is here somewhat condensed, is reprinted in G. Bateson: *Steps to an Ecology of Mind* (Scranton, Pa.: Intext 1972).

1. Warren S. McCulloch: *Embodiments of Mind* (Cambridge: M.I.T. Press; 1965).
2. Jean-Baptiste Lamarck: *Philosophie zoologique, ou exposition des considérations relatives à l'histoire naturelle des animaux, etc.* (Paris: Dentu Libraire; 1809). Translated as *Zoological*

*Philosophy: An Exposition with Regard to the Natural History of Animals* by Hugh Elliot (London: Macmillan and Co.; 1914).
3. William Blake: *The Marriage of Heaven and Hell* (1825–7). Facsimile edition (London: Trianon Press; 1960).

CHAPTER 2

1. *Waste Management and Control*, a report to the Federal Council for Science and Technology by the Committee on Pollution, National Academy of Sciences, National Research Council, Publication 1400 (1966); G. Cook, in *Proceedings: Conference in the Matter of Lake Erie and Its Tributaries,* U.S. Department of Health, Education and Welfare, Cleveland, August 3–6, 1966, Vol. 2; and *Report on Commercial Fisheries Resources of the Lake Erie Basin*, U.S. Department of the Interior, Fish and Wildlife Science, Bureau of Commercial Fisheries, August 1966.
2. G. E. Smith, *Sanborn Field Bulletin 458*, University of Missouri, College of Agriculture, Agricultural Experiment Station, Columbia, Missouri (1942).
3. E. H. W. J. Burden: *The Analyst*, Vol. 86 (1961), p. 421; and L. W. Weinberger, *et al.*: in *Annals of the New York Academy of Science*, Vol. 136 (1966), p. 131.
4. F. E. Allison: *Advances in Agronomy*, Vol. 18 (1966), p. 219.
5. American Association for the Advancement of Science, Committee on Science in the Promotion of Human Welfare. *Cf.* "The Integrity of Science," *American Scientist: 53* (June 1965).

CHAPTER 3

1. Elizabeth Marshall Thomas: *The Harmless People* (New York: Knopf; 1959).
2. Barry Commoner: "Failure of the Watson-Crick Theory as a Chemical Explanation of Inheritance," *Nature 220* (1968), p. 334.
3. J. F. Speyer, *et al.*: *Cold Spring Harbor Symposia on Quantitative Biology* (Cold Spring Harbor, N.Y.: Cold Spring Harbor Laboratory; 1966), Vol. 31, p. 693; and E. B. Freese and E. Freese: *Proceedings of the National Academy of Science*, Vol. 57 (February 1967), p. 650.
4. For instance, in "The Genetic Code," *Cold Spring Harbor Symposia*, Vol. 31, 1967.
5. F. H. C. Crick: *Symposia of the Society for Experimental Biology*, Vol. 12 (1958), p. 138.

6. Alan W. Watts: *The Book: On the Taboo Against Knowing Who You Are* (New York: Collier Books; 1967), pp. 48–50.
7. C. G. Jung: *Septem Sermones ad Mortuos* (London: Stuart & Watkins; 1967).

### CHAPTER 4

1. Theodore Schwartz: *The Paliau Movement in the Admiralty Islands, 1946–54*, Anthropological Papers of the American Museum of Natural History, Vol. 49, Pt. 2 (New York, 1962).
2. Leon Festinger, Henry W. Riecken, and Stanley Schacter: *When Prophecy Fails* (Minneapolis: Minnesota University Press; 1956); and Leon Festinger: *A Theory of Cognitive Dissonance* (Stanford: Stanford University Press; 1962).

### CHAPTER 6

1. Following Judd's conscious generalization theory; *cf.* C. H. Judd: *The Psychology of Secondary Education* (Boston: Ginn and Co.; 1927).
2. G. Hendrix: "A New Clue to Transfer of Training," *Elementary School Journal*, Vol. 48 (December 1947), pp. 197–208.
3. G. Hendrix: "Learning by Discovery," *The Mathematics Teacher*, Vol. 54 (May 1961), pp. 290–9.

### CHAPTER 7

1. Harmon Henkin: "Side Effects," *Environment* (formerly *Scientist and Citizen*), Vol. 2, No. 1 (1969), p. 28.
2. P. H. Klopfer: *Habitats and Territories: A Study of the Use of Space by Animals* (New York: Basic Books; 1969); and P. H. Klopfer and J. P. Hailman: *An Introduction to Animal Behavior: Ethology's First Century* (Englewood Cliffs, N.J.: Prentice-Hall; 1968).
3. Horst Mittelstaedt: "The Analysis of Behavior in Terms of Control Systems," in *Transactions of the Fifth Conference on Group Processes* (New York: Josiah Macy, Jr., Foundation; 1960).

### CHAPTER 9

1. These structures are named after their inventor, Carl Adam Petri, theoretician at the University of Bonn. He called them

"transition nets" and first described them in his doctoral dissertation (1962). This was translated into English by Project ISTP: *Communication with Automata*, translated by Clifford F. Greene, Jr., A Supplement to Technical Documentary Report #1, Prepared for Rome Air Development Center Contract AF30(602)–3324, (summer 1965).

### CHAPTER 10

1. Eugene Wigner in *Transactions of the Fifth Conference on Group Processes* (New York: Josiah Macy, Jr., Foundation; 1960).

### CHAPTER 11

1. J. Y. Lettvin, H. R. Maturana, W. S. McCulloch, and W. Pitts: "What the Frog's Eye Tells the Frog's Brain," *Proceedings of the Institute of Radio Engineers*, Vol. 47 (1959), pp. 1940–52.
2. A. N. Whitehead and B. Russell: *Principia Mathematica*, 3 vols., 2nd edn. (Cambridge: Cambridge University Press; 1910–13).
3. N. Rescher: *The Logic of Commands* (London: Routledge and Kegan Paul; 1966).

### CHAPTER 13

1. "I believe that mathematical reality lies outside us, that our function is to discover or *observe* it, and that the theorems which we prove, and which we describe grandiloquently as our 'creations,' are simply our notes of our observations." G. H. Hardy: *A Mathematician's Apology* (Cambridge: Cambridge University Press; 1941), p. 63.
2. Alan W. Watts: *The Book*, pp. 31–2.

### CHAPTER 14

1. P. H. Klopfer: *Behavioral Aspects of Ecology* (Englewood Cliffs, N.J.: Prentice-Hall; 1962).

### CHAPTER 15

1. "The Life After Death," *The Notebooks of Samuel Butler*, ed. Henry Festing Jones (London: A. C. Fifield; 1912), p. 397.

# INDEX

*Note:* Although a work of this sort—because of its discursive character and the variable use of terms by different participants—does not really lend itself to indexing, it has seemed desirable to offer a key to the more significant concepts referred to, as well as to proper names (except those of participants). Central concepts are indexed even when they have not been specifically mentioned, so that, for instance, all discussions of interactions between systems are indexed under "coupling." See "The Members of the Conference" for a list of key presentations by each participant. Names and concepts discussed in the 1991 Foreword and Afterword are not included in this Index.

339

war, 93
water, 37–40
Watson, J. D., 57
Watts, Alan, 63–4, 260
Wenner-Gren Foundation, ix, 17, 264
Whitehead, A. N., 212, 302

wholes, *see* holism; systems
Wiener, Norbert, 7, 23, 204
Wigner, Eugene, 200
world-view, 29, 45, 56, 94–5, 118–119, 269, 271–2, 275–7; *see also* thought, patterns of
Wynne-Edwards, V. C., 15

Printed in the United States
23266LVS00005BA/7-39